# The Naked Clone

# The Naked Clone

*How Cloning Bans Threaten Our
Personal Rights*

JOHN CHARLES KUNICH

Westport, Connecticut
London

**Library of Congress Cataloging-in-Publication Data**

Kunich, John C., 1953–
   The naked clone : how cloning bans threaten our personal rights / John Charles Kunich
      p.   cm.
   Includes bibliographical references and index
   ISBN 0–275–97964–4 (alk. paper)
   1. Human cloning—Law and legislation—United States. 2. Civil rights—United States.
I. Title

KF3831.K86 2003
342.73'085—dc21          2003042931

British Library Cataloguing in Publication Data is available.

Library of Congress Catalog Card Number: 2003042931

ISBN: 0–275–97964–4

First published in 2003
Praeger Publishers, 88 Post Road West, Westport, CT 06881
An imprint of Greenwood Publishing Group, Inc.
www.praeger.com

Printed in the United States of America

The paper used in this book complies with the
Permanent Paper Standard issued by the National
Information Standards Organization (Z39.48-1984).

10 9 8 7 6 5 4 3 2 1

This book is dedicated to the children of the world, present and future, and to all of the people who love and believe in them.

# Contents

# Preface

Every human being has legal rights. These rights do not depend on whether a person came to be through in vitro fertilization, artificial insemination—or cloning.

Human cloning is inevitable, and the law must adjust. The title of this book, *The Naked Clone*, highlights how far off the mark the legal debate on cloning has been. The widespread public horror that has greeted the dawning of mammalian cloning is being translated into laws, and often outright bans, on the cloning of human beings, particularly reproductive cloning (cloning to produce children). Children will not be born at all because of these bans, and potential parents will be denied the children they could have had. The very processes that could have enabled these children to be born are criminalized and outlawed. The child of cloning—often inaccurately and callously called a "clone"—is therefore rendered naked and alone, in the legal sense. No laws shelter this child who will never be born. No laws cover this child with their protective shield and enable him or her to begin life. And the hopeful parents of this child are left similarly bereft.

The naked clone situation is happening right now. Within the United States, six states have enacted bans on human cloning in some form, and many more are considering it. The United States Congress has come close to enacting a permanent, sweeping ban on both reproductive cloning and therapeutic/research cloning, with the enthusiastic support and encouragement of President George W. Bush. Numerous other nations have already passed their own bans of various types, including the United Kingdom, Germany, Japan, Israel, Spain, Australia, Denmark, New Zealand,

and the Netherlands. And the United Nations has begun preparing an all-encompassing international agreement to halt reproductive cloning world-wide. Religious and political leaders on the global stage, from popes to presidents, have united to demand an end to the age of human cloning before it can even begin.

What has prodded the planet into this crisis mode? The momentous, earthshaking event that started it all was the birth of a sheep named Dolly in July 1996, the bleat heard 'round the world. This first reported success-ful cloning of a mammal from an adult cell shocked people all over the globe into a frenzy of political and legal action. But the facts and the sci-ence of cloning—its capabilities and limitations—swiftly were lost in the dust cloud stirred up by people rushing to do something, anything, to stop cloning before it reached humans. Science fiction and horror movies crowded out rational discourse, and vague notions of repugnance, or "the yuck factor," substituted for reasoned and balanced debate rooted in the rule of law and reality.

I wrote this book to change the direction of the legal debate on cloning, but not only because so many people have gotten their facts on cloning itself so wrong. Much more important are the multiple ways in which bans on cloning can endanger the core constitutional liberties of all Amer-icans. Bans on reproductive cloning jeopardize the privacy and reproduc-tive rights, including abortion, set forth in United States Supreme Court decisions from *Roe v. Wade* onward. Why? Because the *same* constitutional interests are at the heart of reproductive cloning and the rights to marry, have children, use contraceptives, choose whether to abort, and maintain a zone of personal privacy safe from unwarranted governmental intru-sion. Some of these rights were first recognized and later sustained by bitterly divided Supreme Court panels with the narrowest of majorities. As the courts deal with challenges to statutes outlawing reproductive cloning, they will be confronted by extremely difficult and contentious issues equally applicable to these noncloning rights. If bans on cloning to produce children are upheld, this legal precedent could be the stepping stone to the next case, in which the target is no longer cloning but another fragile, intensely personal privacy interest.

The naked clone situation refers specifically and precisely to *reproductive cloning.* However, scientific/medical research into cloning for purposes apart from reproduction is also linked to other vital constitutional rights. Severe restrictions or outright bans on cloning research—"therapeutic cloning"—threaten much than simply the right of a few scientists to conduct research on cloning and stem cells. The First Amendment to the United States Constitution is implicated by bans on cloning research. Such research may be worthy of First Amendment protection because it is the necessary and closely linked precursor to the expression of ideas; ideas must be created before they can be shared. Also, the research itself may be a form of expression, or symbolic speech, in part making a statement that such research is vital and should be free from prior censorship by the government. If government can, with impunity, shut down scientific research *because it abhors the subject matter in question*—the content of the message expressed—this will imperil cherished expressive liberties that are quite remote from the cloning situation. Again, the act of banning an aspect of cloning, if upheld by the courts, might be the basis for far more widespread invasions of our First Amendment rights. The collateral legal damage from these bans could reach far beyond the narrow confines of cloning per se.

One of the legislative options being pursued in the states and in the United States Senate is to enact an outright permanent ban on reproductive cloning while allowing therapeutic cloning to proceed with some restrictions. But this "split ban" generates a perverse incentive, indeed a duty, on the part of researchers: to destroy the nascent cloned human embryos created in the laboratory before they are ever implanted in a woman's womb, under the threat of severe criminal and civil penalties for violation. This "clone-and-kill" situation is without precedent in the United States. It is the first time the law has established an entire class of arguably human beings that American civilian citizens are under *a legal obligation to destroy.* When such a split ban is challenged, the courts will be forced to deal with a situation that many people would find abhorrent, and the precedent they set forth in the cloning cases may lead directly to the overturning of *Roe v. Wade* and other related cases. Could some of the proponents of the split bans be aware of this potential and knowingly advance their cloning legislation with the intention of using it as a type of Trojan Horse to reverse the abortion rights cases? It is a distinct possibility, made clear when one understands the sticky web of interconnected legal issues that binds cloning rights to abortion rights and other privacy interests.

This book, therefore, is about much more than cloning. It is a thorough examination of the immense, but hidden, *legal and constitutional* significance of the bans being considered and enacted state by state and at the federal level. It demonstrates how bans on cloning endanger some of our most personal constitutional rights, by confronting our courts with hard, complex choices involving a wildly unpopular cause. Judges, including justices of the Supreme Court, are not immune to the same misconceptions and fallacies that have spawned intense and overwhelming opposition to human cloning among the general populace. If, as the saying goes, hard cases make bad law, then bans on cloning could be the springboards for some very bad law indeed.

In chapter 1, I briefly summarize and clarify the basic history and scientific facts of cloning—what it is, what it is not, what it can and cannot do. This chapter also includes the main arguments against the cloning of humans. Next, in chapter 2, I discuss the anticloning laws within the United States. I begin with the laws now in place in states from California to Rhode Island, followed by legislative initiatives along these lines in many more states. Chapter 2 also presents the federal approach to cloning thus far, including cloning bans passed by the House of Representatives in 2001 and 2003 and debated by the Senate to a standstill both times. In chapter 3, the various approaches to cloning legislation in other nations of the world are analyzed to provide an international context and to illustrate some options available to the United States in crafting its own cloning laws. Chapter 4 deals with the far-reaching First Amendment implications of bans on therapeutic cloning. This includes a basic introduction to the convoluted subject of First Amendment law, followed by an application of that jurisprudence to cloning research and the probable outcome in court when bans are challenged. In chapter 5, I discuss how bans on reproductive cloning threaten vital liberties from the right to marry and have children to the freedom to choose whether to have an abortion. The many links between cloning bans and an array of other privacy and personal autonomy interests will be made clear. Finally, in chapter 6, I describe the way ahead, a better alternative to the permanent, all-encompassing bans that have typified our legislative response to cloning thus far.

Cloning, on its own merits, could be a way for some people to have their own biologically related children where before that was impossible, just as in vitro fertilization has been for others. And research into cloning could lead to extremely important advancements in medicine and therapy for people with harmful genetic conditions, a variety of deadly diseases, and for those in desperate need of vital organ transplants. If these two points constituted the entirety of the significance of the cloning issue, they would be reason enough to rethink our instinctive impulse to ban that which we hate and fear. But this book is about the hidden legal meaning of human cloning, a meaning with momentous import far beyond that of cloning itself.

*The Naked Clone* is a window into a future whereby today's bans on cloning form the foundation for tomorrow's denial of many other fundamental constitutional rights. That future does not have to be. It is the purpose of this book to let us look into the future and change the path we are on, before tomorrow becomes today.

# Acknowledgments

I thank my research assistant, Deborah Niedfeldt, for her superb work in assisting with the preparation of the manuscript for this book, as well as the staff of *The Kentucky Law Journal*, for their help in editing and publishing a shorter, previous version. I am grateful, above all, to my wife, Marcia K. Vigil, and our daughters, Christina Laurel Kunich and Julie-Kate Marva Kunich, for their unending love, support, inspiration, and encouragement, without which this book would not have been possible.

# CHAPTER 1

# Cloning in Science and Science Fiction

"Whew! What they can't do these days!"

—Jiminy Cricket[1]

## INTRODUCTION

As modern science rips gaping holes in the realm of the impossible, modern law struggles to keep pace. Particularly when revolutionary advancements in science demolish ancient notions of the proper ambit of human action, the legal system has been unprepared to meet the new challenges proactively. Instead of accommodating the new realities, there are powerful people—chiefly political and religious leaders—who have tried to bend the law into a reactive, even reactionary force in the path of full exploration of the inchoate terrain of the freshly possible.

Some of the fuel igniting the legal opposition to scientific forays into the frontiers of imagination is a strong primeval sense that people should not be allowed to "play God." This belief has been both explicitly and implicitly at the core of much of the resistance to genetic engineering of crop plants and domesticated animals.[2] Fundamentally, the idea is that our ability to perform certain tasks should not be coterminous with the legality of doing so, at least with regard to modifying living things. There is a belief, usually implicitly and often explicitly religious in origin, that places some life-related areas of medical and scientific endeavor in the category of taboo, top-sacred, forbidden mystical practices reserved exclusively unto deity.

There is a related concept as well. Reflecting the premise embodied and graphically portrayed in numerous popular horror and science-fiction novels, motion pictures, and television programs, some people are afraid that human attempts to "play God"[3] or "fool Mother Nature" are fraught with overwhelming peril. The powerful message and visceral impact from these fantasies is clear: when we meddle in the secrets of life, we risk unleashing a Frankenstein's monster and visiting a horrific plague upon ourselves and our world.[4]

Legal and popular opposition to genetic engineering, formidable enough in its own right, has been dwarfed by the reaction to the prospect of cloning as applied to human beings. During the brief aftermath of the dawn of the cloning age, governments around the world have hastily acted to place severe restrictions, including outright bans, on the cloning of human beings and/or experimentation along such lines. The United States has been no exception. And the degree of unanimity in opposition to cloning has been astounding, often uniting liberal and conservative, pro-life and pro-choice, and secular and religious people of various persuasions.

Yet science continues to advance. In November 2001, scientists in Massachusetts announced that they had succeeded in creating the world's first cloned human embryos, albeit for only a few hours and only at the stage of four to six cells.[5] Although this privately funded research was not aimed at the actual birth of a cloned human baby, it set off anew a tidal wave of impassioned calls for a comprehensive permanent federal ban on the cloning of humans.[6] Within the next year there were claims, of varying degrees of credibility (none of which were independently corroborated), that a human baby had actually been born through the intervention of cloning. These widely publicized stories added incendiary fuel to the already raging outcry.[7] Passion has its place, but not to the exclusion of logic, reality, and the rule of law. That is why this book was written.

This book will trace the history of modern cloning and the various legal responses domestically and worldwide to recent scientific breakthroughs. It will then explore the constitutionality and the wisdom of the legal measures taken within the United States, particularly as anticloning legislation relates to other rights and liberties. Finally, there will be a proposal for a more appropriate, rational, and constitutionally sound course of action.

I must emphasize that this book is definitely *not* intended to be yet another public policy polemic devoted to supposed moral, ethical, and philosophical problems related to human cloning. There are plenty of books in that category, and I do not intend gratuitously to add one more book to the groaning library shelves straining under the collective weight of these volumes. If you are searching for an examination of cloning from the standpoint of ethics, religion, morality, philosophy, and/or public policy, without regard for the legal and constitutional issues, you would be better off looking elsewhere.[8] Moreover, in light of the quasi-official findings and recommendations of blue-ribbon panels such as the President's Council on Bioethics, that field has largely been mooted.

Rather, my goal in this book is to explore the *legal* issues implicated by the impulse to ban cloning. The constitutional collateral damage that could be caused by the more extreme bans is the primary concern of this book—that in the process of prohibiting human reproductive and/or therapeutic cloning, we may also inadvertently undermine our most personal constitutional rights. The law, especially constitutional law, is an aspect of the cloning controversy that has never been fully analyzed until now.

## THE HISTORY AND FACTS OF CLONING

Popular misconceptions abound concerning cloning.[9] Among the most common fallacious notions are that cloning produces exact copies of an original organism; children of cloning are in some sense less genuine or less worthy than their parents; and cloning is capable of mass-producing legions of superpowered transgenics or superevil menaces, such as an army of Hitlers. Let us dispatch these fallacies as swiftly and painlessly as possible, with the aid of a brief historical and scientific overview.

We need a working definition of cloning for purposes of this book, preferably one that will not cause our eyes to glaze over. Any simple definition is vulnerable to charges of oversimplification and incompleteness, but if it aids our understanding, it is at least a good place to begin. Here is one that with a solid scientific pedigree that will work for us:

Reproductive cloning is defined as the deliberate production of genetically identical individuals. Each newly produced individual is a clone of the original. Monozygotic (identical) twins are natural clones. Clones contain identical sets of genetic material in the nucleus—the compartment that contains the chromosomes—of every cell in their bodies. Thus, cells from two clones [of the same individual] have the same DNA and the same genes in their nuclei.[10]

The term *cloning* itself was once reserved for horticultural practices involving plants, not animals, in which a group of plants are grown from an original plant but do not come from "true seed." Plants can be reproduced asexually through cuttings, for example. Today, there are several modern forms of cloning that usually consist of direct manipulation of genetic material in a process called somatic cell nuclear transfer (SCNT),[11] or dividing an embryonic cell (embryo splitting), although there are other methods of cloning as well.[12]

Hans Spemann, a German embryologist, laid the foundation for all subsequent experiments into animal cloning as part of his work on whether each differentiated cell retains in some sense the full complement of genetic information present initially in the zygote. During the late 1920s, he took a salamander embryo at the sixteen-cell stage and tied off part of a cell with its nucleus; he was able to get the single cell to divide, showing that the nucleus of that early embryo could essentially begin its processes again. He subsequently speculated as to whether more completely differentiated cells had the same capacity; he theorized about the possibility of transferring the nucleus from a differentiated cell, taken from either a later-stage embryo or an adult organism, into an enucleated egg.[13] Spemann wrote: "Decisive information about this question may perhaps be afforded by an experiment which appears, at first sight, to be somewhat fantastical. This experiment might possibly show that even nuclei of differentiated cells can initiate normal development in the egg protoplasms."[14]

In 1952, American embryologists Robert Briggs and Thomas King made significant strides toward actually conducting the "fantastical experiment" Spemann had envisioned when they became the first researchers successfully to transfer nuclei from early embryonic cells of leopard frogs to enucleated leopard frog eggs. The resulting "activated eggs" began to divide and develop, became embryos, and then developed into tadpoles. Other researchers were able to replicate the Briggs and King experiments on different species of frogs, but this work showed that the older and more differentiated a DNA donor cell becomes, the less likely it is that its nucleus will be able to be returned to its early full potential. Notably, during the 1960s and 1970s, the British developmental biologist John Gurdon reportedly produced adult cloned frogs by transferring nuclei both from intestinal cells of tadpoles and adult frog skin cells into enucleated frog eggs.[15]

Cloning research then gradually shifted to the possibility of cloning mammals from adult cells. The major challenge was how to reset the genetic functioning of differentiated, somatic cells, after some early successes in transferring DNA from embryonic nuclei of mice during the 1980s.[16] Famously, this culminated in the work of Dr. Ian Wilmut and his colleagues at the Roslin Institute in Scotland, in which the nuclei of adult mammary cells were used to clone the sheep named Dolly in 1996.[17] During the post-Dolly cloning explosion, scientists have successfully cloned several additional species of mammals, including cattle, goats, pigs, mice, cats, and rabbits.[18]

Embryo splitting, or blastomere separation, has not received as much media (or legislative) attention as SCNT, but it is important to note its existence because it implicates some, but by no means all, of the same issues. Simply put, the process entails the manipulation of a very recently fertilized ovum, the union of egg and sperm. Within about 1.5 days after fertilization, the fertilized ovum begins to divide, forming a blastomere as cell division produces two, four, eight, and then sixteen cells, becoming a blastocyst by about the four-day point.[19] Each of these very early embryonic cells is totipotent, that is, capable of developing into an entire adult organism if separated from the other cells. To clone via embryo splitting, the blastomere is fragmented (into two, four, eight, or sixteen identical cells), and each cell is then cultured to grow into a very small multicell embryo, which must then be implanted into an adult female of the same species.[20] Each embryo is implanted into a separate adult female for gestation. Each surrogate mother then carries one of these embryos to term in the usual manner, and each resultant individual would be genetically identical to the others produced from the same split blastomere.[21] That is, they would be genetically identical to the others split from the same early-stage embryo but *not* identical to any existing postbirth individual.

The process of SCNT generally involves isolating deoxyribonucleic acid (DNA)[22] from the nucleus of a somatic (body) cell (i.e., a differentiated, nongamete cell, not an ovum or spermatozoa) of a donor to be cloned. These somatic cells may first be deprived of nutrients for a period sufficient to halt further cellular development and bring them back to a totipotent state in which they are capable of developing into any type of cell. Then the nucleus is extracted from the donor cell and transplanted into an oocyte (egg cell) that has had its nucleus and chromosomes removed (enucleated). The resulting renucleated cell is then treated (often with a minuscule electrical pulse) in an attempt to fuse the nucleus with the remainder of the cell and activate it. If activation is successful, the cell will begin to divide, essentially in the same manner as with an ovum fertilized by a sperm cell.[23] If the cell develops to the blastocyst (live preimplantation embryo) stage, it is transferred to and implanted in the uterus of a living female (a surrogate mother/gestational mother) of the same species as the donor and recipient cells, with the goal of enabling the female to carry the embryo and eventual fetus until birth, similar to the methods widely used for in vitro fertilization.[24] The resulting individual would be a clone of the DNA donor and would "inherit" its nuclear DNA from only that one genetic parent.[25]

In current practice, this SCNT is not performed only once but many times over, in an effort to overcome low success rates at the stages of blastocyst development, implantation in the female's uterus, and progress to birth. For example, in the famous case of the cloned sheep named Dolly, 277 enucleated eggs were obtained and received nuclei from adult mammary gland cells,[26] and 29 of these cells made it to the blastocyst stage (an 11 percent success rate); of those 29 blastocysts that were then transferred to the uterus of 13 female sheep (ewes), only 1 cloned sheep was eventually born.[27] This reflected a 3 percent success rate among the blastocysts, and a 0.36 rate overall from start to finish.[28] However, another legitimate way of interpreting the same results is that 1 out of 13 ewes that received implanted cloned blastocysts eventually gave birth, a 7.7 percent success rate that compares favorably with those achieved using in vitro fertilization during the first several years of its history.[29]

An individual born through SCNT intervention is not, strictly speaking, genetically identical to the donor of the DNA. Although the nucleic DNA is the same as in the donor, the DNA in the mitochondria (the organelles within each cell that produce energy for cellular functions), or m-DNA, is the same as the m-DNA of the recipient enucleated ovum.[30] Thus, in SCNT, the new individual is *not* an exact copy, even genetically, of either the donor or the recipient; his or her nuclear DNA comes from the DNA donor, while the m-DNA comes from the egg donor. The only ways in which SCNT can yield an individual with *both* nuclear DNA and m-DNA identical to that of the donor is by using the egg donor's own somatic cell DNA to clone herself, or where the egg comes from the nucleus donor's biological mother (because mitochondria are inherited maternally).[31] In contrast, embryo splitting does produce an exact genotypic duplicate—both nuclear and m-DNA—of the original fertilized ovum (the good old-fashioned union of egg and sperm), but *not* a duplicate of any preexisting individual.

This is an important point, and it is worthwhile to emphasize certain key differences between the two major methods of cloning. Embryo splitting is technologically much easier, at present, because there is no need to perform delicate microscopic surgery on a cell or to "reset" a fully differentiated somatic cell and render it totipotent so that it can develop into an entire organism. Also, as mentioned, because embryo splitting begins with a fertilized egg, it clones a new combination of DNA from a male and a female, not any preexisting individual. In no respect does embryo splitting genetically replicate any one already-born individual, any more than does the natural process of fertilization that unites DNA from mother and father to form an offspring. Embryo splitting is essentially a process of artificially twinning (and beyond) an early stage embryo. In contrast, SCNT does transfer the nuclear DNA from a somatic cell of a single post-birth individual, even an adult, and with the exception of differences in mitochondrial DNA, reproduces the nuclear DNA of that one individual precisely.

There is nothing in either the SCNT process or embryo splitting that lends itself to mass production of clones. The renucleated eggs must each be introduced into the uterus of a living female of the same species (e.g., a female sheep in Dolly's case), one by one, each adult female receiving one renucleated egg. Although the blastomere separation (in embryo splitting) and extraction of nucleic DNA from donor somatic cells and the enucleation of recipient eggs (in SCNT) are done in the laboratory, any resulting embryos must be carried to term by live females, one at a time. The horror-story image of hordes of Hitlers being churned out, factory style, is utterly without basis in scientific fact.

There are, however, some noteworthy questions regarding the risks of human cloning—questions that remain without completely satisfactory answers chiefly because of our limited experience with cloning. For instance, early experiments in cloning frogs sometimes produced badly deformed clones.[32] Subsequent attempts to clone cows resulted in some abnormally large calves, as much as double the usual birth weight, and some cloned calves were born with diseases and deformed hearts; 18 to 20 percent of these died soon after birth.[33] However, more recent experiments involving cloned cows have resulted in "vigorous, healthy, and normal" individuals, as healthy as conventional cows, with a pregnancy survival rate akin to those achieved by conventional livestock breeders.[34] But post-Dolly efforts to create cloned, transgenic sheep met with a very low success rate, and among the few lambs that survived to live outside their surrogate mothers, some weighed almost twice the normal amount.[35] Such phenomena have obvious, very serious implications for the health and well-being of the mother as well as the offspring born through the SCNT cloning process.

The reasons underlying these mixed results remain unclear. One hypothesis is that the process of reactivating the donor DNA in the SCNT process sometimes damages it, possibly by activating normally dormant genes that harbor deleterious mutations or undesirable phenotypic potential, or by failing properly to reactivate all necessary genes or to erase previous patterns of gene activity in the enucleated egg.[36]

There are other questions awaiting answers that only time will deliver. One intriguing issue is whether a cloned organism somehow "inherits" the age of its DNA donor.[37] Was Dolly, in effect, born fully grown, with a remaining life expectancy (derived from the adult mammary gland cell that contributed her DNA) far less than that of an ordinary newborn lamb? Or does the act of rendering the donor cells totipotent restore them to the effective age of any gamete, with a full lifespan in store for any eventual cloned individual? Further research, and time, is necessary to resolve such questions. But these important inquiries may be cut short by legal intervention.

Dolly the sheep was born on July 5, 1996, having been produced by a research team headed by Scottish embryologist Ian Wilmut at the Roslin Institute in Edinburgh.[38] Dolly was front-page news because this was the first time fully differentiated adult somatic cells had been used successfully to clone a mammal—although previously mammals had been cloned using early embryonic cells—thereby proving that cellular differentiation can be reversed.[39] Obviously, a key feature was the freedom from reliance on very early, undifferentiated embryonic cells—any normal somatic cells from a fully grown adult were now potentially the source of a clone. In the aftermath of the February 23, 1997, announcement[40] of this stunning advancement, there came much controversy. Popes and presidents, politicians and philosophers, pundits and people on the street all felt compelled to speak out on the latest, greatest issue of the modern age. Most famously, physicist Richard Seed declared his intention on December 5, 1997, to commence the cloning of human beings;[41] others followed suit.[42] At that point, the proverbial organic waste matter hit the oscillating air circulation device, and legal reactions began in earnest.

## INITIAL LEGAL REACTIONS TO THE CLONING OF HUMANS

On several fronts, the legal response to Dolly and her would-be successors was of a type one would expect had the lid to Pandora's box begun to bulge ominously. The day after the Dolly announcement, then-President Clinton directed the National Bioethics Advisory Commission (NBAC) to examine the legal and ethical aspects of cloning and to prepare recommendations to guard against the misuse of cloning technology, all within ninety days![43] Clinton, as an interim measure, also issued a directive to all executive departments and agencies blocking the use of federal funds to clone human beings.[44]

The NBAC Report recommended adoption of federal legislation to ban the use of SCNT cloning to create children but did not advocate that such a ban be made permanent.[45] The NBAC Report recognized that inasmuch as SCNT cloning "could represent a means of human reproduction for some people, limitations on that choice must be made only when the societal benefits of prohibition clearly outweigh the value of maintaining the private nature of such highly personal decisions."[46] Furthermore, "in light of some arguably compelling cases for attempting to clone a human being" via SCNT, "the ethics of policy making must strike a balance between the values society wishes to reflect and issues of privacy and the freedom of individual choice."[47]

Clinton took action on the NBAC Report's recommendations by sending Congress a draft piece of legislation entitled the Cloning Prohibition Act of 1997 (CPA).[48] The CPA would have banned the use of nuclear transplantation technology to create a human being, whether by the private or the public sectors, through the exercise of Congress's power to regulate interstate commerce.[49] The CPA would have made it unlawful for "any person or other legal entity, public or private, to perform or use somatic cell nuclear transfer with the intent of introducing the product of that transfer into a woman's womb or in any other way creating a human being."[50] It defined SCNT as "the transfer of a cell nucleus from a somatic cell into an egg from which the nucleus has been removed,"[51] thereby not including embryo splitting among the forms of prohibited cloning activity, and not precluding the creation of clones from human embryonic cells. By its terms, the CPA would have expired five years after enactment.[52]

Congress never enacted the CPA, nor did it enact any of the other anticloning bills put forth by various legislators up until 2001.[53] These bills took various forms, but generally speaking, they can be grouped into two main types. Some of the bills reflect the view that research involving human embryos is fundamentally wrong and that embryos, as a form of human life, deserve protection from tampering. These bills would have banned any form of human cloning, whether involving research alone or attempts to create an individual from human cloning.[54] The other main type of proposed legislation is concerned with the end result of cloning, rather than research; these bills focus on banning the implantation of cloned embryos, not creation of those embryos.[55]

With this introduction into the legal response to cloning, I will save the remainder for subsequent chapters, in which I will delve into the actual text of the various laws in considerable detail for those interested. In chapter 2, I set forth and analyze the laws enacted in several individual states within the United States with regard to cloning. Chapter 2 also covers the federal response, including the most recent federal legislation and the Food and Drug Administration's foray into the realm of cloning. I examine cloning laws in other nations and internationally in chapter 3. For now, let us return to some of the reasons there has been such a tumult.

## JUSTIFICATIONS ADVANCED FOR ANTICLONING LEGAL MEASURES

There has been no shortage of arguments in favor of banning or drastically restricting efforts to clone human beings. This is one of those subjects on which virtually everyone appears to have an opinion—often a strongly held opinion—and the arguments have taken various forms, which often blend together and resist strict compartmentalization. I will summarize the anticloning arguments here and attempt to categorize them for the sake of facilitating analysis.

### Religious, Moral, and Ethical Grounds

Many of the reasons marshaled in opposition to cloning of humans, or to experimentation on and killing of human embryos, are directly rooted in religious, ethical, or moral beliefs that this is just something people should not do. Whether couched in terms to the effect that such cloning is tantamount to "playing God" and should be reserved for God alone,[56] or phrased in less overtly religious language,[57] this type of argument represents deep personal convictions. The people who hold these beliefs are convinced of the fundamental correctness of their position, and both the people and the sincerity of their beliefs are entitled to great respect.

To some degree, adherents of this view also tend to be pro-life and against liberalized abortion-on-demand. It may be more accurate to state that among the pro-life group, there is also overwhelming opposition to cloning of humans. This is because anticloning sentiment is much more widespread than even the basic pro-life position, which itself is held by a substantial portion of the populace, depending on exactly how the issue is framed. Many pro-choice people are also adamantly opposed to cloning, on the basis of the perceived degradation and exploitation of human beings for unwise or inappropriate purposes.

On the pro-life side of the anticloning coalition, people who believe that it is wrong for persons intentionally to end the life of an unborn human fetus under many or all circumstances also often believe it is wrong, or at least not constitutionally protected, to create human life using "unnatural" or "artificial" means. For some, this belief extends to in vitro fertilization as well.[58] In part, this objection to in vitro fertilization stems from the fact that there are inevitably some failures along the way, with some number—even sizable numbers—of human embryos created and eventually discarded during the process.

At present, this point applies with much greater force to cloning than to in vitro fertilization. As previously mentioned, cloning by SCNT is still a process with a very low success rate, even when cloning frogs or sheep. Until and unless major advancements are made in the technology and technique, it is reasonable to expect that there will be large numbers of failures, that is, discarded or even deformed embryos, for every healthy cloned individual that survives, whether frog, sheep, or human being. Of course, where the objective is not a successful pregnancy and live birth but rather medical or scientific research, as in therapeutic cloning, this problem is greatly intensified.

Experimentation on human beings has long been considered unethical, absent the voluntary consent of the subject with legal capacity to give consent.[59] Moreover, experimentation is not ethical where it would be likely to result in injury, disability, or death of the experimental subject.[60] Some commentators see these principles relating to the dignity and rights of unborn humans as powerful arguments in favor of anticloning legislation.[61]

Among the core problems with this loosely knit web of objections is the inexorable tendency of opposition to cloning to lead to opposition to other things. To the extent anticloning sentiment is rooted in religious doctrine, there are important First Amendment concerns implicated in any marriage of religion and state-sponsored legal action. If religion-based belief is permitted to manifest itself in a ban of cloning, then similar arguments could next target in vitro fertilization, stem-cell research, or abortion. As I will discuss later in this book, there are doctrinal strands that tie cloning to each of these, and more.

Moreover, anticloning sentiment is often not even based on any clearly articulated principles. Opponents of cloning simply refer to the putative immorality of it, as if it were intuitively obvious to everyone, and sometimes offer by way of explanation something on the order of "It just seems wrong." Unfortunately, such vague, emotion-rooted, gut-level aversion is a poor foundation on which to build a set of legal requirements. The same type of sincerely held yet poorly defined abhorrence has led, in the America of not so long ago, to antimiscegenation laws, legal ownership of and commerce in slaves, legally sanctioned racial segregation, denial of equal rights to African Americans, denial of suffrage to women, and many other grave injustices. During the 1960s, a popular slogan among young people was, "If it feels good, do it." That was a poor rule by which to live, and so is its opposite: "If it feels bad, ban it."

## Legal Grounds

Some commentators have posited legal objections to the reproductive cloning of humans. These concerns focus on questions such as the rights of the child of cloning, issues concerning inheritance and parenthood, and related problems.[62] These are ancillary to the other anticloning arguments and are probably insufficient in isolation to justify such legislation. However, because they could form a portion of a broader, more comprehensive justification for a ban, it is appropriate to discuss them briefly here.

For example, legislatures might assert that a reproductive cloning ban is necessary to prevent physical harm to the children of cloning. If these children are at greater risk of birth defects, including deformities, and susceptibility to illness and early death, this could be adduced as evidence in favor of a ban on cloning.[63] Clearly, there is a legitimate public policy cause for concern if the cloning of humans is accompanied by a high probability of serious abnormalities, but this objection argues for temporary restrictions and narrowly tailored regulations while further animal experiments are conducted, rather than a permanent and all-encompassing ban. If the problems eventually can be solved, the restrictions and regulations should allow for that possibility. Low success rates in the union of DNA and enucleated egg, the implantation of the resulting embryo in a woman's uterus, and the carrying of the fetus to term without miscarriage could all form an additional basis for restrictions or temporary moratoria, albeit with less legal justification, for reasons to be discussed later.

Another legal concern involves potential confusion as to family lineage and kinship, and the impact such confusion could have on all the rights and duties implicated in the familial relationship within the legal system. Would the donor of the nuclear DNA be recognized as a relative of the child of cloning, to a greater extent or to the same extent as the donor of the enucleated egg (which contributes the m-DNA as well as cytoplasm to the child of cloning)? Does the contribution of nuclear DNA or enucleated egg by a third party, that is, someone not part of the family unit within which the child will be reared, entitle the contributor to any rights or bind the contributor with any responsibilities regarding the child? These issues are relevant to varying degrees depending on who is donating the nuclear DNA and who is donating the enucleated egg.

Some scenarios present negligible risk of legal dispute as to lineage and kinship, as where parents clone their own child, using the child as the donor of the nuclear DNA and the mother as the source of the enucleated egg. The child born through these means would still have the same biological parents as the first child, with no outside source of DNA or m-DNA.[64] In other situations, as where a person clones himself or herself, perhaps as a method of reproduction for a single person or an infertile or same-sex couple, or a couple wishes to clone an unrelated third party, the kinship issues can be somewhat more complex. Still, the law has proved robust to the challenge of sorting out gestational, genetic, and social parentage in modern varieties of assisted reproduction, such as gamete donation and surrogate motherhood, and cloning is not fundamentally distinguishable from—and may in some respects be *superior* to—other forms of assisted reproduction.[65] Artificial insemination, in vitro fertilization, gamete intrafallopian transfer, and zygote intrafallopian transfer all have become familiar means of assisted reproduction, each with technological and legal advantages and disadvantages,[66] and cloning would be no exception.

## Slippery-Slope Grounds

The prospect of cloning humans seems to have special power to provoke slippery-slope arguments in opposition. Largely because of rampant ignorance concerning the facts of life as applied to cloning, an array of horrific consequences has been posited as a possible if not probable outgrowth of legal cloning of humans.

An oft-repeated concern is that cloning could be employed to mass-produce people, particularly those with tendencies toward violence and evil, such as an army of Hitlers.[67] The (false) assumption, fed by the fantasies of popular entertainments, is that cloning allows for an easy, assembly-line type of replication of people, almost akin to running off limitless copies on a photocopier machine.[68] A corollary of this combines anti-cloning opinion with fear of modern genetic engineering to yield the horrific prospect of legions of transgenically enhanced superwarriors or archterrorists.[69] On this point, suffice it to say that the genes have not as yet been identified that specifically code for such peculiar traits as (1) extraordinary susceptibility to brainwashing and submission to an evil supervillain's commands, (2) affinity for self-destruction, (3) skill in modern weapon usage, (4) Hercules-like physical strength, and (5) Bruce Lee degree of adeptness in martial arts. Maybe someday.

Given the extreme examples of eugenics during the twentieth century, some fear that cloning would be widely used to select for, and select against, particular genetic traits, possibly through governmental coercion. If modern societies produced compulsory sterilization, what would prevent them from harnessing cloning to generate the genotypes and pheno-types they favor?[70]

Another objection posits that legal cloning would usher in an era in which cloning becomes a serious competitor to, if not the predominant form of, human reproduction. Under what might be termed the "sex is dead" scenario, children of cloning would become so numerous relative to the children produced through traditional means that the human gene pool would be impoverished. Certain genotypes would be replicated repeatedly, swamping the gene pool with sameness. Genetic diversity would diminish, leaving the human species with less resources for natural selection and evolution, and thus less capable of evolving resistance to disease or changed environmental factors, or other eventualities calling for a deep and varied reservoir of genetic raw materials.[71] Furthermore, society itself would become less diverse, less interesting, and less genuine as people were replicated from a limited number of popular templates.[72] The "sex is dead" theory and its prophesies that the gene pool will be drained might be persuasive but for the fact that, as compared with con-ventional coital reproduction, cloning will always be (1) much more expensive, (2) much riskier, and (3) much less fun.

## Psychosocial Grounds

Several potential psychosocial problems have been adumbrated, center-ing around the difficulties a child of cloning might encounter.[73] In that there has never been a successful cloning of a human being, one is entirely free and without fear of definitive contrary evidence to postulate a host of psychosocial challenges that might be collectively denominated post-cloning syndrome (PCS).

Persons afflicted with PCS might suffer from a reduced sense of self, or at least a lessened sense of individuality or personal autonomy.[74] A sen-tient human being who learns at some stage of life that he or she was launched on the path toward birth by SCNT rather than good old-fashioned fertilization might feel like a product rather than a person. There would be the knowledge that someone else has the identical com-plement of nuclear DNA (albeit not m-DNA) and perhaps, that others also possess the exact same set of DNA in their nuclei. For these people, there could be psychological trauma in knowing that they are not completely unique in the genetic composition of their nuclei, that is, that they are in roughly the same situation as identical twins have always been.[75]

A related aspect of PCS might be the harm to a person's psyche from knowing that he or she has the same nuclear DNA as a particular individ-ual and presumably is foreordained to the same genetically determined path in life. Assuming the identity of the DNA donor is known to the child of cloning, he or she would be able to view the future to some extent by looking at the donor: "Dad, am I really doomed to look like *you* in thirty-five years? Gross!" Predisposition to a variety of genetically based medical conditions, adult physical appearance, aging patterns, intellectual capacity, and other important phenotypic manifestations of a person's genetic material would be on display. Perhaps foreknowledge of some of these attributes would be disturbing, assuming that the DNA donor represents a future that is frightening or unappealing to the child of cloning.[76] Of course, much the same thing happens in all biological parent-child relationships, and this "living mirror into the future" syndrome has not proved to be an overwhelming burden for most children, although it might be more pronounced for children of cloning.

The opposite problem could eventuate when a person is cloned specifically to manifest a particular trait and then he or she does not fulfill this destiny, whether through injury, illness, or other of life's vicissitudes. The person could experience pressure to conform to the desired life template and suffer feelings of rejection and inadequacy when he or she does not.[77] Particularly where the person is aware that he or she was intended specifically to excel at some special field of endeavor, there may be a sense of being, in essence, a defective product, and parents or siblings might treat the person as such.[78] Again, excessive parental expectations of and pressures on children is hardly a new phenomenon. Parents have always had children and brought them up specifically to carry on in their footsteps, take over the family business, uphold or regain the family honor, and fulfill many other forms of vicarious living. Does any of this sound familiar? No doubt this type of pressure has caused problems for countless generations of children and parents alike, and would do the same in the cloning situation. Whether it would be much worse than, or different in kind from, the time-honored mode of parent-induced stress on children is far from certain.

Potentially, PCS could entail some psychological problems (and advantages) arising out of a parent's excessive insight into the feelings and thoughts of a child of cloning. If the DNA donor and recipient experience some mysterious mental or emotional link, similar to that often reported by identical twins, some children might be disturbed by heightened parental awareness of their innermost selves and view it as a sort of psychic invasion of privacy. Conversely, many identical twins enjoy their special intangible closeness, and if parents and children of cloning have a similar experience, it could be helpful in bridging the gap between the generations and ameliorating the difficult misunderstandings that so often plague the parent-child relationship, particularly during adolescence.

It is possible that PCS could also entail psychological distress generated by the treatment the child of cloning receives from others in society. It may be that these children would be the target of insults and cruel jokes and that some "normal" people would shun them or otherwise make them feel unwelcome. They might be ostracized because of their genetic origin. Such unfair and discriminatory actions might be especially common, and especially damaging, during the childhood years when youthful people can be prone to single out others who are perceived as different. This, of course, presupposes that people beyond the immediate family would be aware that a particular child began life through the cloning process. But this would not be the case unless someone in the family chose to reveal the information publicly—there would be no way someone could discern a clonal origin merely by looking at a person. Even striking physical similarities between the DNA donor and the child of cloning—the "spitting image" or "chip off the old block" phenomenon—could plausibly be attributed to traditional family resemblance, just as has always been recognized. Public disclosure of a clonal origin would be a matter within the discretion of the family, absent an ethical breach by a health care provider with knowledge of the situation or DNA analysis.

It also has been suggested, paradoxically, that cloning would at once diminish parental ties and expand parental control over the genetic destiny of children. The NBAC Report included a "concern about a degradation in the quality of parenting and family life," with impersonalization of the parent-child relationship and children being only conditionally accepted by their parents, because of the supposed manufacturing-like aspects of the cloning process.[79] This view holds that children of cloning might be viewed as manufactured products or possessions, not as people, with less-than-usual tolerance of deviations from parental expectations or, to use the language of manufacturing and contracts, specifications.[80] It also decries the "total parental control over the genetic destiny of the child" that cloning offers.[81]

One extreme and disturbing variant of this type of objection centers around child sexual abuse. In situations whereby a couple clones one member of the pair, the fear is that at some point, the other member of the parental pair will become sexually attracted to the child of cloning. Because the child is genetically almost identical to the person's sexual partner, and because presumably the person was at least at one time enticed by the other's physical attributes, this situation is postulated as a recipe for incest and other forms of child sexual abuse.[82] However, this argument downplays some key facts: (1) the parent would be at least one generation older than the child, and much older than when he or she first became attracted to his or her partner; (2) the child would be reared by the parents throughout life, and only gradually come to resemble the non-cloned parent's partner as he or she appeared at the age of initial attraction, by which time both parents would be very much in the parental mode with regard to the child; (3) we are attracted to people not only because of their physical appearance but by a host of other features largely unrelated to genotype; (4) our preferences in sexual partners evolve over time; and (5) we can be parents of very attractive children, cloned or not, and yet be completely capable of resisting any spark of an impulse to treat them as potential sex partners, for powerful reasons of morality, religion, and aversion to criminal penalties.

The President's Council on Bioethics, formed by President George W. Bush, summarized its opinions concerning reproductive cloning, or, as they call it, cloning-to-produce-children, as follows in its 2002 report:

*Problems of identity and individuality:* Cloned children may experience serious problems of identity both because each will be genetically virtually identical to a human being who has already lived and because the expectations for their lives may be shadowed by constant comparisons to the life of the "original."

*Concerns regarding manufacture:* Cloned children would be the first human beings whose entire genetic makeup is selected in advance. They might come to be considered more like products of a designed manufacturing process than "gifts" whom their parents are prepared to accept as they are. Such an attitude toward children could also contribute to increased commercialization and industrialization of human procreation.

*The prospect of a new eugenics:* Cloning, if successful, might serve the ends of individualized eugenic enhancement, either by avoiding the genetic defects that may arise when human reproduction is left to chance, or by preserving and perpetuating outstanding genetic traits, including the possibility, someday in the future, of using cloning to perpetuate genetically engineered enhancements.

*Troubled family relations:* By confounding and transgressing the natural boundaries between generations, cloning could strain the social ties between them. Fathers could become "twin brothers" to their "sons"; mothers could give birth to their genetic twins; and grandparents would also be the "genetic parents" of their grandchildren. Genetic relation to only one parent might produce special difficulties for family life.

*Effects on society:* Cloning-to-produce-children would affect not only the direct participants, but also the entire society that allows or supports this activity. Even if practiced on a small scale, it could affect the way society looks at children and set a precedent for future nontherapeutic interventions into the human genetic endowment or novel forms of control by one generation over the next. In the absence of wisdom regarding these matters, prudence dictates caution and restraint.[83]

The conclusion was that "For some or all of these reasons, the Council is in full agreement that cloning-to-produce-children is not only unsafe but also morally unacceptable, and ought not to be attempted."[84] Their opinion essentially mirrors the various anticloning arguments I have outlined in this chapter.

## WHY WOULD ANYONE WANT TO CLONE A HUMAN?

Given this rather extensive list of arguments against the cloning of humans, one might presume that it is chiefly a dead issue—few would want to clone a person if these arguments are valid.[85] Yet cloning is very much a live issue, both figuratively and literally. There are several reasons certain people would wish to have a child through the intervention of cloning technology.[86]

Initially, of course, some people are interested in becoming the first successfully to clone a human being, or the first person to be cloned. Whether driven by scientific zeal, a desire for fame and a place in history, the yearning for riches, or some combination thereof, there is a special allure associated with being the first to cross a chasm of this magnitude. But this impetus would quickly dissipate once the chasm is conquered. Few remember the second or third person to master any significant scientific or technological challenge. So let us consider what other reasons might persist beyond the pioneering phase of human clonal research.

There may be a desire by family members to clone a beloved dying relative, especially a child. The impetus to clone would be particularly strong where the family is unable to have another child through traditional procreation, but it would be a natural reaction of loving parents to the impending death of any child under any circumstances. Parents of a child critically injured in an accident or attack, or stricken with a devastating communicable disease, may have a powerful urge for something approaching a second chance. By cloning the dying child, the parents could feel that they are in some measure providing their child with a second chance at a full life. Simultaneously, they would afford themselves a second chance to experience parenting and relating to their child, this time for many more years. Obviously, the new child would have a new brain, with no recollection of any experiences from the life of the first child, but the genetic identity of the two would be a powerful factor moving grief-stricken parents toward the cloning decision.

Couples or individuals may also want to use cloning as a means of having children, apart from any desire to replace a lost loved one. Presumably, cloning would be an attractive option mostly in situations that do not present many alternatives; it would be a rarity, not the norm.[87] Given the prohibitively high expense and low success rate likely to be associated with cloning for the foreseeable future, people are not apt to attempt cloning unless it is the only way to have, as it were, "children of their own." If there is a social stigma that arises against cloning, that would be a further disincentive. Prospective parents would probably exhaust their options regarding conventional procreation, adoption, and in vitro fertilization before turning to cloning, absent a strong personal philosophical drive to explore a new reproductive frontier.

One exception might be in the case of a couple, one member of whom is a carrier of a genetic disease, and who do not want to accept the risk of transmitting the disease or the gene to their children.[88] They could clone the member who lacks the disease-linked gene and thus ensure that their child will not possess the undesired gene, or, if they already have a child who is free of the gene, they could clone that child.[89] Situations in which the combination of two recessive copies of a gene that were each carried unexpressed by the two parents constitute one of the most common classes of genetic disorders, encompassing serious conditions such as sickle cell anemia, cystic fibrosis, Tay-Sachs disease, and phenylketonuria (PKU), and cloning would greatly reduce the incidence of these harms.[90] Cloning would also significantly lower the risk of the other most prevalent variety of genetic abnormalities, Down's syndrome (the presence of an abnormal number of chromosomes).[91] Thus, in contradistinction to the fears that cloning would be unacceptably dangerous, with myriad dead or deformed embryos and babies among the casualties, cloning may actually be safer and less risky than even coital reproduction under some circumstances.[92]

Another exception could involve couples, at least one member of which cannot produce viable gametes. Cloning would enable these couples to refrain from relying on anonymous donors of sperm (as in a sperm bank) or egg donors from outside the couple and would allow the couple to use only the genetic material of one member of the couple. Moreover, if the male contributes the DNA and the female the enucleated ovum, the resulting child would have the father's nuclear DNA and the mother's m-DNA, permitting both members to contribute to the child's genetic makeup. Likewise, both members of lesbian couples could contribute to their child's genetic structure by having one woman donate the DNA and the other the enucleated egg.

The majority of people exploring the cloning option would comprise infertile heterosexual couples, single persons, and homosexual life partners,[93] just as they do for the more well-established alternatives to conventional reproduction. The same basic yearnings that drive people to adopt, to become foster parents, to employ surrogate mothers, or to attempt in vitro fertilization would apply to the decision to clone. But this is not to say that all the alternatives have identical appeal to all people. Many choose to adopt despite an ability to procreate because of a desire to help a child in need who has already been born, as my wife and I have done with our own daughters from the Peoples' Republic of China. In vitro fertilization is attractive to people who wish to have the genes of both members of the couple represented in the couple's children but who cannot do so without the aid of this technique. Cloning would be a way for single persons not in a coupled relationship to contribute their genes to their own children, or for one member of same-sex couples to do the same.[94]

Each of these forms of having children satisfies certain profound human needs, each in its own way. The tendency of people to prefer one means over the others may be influenced by religious beliefs, societal norms, and the importance to each person of passing one's own genes on to the next generation. This last variable is paramount for some, whether rooted in a belief in the primacy of genes as the determinants of one's life or in a conviction that a child is more fully one's "own" if that child possesses the genes of the parent(s). This position can attain its fullest expression on the individual level in the case of cloning because no one's genes other than those of the DNA donor will be present in the child.

Adherents of genetic determinism may offer another reason in support of the cloning of humans: this technique maximizes our ability to ensure that certain admired persons have the opportunity to transmit their genes across the generational boundary. Of course, which persons are admired is very much a personal decision in the eyes and mind of the beholder. For some, there is no doubt (presumably after long and careful study, comparison, and analysis) that the one person on earth whose genes absolutely must be replicated is, in fact, that person. Perhaps a substantial number of other people would agree in principle regarding some subset of such me-first potential cloners—Nobel laureates, Pulitzer Prize winners, and decorated heroes, for instance. In other cases, a person's lofty view of his or her own unique merit may be shared by no one else, yet that person may be totally committed to donating genetic self-copies to the world of tomorrow.

A variant of this theme would involve not a sense of egocentric superiority so much as a desire for physical immortality. Some people, in coming to terms with their own mortality, might conclude that they possess the means to live on through cloning themselves. Either owing to a misguided misunderstanding of cloning or a powerful adherence to genetic determinism or genetic essentialism,[95] these persons could decide to clone themselves as a form of proactive reincarnation. Such belief in the primacy of genetics may be quite misguided,[96] but it can also be tenacious[97] and may lead to a cloning decision. This could be conceptualized as a contemporary manifestation of the poet's plea that we "do not go gentle into that good night" but rather "rage, rage against the dying of the light."[98] If already terminally ill, the DNA donor might entrust the clonally originated child to the care of a close relative or friend, with the injunction to bring up the child so as to honor and emulate the donor. Or if the donor still enjoys sufficiently good health and the time to rear the child, the donor can personally teach the child in the manner deemed appropriate, complete with information about the donor's own family history and traditions, likes and dislikes, and various other life patterns.

Possibly some devoted followers of particular individuals might feel so strongly about their idol's value that they would be willing to pay to clone them or serve as their surrogate mothers. This would have to be an especially potent form of devotion because of the great expense involved and the requirement of finding a willing surrogate mother to carry every SCNT embryo to term, one embryo per surrogate at a time. Presumably, the consent and cooperation of the object of such hero worship would be essential to supply the requisite DNA in a viable form. It is highly unlikely that anyone could be cloned without his or her knowledge and consent, absent the collusion of health care providers with access to living somatic cell samples.[99]

One can imagine some sinister examples in which a modern-day despot, zealot, terrorist, or archcriminal either attempts to create multiple self-clones or is urged to do so by disciples. Particularly charismatic, delusional, powerful, ruthless, and/or wealthy figures might be able to spearhead a successful self-cloning campaign on a limited scale. One might denominate this the Hitler Syndrome or the Osama bin Laden Plot, with the name of the ultravillain subject to whatever current events and cultural debates are dominant. On a less-ominous note, certain celebrities might enjoy an extreme strain of hero worship in which their fans provide funds and wombs for their cloning. Sometimes, such pronounced devotion does not blossom until after the death of the idol; in these cases, cloning would be impossible unless somehow the necessary cell samples had been obtained in advance by forward-looking persons. Thus, what we might call the Elvis Option would often be impracticable, notwithstanding the posthumous devotion some celebrities attract.

Additional utilitarian motivations for cloning may exist. For example, some people might want to create a clone of themselves for the primary or secondary purpose of securing a compatible potential donor of organs such as kidneys. Because of the genetic identity of donor and child of cloning, there should be drastically diminished risks of rejection of the transplanted organ in these situations. One presumes that this use of cloning would be limited to nonessential organs, blood, and bone marrow and that the law would never allow a living, viable, child of cloning individual to have his or her heart or liver harvested for the benefit of the donor, exactly as such abominable practices are now illegal for any children; no amendment of the law whatsoever is necessary to protect children of cloning from harmful or involuntary organ harvestation. Aside from the extreme polar situation wherein a person creates a self-clone for the express purpose of killing the child of cloning and cannibalizing him or her for vital organs, and presuming both the proper normal care and education of the child and the voluntary and informed consent on the part of the child to the donation of any nonessential organs and other bodily components, this could be viewed as a legitimate reason for cloning. As an actuating motive, it lacks the emotional appeal of the naked clone scenario soon to be discussed, but it may be an understandable rationale, especially in the case of individuals with particularly acute vulnerability to certain serious medical conditions.

It is possible that cloning could also be employed to clone only specific tissues or organs, not as part of an entire freestanding postbirth organisms but as discrete and isolated entities. Indeed, in early 2002 there were some preliminary reports that researchers in Massachusetts had used cells derived from cloned cow embryos to grow kidney-like organs that function and are not rejected when implanted into adult cows.[100] If verified and perfected, such methodology could allow the use of cloning to produce "personalized, genetically matched organs for transplantation," or, more precisely, reimplantation into the same individual from which the organ's DNA was originally extracted, and might dramatically reduce the need to rely on organ donors in the future.[101] Similarly, cloning may be highly useful in stem-cell research, which could hold the key to unlocking many intractable medical problems. Such therapeutic cloning may be an enormously powerful tool for medical science.

All of the motivations discussed here would necessarily entail use of the SCNT and not the embryo-splitting method of cloning. This is because only the SCNT technique allows the cloning of an individual who has already been born. Embryo splitting can create multiple people with the identical genotype, but the source must be embryonic cells of a very early stage. Once an embryo develops beyond the blastomere phase and consists of more than just a few cells, embryo splitting is no longer an option—and this is certainly true for later-stage fetuses, newborns, babies, toddlers, children, adolescents, and adults. Moreover, most if not all of the reasons that people might want to clone do not apply to the embryo-splitting method. Rather than replicating the genes of a known person—whether self, life partner, a child, or an admired individual—the embryo-splitting technique clones an embryo, essentially making multiple children (identical twins, triplets, quadruplets, etc.) out of what ordinarily would only become one child. And an embryo, of course, is produced through the union of egg and sperm cells, with an equal genetic contribution from both mother and father, that is, a new, unique genotype, not a replication of any one person's genes.

Some of the aforementioned reasons for cloning humans are of broader and deeper appeal than others. Many people may empathize with bereaved parents over their desire for their dead child to live again, in a manner of speaking. There is also a poignancy in the longing of people to have children to love and nurture, despite the obstacles nature or society has placed in their path. The other goals of cloning might not be as popular, either in terms of the number of people who would be ready to implement them at their own expense and risk or in the level of approval they would attract in public opinion. Some would be unambiguously unpopular, to say the least. But this chapter has established that there are reasons people might want to clone human beings, and that these reasons are both complex and varied.

The next two chapters take an in-depth look at the legislation that either bans or severely circumscribes the cloning of humans, first state by state, next on the national level within the United States, and finally in other nations of the world. These chapters prepare us to analyze the wisdom and, with regard to the laws within the United States, the constitutionality of the restrictions they have imposed.

## NOTES

1. In the animated film *Pinocchio* (1940), Jiminy Cricket uttered these words of astonishment when he witnessed the Blue Fairy bringing a wooden puppet, Pinocchio, to life. Despite persistent rumors, there is no credible evidence that Pinocchio himself was a clone of his maker, Geppetto.

2. *See* John Charles Kunich, *Mother Frankenstein, Doctor Nature, and the Environmental Law of Genetic Engineering,* 74 S. CAL. L. REV. 807, 813–17 (2001) (describing vocal, even violent, public opposition to transgenic technology despite the paucity of scientific evidence against it).

3. The specter of irresponsible scientists "playing God" was highlighted in the remarks of physicist Richard Seed when he announced his intention to open a clinic to clone humans. He stated, "In the first two chapters of the Old Testament, we learned that God made man in his own image. He intended the union of man and God. Is this union spiritual or in body? I think it is talking about the body. That we would become God in body and spirit." Seed indicated that cloning is the first step toward "indefinite life extension" in which man becomes one with God, with almost as much power as God. Despite the implausibility of a physicist undertaking to win the race to the first cloned human, Seed's remarks were quite successful in attracting the spotlight of public attention. *See* Gene Weingarten, *Strange Egg: A House Call to the Mysterious Doctor Seed, the Man Who Wants to Clone Humans,* WASH. POST, Jan. 25, 1998, at F1.

4. Kunich, *supra* note 2, at 813–17.

5. Rick Weiss, *First Human Embryos Are Cloned in U.S.,* WASH. POST, Nov. 26, 2001, at A1. Researchers at Advanced Cell Technology in Worcester, Massachusetts, performed the research as a step in the process of generating embryonic stem cells that could be used to create various human tissues for therapeutic purposes. *Id.*

6. *Id. See* Rick Weiss, *Mass. Firm's Disclosure Renews Cloning Debate; Bush Reiterates Support for Ban on Use of Embryos,* WASH. POST, Nov. 27, 2001, at A3 (discussing reaction to the announcement from President George W. Bush, other political leaders worldwide, the Vatican, and other religious organizations).

7. *See* Clifford Krauss, *Earthlings, the Prophet of Clone is Alive in Quebec,* N.Y. TIMES, Feb. 24, 2003, at A4; Richard Jerome et al., *Maybe Baby; History or Hoax? A Bizarre Sect That Believes in Space Aliens Announces the Birth of the First Human Clone, a Girl Named Eve,* PEOPLE, Jan. 13, 2003 at 58; Tim Friend, *Proof Still Not Given of First Human Clone,* USA TODAY, Jan. 6, 2003 at 2A.

8. *See, e.g.,* Andrea L. Bonnicksen, CRAFTING A CLONING POLICY: FROM DOLLY TO STEM CELLS (Georgetown University Press, 2002); Glenn McGee (ed.), THE HUMAN CLONING DEBATE (Berkeley Hills Books, 2002); GREGORY E. PENCE (ed.), FLESH OF MY FLESH: THE ETHICS OF CLONING HUMANS, A READER (Rowman and Littlefield, 1998); Lori B. Andrews, THE CLONE AGE: ADVENTURES IN THE NEW WORLD OF REPRODUCTIVE TECHNOLOGY (Henry Holt, 1999); Leon R. Kass and James Q. Wilson, THE ETHICS OF HUMAN

CLONING (AEI Press, 1998); Andrew Kimbrell, THE HUMAN BODY SHOP: THE CLONING, ENGINEERING, AND MARKETING OF LIFE (Regnery, 1998); and Francis Fukuyama, OUR POSTHUMAN FUTURE: CONSEQUENCES OF THE BIOTECHNOLOGY REVOLUTION (Farrar, Straus and Giroux, 2002).

9. *See* Katheryn D. Katz, *The Clonal Child: Procreative Liberty and Asexual Reproduction*, 8 ALB. L. J. SCI. & TECH. 1, 15–23 (1997) (setting forth and debunking several popular misconceptions regarding both the meaning and the application of cloning of humans).

10. *See* Committee on Science, Engineering, and Public Policy, SCIENTIFIC AND MEDICAL ASPECTS OF HUMAN REPRODUCTIVE CLONING 24 (National Academy Press, 2002) (HUMAN REPRODUCTIVE CLONING).

11. SCNT was the method employed by the Advanced Cell Technology team to generate the first cloned human embryos in late 2001. *See* Weiss, *supra* note 5.

12. Anne Lawton, *The Frankenstein Controversy: The Constitutionality of a Federal Ban on Cloning*, 87 KY. L. J. 277, 284–89 (1998/1999) (outlining the various types of cloning—molecular or gene cloning, cellular cloning, blastomere separation or embryo splitting, and somatic cell nuclear transplantation cloning). Of these techniques, only embryo splitting and SCNT have a potential application to the cloning of humans. *Id.*

13. Hans Spemann, EMBRYONIC DEVELOPMENT AND INDUCTION (Garland 1988).

14. Lawton, *supra* note 11, at 284–89.

15. President's Council on Bioethics, *Human Cloning and Human Dignity: An Ethical Inquiry*, chapter 2 (July 2002), <http://www.bioethics.gov/Reports/cloningreport/index.html>.

16. *Id.*

17. The advent of Dolly the cloned sheep has inflicted upon us many puns and arguably clever plays on words, often involving variations on the theme of "Hello, Dolly!" and whether there should be more than one "ewe."

18. President's Council on Bioethics, *supra* note 14.

19. Lawton, *supra* note 11, at 287.

20. *Id. See* HUMAN REPRODUCTIVE CLONING, *supra* note 9, at 25–26.

21. *Id.* Embryo splitting has been employed successfully to produce normal adult sheep and cows. Additionally, researchers have cloned human embryos, mostly at the two-cell blastomere stage, but none of the resulting embryos were permitted to develop for longer than six days. *Id.*, at 288. *See also* Kathy A. Fackelmann, *Researchers 'Clone' Human Embryos*, 144 SCI. NEWS 276, 276 (1993); Gina Kolata, CLONE: THE ROAD TO DOLLY AND THE PATH AHEAD 175–78 (William Morrow & Co. 1998).

22. *See* Lawton, *supra* note 11, at 281–83, for a concise summary of the basics of the role of DNA in reproduction.

23. *See* HUMAN REPRODUCTIVE CLONING, *supra* note 9, at 25.

24. *See* National Bioethics Advisory Committee, CLONING HUMAN BEINGS: REPORT AND RECOMMENDATIONS OF THE NATIONAL BIOETHICS ADVISORY COMMISSION 13–38 (National Bioethics Advisory Commission, 1997) (NBAC Report).

25. *See* HUMAN REPRODUCTIVE CLONING, *supra* note 9, at 25.

26. Dr. Ian Wilmut, the principal researcher who brought the cloned sheep into being using the nucleus from an adult sheep's mammary glands, whimsically named her Dolly in honor of the country singer Dolly Parton. He explained that he could think of no mammary cells more widely known than those of Ms. Parton. *See* Michael Specter and Gina Kolata, *A New Creation: The Path to Cloning—A Special Report; After Decades of Missteps, How Cloning Succeeded,* N.Y. TIMES, Mar. 3, 1997, at A1.

27. NBAC Report, *supra* note 23, at 22.

28. *Id.*

29. *See* Lee M. Silver, REMAKING EDEN 103–4 (Avon Books 1997).

30. *See* Shirley Tilghman, *Address to the National Bioethics Advisory Commission* (Mar. 13, 1997), <http://www.all.org/nbac/970313a.htm>.

31. *See* HUMAN REPRODUCTIVE CLONING, *supra* note 9, at 25.

32. Francis C. Pizzulli, Note, *Asexual Reproduction and Genetic Engineering: A Constitutional Assessment of the Technology of Cloning,* 47 S. CAL. L. REV. 476, 484–85 (1974). Frogs long have been subjects for cloning and other embryological experiments because they produce thousands of relatively large, easily manipulated eggs at a time. As long ago as 1952, researchers removed the nuclei from a frog ovum and replaced it with the nucleus from an older embryonic cell, producing 27 tadpoles from 197 renucleated eggs. Some success was also achieved using the intestines of tadpoles for the donor nuclei, but not with the differentiated cells of adult frogs. *See* Lawton, *supra* note 11, at 289–92.

33. BBC, *Horizon: Dawn of the Clone Age* (television broadcast, Sept. 10, 1997), <http://www.bbc.co.uk/horizon/cloneagetrans.shtml>.

34. Recent researchers have claimed an 80 percent success rate among those cloned cows that survived gestation, although many embryos were spontaneously aborted during gestation. These surviving cows were reported to be as healthy and normal as any others. *See* John Whitfield, *Cloned Cows in the Pink,* Nature Science Update, <http://www.nature.com/nsu/011129/011129-1.html, 2001>; K. Inoue et al., *Faithful Expression of Imprinted Genes in Cloned Mice,* 295 SCIENCE 11, 11 (2002).

35. *See* Nick Thorpe, *Scientists Baffled by Oversized Sheep Clones,* SCOTSMAN, 28 July 1997, at 1.

36. *See* Tilghman, *supra* note 29; Sharon Begley, *Little Lamb, Who Made Thee?* NEWSWEEK, Mar. 10, 1997, at 53, 59; Helen Pearson, *Cause of Sickly Clones Contested,* Nature Science Update, <http://www.nature.com/nsu/020107/020107-10.html>.

37. *See* Terence Monmaney, *Prospect of Human Cloning Gives Birth to Volatile Issues,* L.A. TIMES, March 2, 1997, at A1.

38. See Rick Weiss, *Scottish Scientists Clone Adult Sheep: Technique's Use with Human Is Feared,* WASH. POST, Feb. 24, 1997, at A1; Ian Wilmut et al., *Viable Offspring Derived from Fetal and Adult Mammalian Cells,* 385 NATURE 810, 813 (1997).

39. *See* Lawton, *supra* note 11, at 296. For many years, prevailing scientific thought held that the process by which cells—capable of developing into anything in the early embryonic stage—gradually differentiate into specific types of cells was irreversible. Thus, a mature muscle cell was believed incapable of ever producing anything other than other muscle cells, whereas any blastomere cell could be made to develop into fully formed adults. *Id.*

40. *See* Weiss, *supra* note 37.

41. *See* Richard Saltus, *Would-Be Cloner Plans to Start with Himself,* BOSTON GLOBE, Sept. 6, 1998, at A6.

42. Dr. Severino Antinori of Italy is among the embryologists who have announced their intention to clone humans. *See* Steve Farrar, *Maverick Fertility Expert Plans First Human Clone,* SUN. TIMES (LONDON), Oct. 25, 1998, at 1. Unlike physicist Richard Seed, who apparently lacked the requisite knowledge and means to carry out his ambitious and headline-grabbing plan, Antinori is recognized as a pioneer fertility specialist who has enabled a sixty-two-year-old woman to become pregnant. Antinori, together with a professor of reproductive physiology, Dr. Panayiotis (Panos) Zanos, has vowed to pursue human cloning in an unnamed Mediterranean nation. Zanos appeared on CNN in August 2002, with a Kentucky couple whom he planned to assist with cloning, after the couple had unsuccessfully tried to have a baby through standard in vitro fertilization. *See* Rick Weiss, *U.S. Fertility Expert Announces Efforts to Clone a Human; Consortium Led by Renegade Doctor Says It Will Help Infertile Couples,* WASH. POST, Jan. 27, 2001, at A3; Nancy Gibbs, *Baby, It's You! and You, and You...,* TIME, Feb. 19, 2001, at 46; Tim Friend, *Scientist Says He Will Begin Human Cloning,* USA TODAY, Aug. 14, 2002.

43. NBAC Report, *supra* note 23, at Letter from the President.

44. *Memorandum on the Prohibition on Federal Funding for Cloning of Human Beings,* 33 WEEKLY COMP. PRES. DOC. 281 (Mar. 4, 1997).

45. NBAC Report, *supra* note 23, at 109. The commission believed that a limited ban was justified because of serious questions regarding cloning of humans but that any such ban should have an expiration date so as not to constitute an unnecessary infringement on citizens' right to procreate. *Id.*

46. *Id.,* at 107.

47. *Id.*

48. Cloning Prohibition Act of 1997, H.R. Doc. No. 105-97 (1997).

49. *Id.* 2(c), at 6.

50. *Id.* 5, at 7.

51. *Id.* 4(c), at 6–7.

52. *Id.* 8, at 8.

53. *See generally* Jennifer Cannon and Michelle Haas, *The Human Cloning Prohibition Act: Did Congress Go Too Far?* 35 HARV. J. ON LEGIS. 637 (1998).

54. *See, e.g.,* the Bond Act, S. 368, 105th Cong. 1(a) (1997); Human Cloning Research Prohibition Act, H.R. Rep. No. 105–239, at 2 (1997) (stating the amended version of H.R. 922 2(a)); Human Cloning Prohibition Act, H.R. 923, 105th Cong. (1997); Human Cloning Prohibition Act of 1998, S. 1599, 105th Cong. (1998); and the Bond/Lott Act/Human Cloning Prohibition Act, S. 1601, 105th Cong. (1998). *See also* Lawton, *supra* note 11, at 304–10.

55. *See, e.g.,* both versions of the Kennedy/Feinstein Act/Prohibition on Cloning of Human Beings Act of 1998, S. 1602, 105th Cong. (1998); S. 1611, 105th Cong. (1998). The CPA would also fall within this category. *See also* Lawton, *supra* note 11, at 310–11.

56. *See, e.g.,* Allen Verhey, *Theology after Dolly,* CHRISTIAN CENTURY, March 19–26, 1997, at 285.

57. *See, e.g.,* Leon R. Kass, *The Wisdom of Repugnance,* NEW REPUBLIC, June 2, 1997, at 17 (detailing the ethical case against the cloning of humans); Catholic

Medical Association, *Human Cloning: Position Paper of the Catholic Medical Association, reprinted in* 15 ISSUES L. & MED. 323, 323–24 (2000) (describing the cloning of human beings as a "violation of the natural moral law").

58. *See* Clarke D. Forsythe, *Legal Perspectives on Cloning: Human Cloning and the Constitution,* 32 VAL. U. L. REV. 469, 539–40 (1998).

59. *See* United States v. Brandt (The Medical Case), 2 Trials of War Criminals before the Nuremberg Military Tribunals under Control Council Law No. 10, at 181–82 (1949).

60. Warren T. Reich (ed.), 5 ENCYCLOPEDIA OF BIOETHICS, 2763 (rev. ed., MacMillan 1995).

61. *See, e.g.,* Forsythe, *supra* note 57, at 532–34.

62. *See, e.g.,* Mona S. Amer, *Breaking the Mold: Human Embryo Cloning and Its Implications for a Right to Individuality,* 43 U.C.L.A. L. REV. 1659, 1684–88 (1996).

63. Note, *Human Cloning and Substantive Due Process,* 111 HARV. L. REV. 2348, 2362–63 (1998); *see* Lori B. Andrews, *Is There a Right to Clone? Constitutional Challenges to Bans on Human Cloning,* 11 HARV. J. LAW & TECH. 643, 649–52 (1998).

64. *See* John A. Robertson, *Liberty, Identity, and Human Cloning,* 76 TEX. L. REV. 1371, 1383–84 (1998).

65. *Id.,* at 1424–30. For example, when cloning is utilized, there should generally be no question as to the identity and legal rights and duties of the DNA donor. This is not always the case with other forms of assisted reproduction, in which gametes may be obtained from anonymous and extrafamilial sources. *See, e.g.,* Thomas S. v. Robin Y., 618 N.Y.S.2d 356, 357–62 (App. Div. 1994) (order of filiation granted to a homosexual man who fathered a daughter by donating spermatozoa to a lesbian couple for artificial insemination); Jaycee B. v. Superior Ct., 49 Cal. Rptr. 2d 694, 696 (4th Dist. 1996) (dealing with an arrangement by which a married couple hired a surrogate mother to carry and give birth to a baby developed from an embryo created from the ovum and spermatozoa of anonymous donors, and the divorce of the married couple prior to the child's birth). *See* William N. Eskridge Jr. and Nan. D. Hunter, SEXUALITY, GENDER, AND THE LAW 827 (Foundation Press 1997) (discussing some of the complex parentage problems spawned by the use of artificial insemination and in vitro fertilization).

66. *See* Robert Blank and Janna C. Merrick, HUMAN REPRODUCTION, EMERGING TECHNOLOGIES, AND CONFLICTING RIGHTS 86–88 (1995); Katz, *supra* note 8, at 23–28; Elizabeth A. Pitrolo, Comment, *The Birds, the Bees, and the Deep Freeze: Is There International Consensus in the Debate over Assisted Reproductive Technologies?* 19 HOUS. J. INT'L. L. 147, 168–204 (1996).

67. *See* Michael A. Goldman, *Human Cloning: Science Fact and Fiction,* 8 S. CAL. INTERDIS. L. J. 103, 103 (1998).

68. Robertson, *supra* note 63, at 1423–24.

69. *See, e.g.,* Aldous Huxley, BRAVE NEW WORLD, 10–12 (Buccaneer Books 1932) (in which the novel describes the transgenic subservient class of citizens created by despots to do their bidding). The successful Star Wars motion picture *Episode 2: Attack of the Clones* (2002) is another in this long series of entertaining but wholly impossible fantasies regarding the awesome power and potentially catastrophic and/or hilarious abuse of cloning technology. *See also* such films (if you really must) as *The 6th Day* (2000), *Multiplicity* (1996), *The Boys from Brazil* (1978), and *Blade Runner* (1982), among many others. On the lighter side, the popular ani-

mated television comedy series *The Simpsons* poked fun at "the horrors of human cloning" in its Halloween episode that aired on November 3, 2002, on the Fox network.

70. *See* Philip R. Reilly, THE SURGICAL SOLUTION: A HISTORY OF INVOLUNTARY STERILIZATION IN THE UNITED STATES 94, 105–10 (Johns Hopkins University Press 1991) (discussing the involuntary sterilization of some 60,000 people in the United States, 1907–63, and approximately 3.5 million in Nazi Germany, 1933–45).

71. *See* George B. Johnson, Editorial, *What Rights Should a Cloned Human Have?* ST. LOUIS POST-DISPATCH, March 20, 1997, at B7; Pizzulli, *supra* note 31, at 560.

72. Pizzulli, *supra* note 31, at 559. It has become nearly obligatory in the scholarly literature on cloning to mention Michael Jordan as a likely candidate for repeated cloning. *See, e.g.,* Robertson, *supra* note 63, at 1384; Andrews, *supra* note 62, at 648. Ever the contrarian, I might offer instead the possibility of baseball superstar and new single-season home run champion Barry Bonds, although old-fashioned sexual reproduction has evidently been quite adequate to allow him to surpass beyond anyone's wildest dreams even the stellar major league record established by his father, Bobby Bonds. *See also* the similar examples of Ken Griffey Jr. and Sr., Bret and Bob Boone, and other cases in which the noncloned sons of major league baseball players far surpassed their fathers' outstanding achievements.

73. *See* Andrews, *supra* note 62, at 652–56 (hypothesizing several psychological drawbacks related to cloning and crediting their credibility); Vernon J. Ehlers, *The Case against Human Cloning,* 27 HOFSTRA L. REV. 523, 526–27 (1999).

74. NBAC Report, *supra* note 23, at ii, 66–68.

75. Robertson, *supra* note 63, at 1411–18 (describing and analyzing these objections to cloning and concluding that they are not likely to constitute sufficient justification for a ban).

76. *See generally* Lori B. Andrews, *Prenatal Screening and the Culture of Motherhood,* 47 HASTINGS L. J. 967 (1996) (examining evidence that access to genetic screening information about oneself can be psychologically harmful to a person).

77. Andrews, *supra* note 62, at 653.

78. Christine Willgoos, *FDA Regulation: An Answer to the Question of Human Cloning and Germline Gene Therapy,* 27 AM. J. L. and MED. 101, 107–8 (2001).

79. NBAC Report, *supra* note 23, at ii.

80. Forsythe, *supra* note 57, at 536–50.

81. *Id.,* at 536.

82. *See* Fukuyama, *supra* note 7.

83. President's Council on Bioethics, *supra* note 14.

84. *Id.*

85. *See* Dorothy C. Wertz, *Twenty-one Arguments against Human Cloning, and Their Responses,* THE GENE LETTER (Aug. 1998), <http://www.geneletter.com/archives/twentyonearguments.html> (listing numerous arguments in opposition to the cloning of humans and offering rebuttals to each); Katz, *supra* note 8, at 12–13.

86. *See* HUMAN REPRODUCTIVE CLONING, *supra* note 9, at 27.

87. *See* Lee M. Silver, *Popular Cloning versus Scientific Cloning in Ethical Debates,* 4 N.Y.U. J. LEGIS. & PUB. POL'Y 47, 53 (2000/2001).

88. NBAC Report, *supra* note 23, at 80.

89. Robertson, *supra* note 63, at 1379; Andrews, *supra* note 62, at 647–48.

90. *See* Kolata, *supra* note 20, at 239–42; Silver, *supra* note 28, at 103–4.

91. *See* Silver, *supra* note 28, at 103–4.

92. *See* Katz, *supra* note 8, at 12.

93. Some gay activists, such as the Clone Rights United Front, have protested anticloning legislation, seeing cloning as an opportunity for same-sex couples to experience the procreative process. *See* <http://www.clonerights.com/>; Anita Manning, *Pressing a "Right" to Clone Humans, Some Gays Foresee Reproduction Option,* USA TODAY, March 6, 1997, at 1D; Christopher Rapp, *Heterosexual Reproduction Is Now Obsolete,* HETERODOXY MAGAZINE, <http://www.clone rights.com/hetrodoxy.htm>. Some lesbians have noted the advantage of reproduction without the direct involvement of men, including anonymous sperm donors who may have undesirable genetic traits. *Id. See* Lee M. Silver, *Popular Cloning versus Scientific Cloning in Ethical Debates,* 4 N.Y.U.J. LEGIS. & PUB. POL'Y 47, 54 (2000/2001).

94. Robertson, *supra* note 63, at 1381–82 (mentioning additional possible reasons for cloning).

95. *See* NBAC Report, *supra* note 23, at 32; Steve Jones, *Arguing Ethics, Forfeiting Progress,* N.Y. TIMES, Mar. 14, 1998, at A17.

96. *See* Robert Wachbroit, *Should We Cut This Out? Human Cloning Isn't as Scary as It Sounds,* WASH. POST, Mar. 2, 1997, at C1 (describing genetic determinism as "not only false, but pernicious; it invokes memories of pseudoscientific racist and eugenic programs premised on the belief that what we value in people is entirely dependent on their genetic endowment or the color of their skin").

97. According to some polls, 30 to 40 percent of Americans believe in genetic determinism. *See* Ronald Bailey, *The Twin Paradox: What Exactly Is Wrong with Cloning People?* REASON, May 1997, at 52.

98. Dylan Thomas, COLLECTED POEMS OF DYLAN THOMAS 1934–1952 (W.W. Norton & Co. 1971).

99. It might also be possible, after a great deal of advancement in the technology of cloning, with the assistance of employees with access to minute quantities of DNA contained in shed skin or saliva as found on objects the source had touched. *See* Robertson, *supra* note 63, at 1446. (speculating that eventually, minuscule amounts of DNA from such sources as saliva residue on postage stamps might be usable for cloning).

100. Rick Weiss, *Advance in Transplant Cloning Claimed,* WASH. POST, Jan. 30, 2002, at A1.

101. *Id.* In addition to obviating the need to search for available organs, this technology would presumably eliminate most of the risk of rejection attendant upon the transplant of organs from one genetically unique individual to another.

# CHAPTER 2

# Cloning Law in the United States

## CLONING LEGISLATION STATE BY STATE

Historically, the United States has employed a federalism approach to many aspects of the law. This means that within certain boundaries set by the federal government, the states are free to legislate and regulate on many issues as they see fit. The people in some states tend to be more liberal or conservative than those in other states; they also may tend to possess other distinctive viewpoints and characteristics, which can be reflected in the laws of their state. The issue of the cloning of human beings has been an interesting example of federalism at work during the past few years as the law has struggled to stay abreast of the mercurial pace of scientific and technological advances.

Six state legislatures have already enacted specific cloning-ban legislation and in this regard have been ahead of the United States Congress. California was the first,[1] followed by Rhode Island,[2] Michigan,[3] Louisiana,[4] Virginia,[5] and Iowa,[6] in either banning the cloning of humans or imposing a moratorium on cloning within the state, with varying treatment of the SCNT and embryo-splitting techniques. At least nineteen other states[7] have since taken action at least to consider formally similar legislation, and three more[8] have passed resolutions urging the United States Congress and President Bush to enact a federal ban. Also, Missouri has prohibited the use of state funds for cloning.[9]

The following section examines the main provisions of each of the anti-cloning statutes currently on the books, state by state, followed by a brief discussion of some of the legislation still under consideration. A complete, verbatim recitation of the full text of each statute is included in appendix 1.

In this way, readers who prefer can focus on a brief summary and analysis provided here to place the law of each state in context. Other readers who require the full text of a given state's law can turn to appendix 1 for such details.

## State Legislation Already Enacted

### *California*

The California law, taken in its entirety, prohibits anyone from using SCNT (but not, by its terms, embryo splitting) to clone (or attempt to clone) a human being and from purchasing or selling an ovum, zygote, embryo, or fetus for the purpose of cloning a human being. Cloning is defined so as to mean only reproductive cloning and not cloning for research alone. It is the creation of a "human fetus" with a view toward creation of a "human being" through SCNT cloning methods that is expressly prohibited.

The law authorizes the California director of health services to levy administrative penalties of $1 million for violation on a corporation, firm, clinic, hospital, laboratory, or research facility and $250,000 on an individual. If the person or entity obtains pecuniary gain from cloning humans, an even larger penalty is authorized: twice the amount of pecuniary gain.

The California legislation also provides that violation constitutes unprofessional conduct for purposes of the Medical Practice Act. It requires city business licenses and county business licenses to be revoked for violation of the prohibition on cloning.

This law only bans reproductive cloning, not therapeutic/research cloning. The legislature explicitly stated in its original 1997 law: "It is not the intent of the Legislature that this moratorium apply to the cloning of human cells, human tissue, or human organs that would not result in the replication of an entire human being." This view was reiterated in the 2002 amendments. Thus, only SCNT cloning that could result in the birth of a live human baby is prohibited. There is no other California law that prohibits experimentation on human embryos either, whether for purposes of therapeutic cloning or otherwise.

In its initial legislation, California built in a sunset provision. The law was automatically to be repealed on January 1, 2003, unless new legislation extended its terms. However, in its 2002 amendments, California made its prohibition on human reproductive cloning and related provisions permanent. There is no longer any automatic expiration date for the California prohibition on reproductive cloning, so it is now a permanent ban, not a moratorium.

One other change enacted in 2002 requires the California Department of Health Services to establish an "advisory committee" to advise the legislature and the governor on human cloning and other human biotechnology issues. This advisory committee must include at least one representative from the areas of medicine, religion, biotechnology, genetics, and law, and from the general public, as well as at least three independent bioethicists of specified qualifications. The Department of Health Services will be required to make annual reports of the committee's activities beginning no later than December 31, 2003.

### Rhode Island

The Rhode Island law relevant to reproductive cloning appears to allow for therapeutic cloning under some circumstances, but, as we shall see, this is debatable.

Rhode Island is the only state to ban reproductive cloning by both the SCNT *and* embryo-splitting methods. Oddly, either the actual or *attempted* reproductive cloning by SCNT is prohibited, whereas the use of embryo splitting is only disallowed to "create genetically identical human beings by dividing a blastocyst, zygote, or embryo." It is difficult to discern a legitimate policy rationale for this disparity—the difference may be attributable to inartful drafting rather than actual legislative intent.

Rhode Island provides for administrative/civil (noncriminal) penalties for violation of its anticloning law that are the same as in California: $250,000 for individual violators and $1 million for violation by a "corporation, firm, clinic, hospital, laboratory, or research facility." Rhode Island also adopts the double forfeiture of pecuniary gains derived from reproductive cloning and, in its sunset clause, provides for automatic expiration of the ban five years after its effective date (i.e., on July 7, 2003) unless reauthorized. There are no specific provisions for license forfeiture by violators, unlike the laws of several other states.

It is interesting that Rhode Island has a separate law relevant to human embryo experimentation, which could be read as prohibiting therapeutic cloning notwithstanding assurances to the contrary in its reproductive cloning law. Rhode Island prohibits the use of "any live human fetus, whether before or after expulsion from its mother's womb, for scientific, laboratory research, or other kind of experimentation."[10] A legal analysis commissioned by the National Bioethics Advisory Commission concluded that this law "ban[s] research on *in vitro* embryos altogether,"[11] and President George W. Bush's Council on Bioethics agreed.[12] Thus, there is some confusion as to the legal status of therapeutic cloning in Rhode Island.

### Michigan

Michigan's cloning law appears, on its own terms, to ban reproductive and also at least some therapeutic cloning of humans.[13] By defining

human cloning as including "the use of human somatic cell nuclear transfer technology to produce a human embryo," which in turn is defined as
"a human egg cell with a full genetic composition capable of differentiating and maturing into a complete human being," it seems that Michigan
has banned therapeutic cloning, even of preimplantation embryos.[14]
Michigan joins all other states except Rhode Island in singling out the
SCNT method for prohibition, while not mentioning embryo splitting.
There are also criminal penalties (as provided in Michigan Penal Code
750.430a), and administrative and civil penalties of up to $10 million are
authorized for violations. There is no sunset provision in Michigan's ban
on reproductive cloning. As in Louisiana, Iowa, Virginia, and California,
the ban is permanent, absent subsequent legislation to the contrary.

### Louisiana

Louisiana's anticloning law is similar to California's in several respects.
It bans only SCNT cloning, not embryo splitting; it does not, on its face,
prohibit therapeutic cloning, only reproductive cloning (including the
attempt to achieve this). But, as will be noted shortly, there is some doubt
on the legal status of therapeutic cloning in Louisiana. Louisiana law
expressly bans the purchase or sale of an ovum, zygote, embryo, or fetus
with the intent to clone a human being. Violation is grounds for forfeiture
of licenses, as well. As with Rhode Island, Louisiana's cloning law has a
sunset provision; its ban on reproductive cloning is slated to expire on July
1, 2003.

However, Louisiana goes far beyond California in the amount of
administrative penalties authorized for violation: $10 million for violation
by a corporation, firm, clinic, hospital, laboratory, or research facility, and
$5 million for individual persons who violate the ban. Double damages in
the event of pecuniary gain are allowed, if greater than the previous
amounts, as in California and other states.

Louisiana has several other provisions in its law that are very draconian. The use of state funds to assist in reproductive cloning is prohibited,
and the Louisiana law bars any health facility or agency from allowing
any individual to clone or attempt to clone a human being in a facility
owned or operated by the health facility or agency. In addition to the stiff
administrative penalties, Louisiana also provides for criminal punishment
consisting of imprisonment of up to ten years and/or fines of up to $10
million. Thus, in several respects, Louisiana has enacted the most sweeping and onerous anticloning legislation in the United States to date,
although, unlike Iowa, it does not ban therapeutic cloning.

As in Rhode Island, there is a complication. Louisiana's law in an
entirely different section recognizes a human embryo outside the womb
as a "juridical person" and prohibits the destruction of a viable fertilized

ovum.[15] It also provides that "[t]he use of a human ovum fertilized in vitro is solely for the support and contribution of the complete development of human in utero implantation. No in vitro fertilized human ovum will be farmed or cultured solely for research purposes or any other purposes."[16] President Bush's Council on Bioethics viewed these provisions as appearing to prohibit "cloning-for-biomedical-research."[17]

## Virginia

The Virginia law evidently permits therapeutic cloning but bans reproductive cloning of humans (although the law does not define the term *human being* and thus might be interpreted as applying to the creation of a preimplantation human embryo if such were deemed a human being). It is also odd that the provision allowing for some research fails to mention embryos, while listing molecules, cells, DNA, and tissues. Does the Virginia law therefore forbid therapeutic cloning of embryos? It is unclear, but that does not seem to have been the intent of the legislature.

The Virginia statute is consistent with all other anticloning states except Rhode Island in only banning the use of the SCNT technique for reproductive cloning, while not mentioning embryo splitting. There is no sunset provision for this ban.

Virginia provides comparatively lenient sanctions for violation: civil penalties of up to $50,000. There are no criminal penalties and no provision for revocation of licenses, nor is there any provision for double forfeiture of profits derived from reproductive cloning activities.

## Iowa

Iowa joined the group of states with anticloning laws on the books on April 26, 2002. The Iowa statute is among the most aggressive. It explicitly bans both therapeutic and reproductive cloning (using only SCNT, but not embryo splitting), and it includes both criminal and civil penalties, with double forfeiture of pecuniary gains and license revocation. There is no sunset provision.

## State Legislation under Consideration

In addition to these six states, at least nineteen others have been actively considering anticloning legislation but have not actually enacted it as of the date of this writing. I will briefly summarize these initiatives here, in alphabetical order. Bear in mind that *none* of the following bills had become law in early 2003. In some cases, alternative bills may be introduced and subsequently enacted, or further amendments may be made to the bills. Of course, it is entirely possible that some or all of these bills will never become law. I include some mention of them here to provide a modicum of insight into the number of states actively considering cloning bans and the variety of measures under consideration.

Alabama has debated a ban on the use of SCNT for reproductive cloning. Arizona has considered both civil and criminal penalties for using SCNT to produce a human clone at "any stage," which appears to ban therapeutic as well as reproductive cloning; Colorado's proposal would ban both reproductive and therapeutic cloning using SCNT. Delaware has debated a ban on all human reproductive cloning technologies, not just SCNT. The Florida proposal would criminalize the use of SCNT for human cloning "at any stage," which again could reach therapeutic cloning. Illinois would impose a five-year moratorium on using SCNT for either reproductive or therapeutic cloning. Indiana considered criminalizing "participating" in SCNT cloning, plus a variety of administrative and licensing sanctions. Kansas has weighed a criminal ban on using SCNT for reproductive cloning. Kentucky's proposal would criminalize the use of SCNT for cloning "at any stage." Massachusetts considered a ban on the use of SCNT to create a human embryo at any stage and thus would ban reproductive and most forms of therapeutic cloning. Missouri would ban reproductive cloning, with some ambiguity in the language of the proposed statute as to whether the ban would apply to embryo splitting as well as SCNT. The Nebraska proposal would only ban reproductive cloning via SCNT. New Hampshire has considered a permanent ban on the use of SCNT for either reproductive or therapeutic cloning. New Jersey considered a ban only on reproductive cloning using SCNT. New York has debated a permanent ban on both reproductive and therapeutic cloning (a human embryo at any stage) using SCNT, as well as the use of public funds for human cloning. Oklahoma would ban SCNT reproductive cloning only. South Carolina's proposal appears to ban both reproductive and therapeutic cloning via SCNT. Tennessee would ban only reproductive SCNT cloning. Wisconsin would do likewise.

With the exception of the Illinois proposal, *all* of these would be permanent bans (with no sunset clause). This illustrates that the example of Louisiana and Rhode Island of establishing self-expiring moratoria rather than outright permanent bans has not been widely considered worthy of emulation in other states. Indeed, California illustrates a trend in this direction, by initially enacting only a self-expiring moratorium but then amending it in 2002 to make its ban on reproductive cloning permanent. Also, all of these other states except Delaware, and with the possible additional exception of Missouri, would only ban SCNT and not embryo-splitting cloning. And many of these states have considered banning not only reproductive cloning but also most if not all forms of therapeutic cloning as well, in which a human embryo at any stage, even preimplantation, is created through use of SCNT technology.

I do not want to devote much time to an analysis of these initiatives, inasmuch as they are not necessarily in final form and indeed may not ever be enacted into law in any form. However, it is notable that these examples mean that no fewer than nineteen more states have recently considered joining California, Rhode Island, Michigan, Louisiana, Virginia, and Iowa in enacting anticloning bans. There is clearly a strong movement afoot within the United States at the state level to "do something" about the cloning of humans. Most of these nineteen additional legislative initiatives are along the general lines of the statutes already on the books, almost always banning SCNT reproductive cloning while not dealing with embryo splitting, but there appears to be more impetus to ban therapeutic cloning as well as reproductive cloning than before, and a definite trend toward permanent rather than temporary bans.

At least seven states (Arizona, Colorado, Florida, Illinois, Kentucky, Massachusetts, and New Hampshire) have considered significant restrictions or bans on therapeutic as well as reproductive cloning. As already indicated, to date only Michigan and Iowa have actually enacted an explicit ban on therapeutic cloning of humans, although when other separate embryo-research laws are considered, Louisiana and Rhode Island are, in effect, added to this list. The New Hampshire proposal, in particular, makes a point of decrying therapeutic cloning as inextricably linked to reproductive cloning and equally deserving of legal condemnation.[18]

Independent of laws explicitly aimed at cloning, however, several additional states have laws that in effect regulate or prohibit experimentation involving human embryos. As with Louisiana and Rhode Island, these human-embryo statutes could be read as essentially banning at least some types of therapeutic cloning. Moreover, until and unless these states also enact legislation regarding reproductive cloning, it is only therapeutic cloning that is forbidden in these jurisdictions. I include excerpts from these statutes here, for sake of completeness.

Maine's law, enacted in 1992, prohibits the "use [of]...any live human fetus, whether intrauterine or extrauterine...for scientific experimentation or for any form of experimentation."[19] A legal analysis commissioned by the National Bioethics Advisory Commission concluded that this law "ban[s] research on *in vitro* embryos altogether."[20]

A 1996 Massachusetts law bans the "use [of] any live human fetus whether before or after expulsion from its mother's womb, for scientific, laboratory, research or other kind of experimentation."[21] The section defines "fetus" as including "an embryo."[22]

Minnesota's 1998 law prohibits using or permitting the use of "a living human conceptus for any type of scientific, laboratory research or other experimentation except to protect the life or health of the conceptus."[23] The statute defines "human conceptus" as "any human organism, conceived either in the human body or produced in an artificial environment other than the human body, from fertilization through the first 265 days thereafter."[24]

North Dakota's 1997 law provides that "A person may not use any live human fetus, whether before or after expulsion from its mother's womb, for scientific, laboratory, research, or other kind of experimentation."[25] The NBAC believed this "would ban embryo stem cell research using either IVF embryos or aborted conceptuses."[26]

Pennsylvania's law, enacted in 2000, bans and criminalizes "knowingly perform[ing] any type of nontherapeutic experimentation or nontherapeutic medical procedure...upon any unborn child."[27] "Unborn child" is defined as "an individual organism of the species Homo sapiens from fertilization until live birth."[28]

South Dakota's law, enacted in 2000, provides that it is a crime to "conduct nontherapeutic research that destroys a human embryo" or to "conduct nontherapeutic research that subjects a human embryo to substantial risk of injury or death."[29] It is also unlawful to "use for research purposes cells or tissues that [a] person knows were obtained" by doing such harm to embryos.[30] "Human embryo" is defined under this law as "a living organism of the species Homo sapiens at the earliest stages of development (including the single-celled stage) that is not located in a woman's body."[31] Thus, South Dakota law bans not only the destruction of the human embryo to obtain stem cells (regardless of the source of funding) but also research using the resulting cells (regardless of whether the cells were harvested in that state or elsewhere).

It is also important to note that no fewer than fourteen of the nineteen states that have recently considered but have not yet enacted anticloning legislation (Alabama, Arizona, Colorado, Florida, Illinois, Indiana, Kansas, Kentucky, Missouri, New Hampshire, New York, Oklahoma, South Carolina, and Tennessee) have debated criminalizing at least some human cloning activities. This is somewhat indicative of the intensity of anticloning sentiment in those states and the extent to which such sentiment is widespread across the nation. To go beyond civil and administrative penalties into the criminal realm is a major step.

In light of the legislative action at the state level, we can now examine the response of the federal government to the cloning issue. We shall see that the example of some of the more aggressive anticloning state statutes has been pursued at the federal level, within both the executive and legislative branches.

## THE FEDERAL RESPONSE TO CLONING

The 107th Congress took the most sweeping and far-reaching steps to date toward actual enactment of anticloning legislation. On September 30, 2001, the House of Representatives passed the Human Cloning Prohibition Act of 2001 (HCPA) by a vote of 265 to 162, with 63 Democrats and 2 Independents joining 200 Republicans in favor of the bill.[32] By a vote of 251 to 176, the House also rejected an amendment that would have allowed private companies to create cloned human embryos (but not human babies) and develop therapies from their cells.[33] The act would outlaw the creation of cloned human embryos for any purpose, whether to make cloned babies or to produce potentially therapeutic stem cells, and would ban the importation of any medical treatments created abroad from closed human embryo cells.[34] This action followed the lead of President George W. Bush and his administration; the administration had announced on June 20, 2001, that it favored the most far-reaching of several competing bills to criminalize the cloning of humans.[35]

The full text of the HCPA as passed by the House in 2001 is given in appendix 1.

The HCPA definition of human cloning as "human asexual reproduction, accomplished by introducing nuclear material from one or more human somatic cells into a fertilized or unfertilized oocyte whose nuclear material has been removed or inactivated so as to produce a living organism (at any stage of development) that is genetically virtually identical to an existing or previously existing human organism"[36] appears to describe the SCNT, but not embryo-splitting techniques of cloning. In contrast to some of the earlier bills mentioned in chapter 1, and contrary to the recommendations in the NBAC Report, the HCPA is a permanent ban with no expiration date.

The HCPA would make it unlawful for any person or entity, public or private, in or affecting interstate commerce, knowingly (1) to perform or attempt to perform human cloning, (2) to participate in an attempt to perform human cloning, or (3) to ship or receive for any purpose an embryo produced by human cloning or any product derived from such embryo.[37] It would also prohibit "any person or entity, public or private, knowingly to import for any purpose an embryo produced by human cloning, or any product derived from such embryo."[38] Violations are punishable by imprisonment for up to ten years, or a fine, or both.[39] In addition, civil penalties are available in the case of a violation that involves the "derivation of a pecuniary gain." Such civil penalties are set at a minimum of $1 million, with a ceiling of "not more than an amount equal to the amount of the gross gain multiplied by 2, if that amount is greater than $1,000,000."[40] These provisions are virtually identical to those found in some of the more far-reaching cloning bans enacted by certain states, as I discussed in the previous sections of this chapter. Undoubtedly, the drafters of the HCPA took their lead from the example of these states on cloning legislation, as traditionally happens under the "laboratory of the states" approach of federalism.

In terms of possible restrictions on scientific research, the HCPA provides that "Nothing in this section restricts areas of scientific research not specifically prohibited by this section, including research in the use of nuclear transfer or other cloning techniques to produce molecules, DNA, cells other than human embryos, tissues, organs, plants, or animals other than humans."[41] This language would ban "therapeutic" cloning that produces a human embryo, irrespective of whether that embryo would ever be implanted into a woman or allowed to develop beyond a very early stage. In this regard, the HCPA is one of the most aggressive pieces of legislation on cloning to date—it would permit very limited uses of cloning at the cellular level but nothing at all involving a human embryo.

In the aftermath of passage of the HCPA by the House of Representatives in mid-2001, and repeated public expressions of approval by President George W. Bush, the issue moved to the United States Senate. Meanwhile, widely publicized news reports of further progress on cloning technology continued to stir the bubbling pot of controversy.

The Senate did not take swift action, no doubt partially because of the crisis arising out of the attacks of September 11, 2001, and their aftermath. Eventually, the Senate considered its own anticloning legislation during the early months of 2002. Republican senator Sam Brownback of Kansas and Democratic senator Mary Landrieu of Louisiana led the efforts to pass a sweeping, comprehensive ban identical to the HCPA passed by the House. There was one major competing bill of a less extreme variety also before the Senate, as well as some others that did not attract significant support. I will not quote the Brownback-Landrieu bill, S. 1899, here because it is the same as the HCPA previously cited in this chapter, although as time slipped away and the prospects of passage of the bill as drafted became gloomy, there were attempts to modify it to a two-year moratorium rather than a permanent ban.[42] As with the House version of the HCPA, Brownback-Landrieu would place both criminal and substantial civil penalties on the actual or attempted cloning of humans, including both reproductive and therapeutic cloning resulting in cloned human embryos at any stage of development. Additional prohibitions on the importation of cloned human embryos were intended to avert potential enforcement problems wherein a ban could be easily circumvented by shifting key portions of the cloning process to other countries.

Ultimately, Senator Brownback tried to rescue his bill late in the session by attaching key portions of it to other bills as amendments. However, this move was blocked by other senators who did not want to deal with cloning in such an indirect manner, or who favored an alternative bill, or who did not want to jeopardize other legislation by encumbering it with unrelated amendments.[43]

The primary competitor to Brownback-Landrieu in the Senate during early 2002 was S. 2439, championed by Democratic senator Diane Feinstein of California.[44] The full text of that bill is included in appendix 1.

This alternative to Brownback-Landrieu attracted significant support in the Senate late in the spring 2002 session, especially among Democrats. It mirrors the HCPA in some key respects, including a firm prohibition on reproductive SCNT cloning and provision for stiff criminal and civil penalties, as well as forfeiture of property for certain violations. As with the HCPA, it does not preempt the states from legislating in this field. In fact, it goes further than the HCPA or any cloning legislation considered to date by any state in providing for treble as opposed to double forfeitures of pecuniary gains, as well as forfeiture of real or personal property involved in violations. However, the Feinstein bill explicitly draws a distinction between reproductive and therapeutic cloning and attempts to safeguard the latter while banning the former; it is this feature that made it an attractive alternative to Brownback-Landrieu for many. Reportedly, each major alternative attracted the unofficial support of approximately forty senators, considerably fewer than the number needed for passage had it come to a vote.

It is interesting that both bills, as well as virtually all state laws on point, only address the SCNT and not the embryo-splitting method of cloning. There are virtually never any formal indications from the legislatures as to why this is so, but we can posit some possible justifications. Embryo splitting may be considerably safer, with a much lower failure rate, than SCNT because it does not require drastic manipulation of a mature somatic cell. There would likely be few if any problems of birth defects, gigantism, accelerated aging, or the like. Embryo splitting also avoids the moral or psychological issues arguably implicated by "replicating" a preexisting person rather than just artificially twinning a normal embryo. For some reason, it does not strike people as wrong to twin, triplet, or beyond a new embryo, but it is abhorrent to transfer DNA from someone who has already been born and use it to have a baby. In any event, the legislative action to date has been limited almost entirely to SCNT and not embryo splitting.

Ultimately, neither Brownback-Landrieu nor the Feinstein alternative nor any other cloning legislation was voted on in the Senate during 2002. As a result, despite the passage of the HCPA by the House and public exhortations from President Bush, there was no federal statute regarding the cloning of humans enacted during the 107th Congress. And so, in effect, despite the apparent absence of any United States Senator who publicly supports reproductive cloning, it was still not banned by any federal law.

The same deep divisions and disagreements that mired legislation in the Senate also appeared in the report issued by President George W. Bush's Council on Bioethics in July 2002.[45] This lengthy, detailed document ultimately did not make a clear, unambiguous recommendation. Instead, the council proffered two proposals. Both proposals advocated an immediate and permanent ban on reproductive cloning, or what the report calls "cloning-to-produce-children." In fact, the council was unanimous (17 to 0) in urging a ban on reproductive cloning. One proposal, which garnered the support of ten members, also recommended a four-year moratorium on therapeutic cloning.[46] The other proposal, supported by seven members, argued for continuing to allow research into human cloning to proceed, but with regulation.[47] This remarkable split decision came after months of work and debate by these seventeen luminaries and followed closely on the heels of the stalled legislation in the Senate.

In the aftermath of the November, 2002 election, with Republicans suddenly gaining control of the Senate and adding to their previous majority in the House, the prospect for enactment of a federal cloning ban brightened considerably. During the 108th Congress, there was initial speculation that a much higher priority would be placed on cloning legislation, with the Bush administration continuing to lead the way.[48]

The Human Cloning Prohibition Act was indeed swiftly reintroduced in both chambers of the new Congress. The text of the 2003 version is substantially identical to that of the HCPA of 2001, as contained in this book.[49] Once again, the House of Representatives voted by an overwhelming margin (241 to 155) to outlaw all forms of human cloning, including both theraputic and reproductive cloning.[50] And once again, the Senate considered its own very similar version of the same legislation (S. 245) as well as a competing bill that would be more tolerant of theraputic cloning.[51] But in mid-2003, despite contunied urging from the Bush administration, these competing cloning bans remained stalled in the Senate even as fears of military quagmire in Iraq evaporated. Thus, in a second consecutive Congress, cloning narrowly dodged a legislative bullet, notwithstanding virtual unanimous public opposition to reproductive cloning among federal lawmakers.[52]

Even absent such new federal legislation, the Food and Drug Administration (FDA) has for years asserted that it has the authority to regulate cloning and has claimed that FDA approval is required prior to any attempt to clone a human being within the United States.[53] The FDA position was that "human cloning is a form of cellular or genetic therapy that requires prior approval by FDA reviewers."[54] The FDA has based its claim on its guidelines for medical "biological products" that contain cells substantially altered through "more than minimal" manipulation, as well as the theory that such products are "drugs" and that cloning procedures can be regulated as involving "medical devices."[55] This is, at best, a tenuous link to cloning, and the FDA may be overreaching.[56] The FDA position has been much criticized, and even the FDA has admitted that it is not ideally suited to dealing with the cloning issue.[57]

Under the Public Health Service Act, a "biological product" is defined as, inter alia, a "virus, therapeutic serum, toxin, antitoxin, vaccine, blood, blood component or derivative,...or analogous product."[58] Before the FDA could regulate cloned human embryos under this definition, they would have to be deemed an "analogous product," presumably one used to treat the disease of infertility. The definition appears on its face to be designed to address entities that are either obviously nonhuman or only a bodily component, things very different from human embryos.[59] And the equation of human beings, or human embryos, with products is itself one of the bases for anticloning arguments, as will be shown in chapter 5, and thus it would be questionable for governmental adoption of this concept to form the foundation for federal regulation of cloning. Official government commodification of human beings, in the process of defending people from the supposed indignity of being commodified by cloning, is at least one layer of irony beyond the straight-face test.

The FDA has, in essence, developed a creative and decided unconventional definition of a key term, "biological product," for the express purpose of conferring regulatory jurisdiction upon itself. This was evidently an attempt to step into the void wherein no administrative agency had clear authority to regulate the cloning of humans. If nature abhors a vacuum, bureaucrats abhor it more. This bold assertion of authority where none would normally exist is akin to the manner in which the Environmental Protection Agency (EPA) has claimed the power to regulate genetically modified organisms as either chemical substances or entities with pesticidal properties under the Toxic Substances Control Act and the Federal Insecticide, Fungicide, and Rodenticide Act.[60]

Nonetheless, the FDA has continued to assert its jurisdiction over the cloning of humans.[61] On March 28, 2001, the FDA sent a "Dear Colleague" letter[62] to researchers and related associations reminding them that "clinical research using cloning technology to clone a human being is subject to FDA regulation" and that

before such research may begin, the sponsor of the research is required to: submit to FDA an IND [investigational new drug application] describing the proposed research plan; obtain authorization from a properly constituted institutional review board (IRB); and obtain a commitment from the investigators to obtain informed consent from all human subjects of the research. Such research may proceed only when an IND is in effect. Since the FDA believes that there are major unresolved safety questions pertaining to the use of cloning technology to clone a human being, until those questions are appropriately addressed in an IND, FDA would not permit any such investigation to proceed.

The letter goes on to aver that the

FDA may prohibit a sponsor from conducting a study proposed in an IND application (often referred to as placing the study on "clinical hold") for a variety of reasons. If the Agency finds that "human subjects are or would be exposed to an unreasonable and significant risk of illness or injury," that would be sufficient reason to put a study on clinical hold. Other reasons listed in the regulations include "the IND does not contain sufficient information required to assess the risks to subjects of the proposed studies," or "the clinical investigators are not qualified by reason of their scientific training and experience to conduct the investigation."

The legitimacy of the FDA's assertion of this jurisdiction over cloning research is dubious. On an obvious level, it is something of a stretch to claim authority to regulate the cloning of humans using methods established for evaluating "investigational new drugs." Cloned human embryos may be many things (potential babies, sources of stem cells, future sports superstars in the making, etc.), but they are not drugs. Additionally, there may be a problem with the constitutional foundation on which this assertion of FDA authority is predicated, that is, the Commerce Clause.

The FDA has used its power, derived from the Commerce Clause, to regulate which drugs doctors can prescribe. One fairly recent Supreme Court decision has cast some doubt on whether the Court would uphold the FDA's authority to regulate in something so far afield from its normal purview as human cloning. In *United States v. Lopez*,[63] the Supreme Court seems to indicate a willingness to reduce the federal government's use of the Commerce Clause to justify its reach into state authority. This could plausibly foreshadow an invalidation of the FDA's reach into human-cloning research, particularly given the considerable differences between such research and the type of food- and drug-related work that is the FDA's traditional field of regulation. However, in light of the fact that the courts have permitted the FDA to operate in general, they are unlikely to use the Commerce Clause as the means to strike down this federal effort to regulate the creation and use of embryo cells for medical purposes.

Thus, at least for the time being, the FDA will very likely persist in applying its "investigational new drug application" requirements to cloning research, just as the EPA has used the Toxic Substances Control Act and the Federal Insecticide, Fungicide, and Rodenticide Act to regulate genetically modified organisms as if they were chemicals or pesticidal substances. Although critics may quibble with the legitimacy of the FDA's assertion of authority over cloning, the fact remains that it has asserted such authority and thus must be reckoned with, at least until and unless its authority is successfully challenged in court.[64] It may not be an elegant solution, but at present the federal government lacks for any better alternative.

## APPENDIX 1
## STATE LAWS AND FEDERAL BILLS APPLICABLE TO HUMAN CLONING

### STATE LAWS CURRENTLY IN EFFECT

#### California

The original legislation, enacted in 1997, provided as follows:

SECTION 1. It is the intent of the Legislature to place a five-year moratorium on the cloning of an entire human being in order to evaluate the profound medical, ethical, and social implications that such a possibility raises. It is not the intent of the Legislature that this moratorium apply to the cloning of human cells, human tissue, or human organs that would not result in the replication of an entire human being. During this moratorium period, the State Director of Health Services should be called upon to establish a panel of representatives from the fields of medicine, religion, biotechnology, genetics, law, bioethics, and the general public to evaluate those implications, review public policy, and advise the Legislature and the Governor in this area.

SECTION 2. Section 2260.5 is added to the Business and Professions Code, to read:

2260.5. (a) A violation of Section 24185 of the Health and Safety Code, relating to human cloning, constitutes unprofessional conduct.

(b) This section shall remain in effect only until January 1, 2003, and as of that date is repealed, unless a later enacted statute, that is enacted before January 1, 2003, deletes or extends that date.

SECTION 3. Section 16004 is added to the Business and Professions Code, to read:

16004. (a) Any license issued to a business pursuant to this chapter shall be revoked for a violation of Section 24185 of the Health and Safety Code, relating to human cloning.

(b) This section shall remain in effect only until January 1, 2003, and as of that date is repealed, unless a later enacted statute, that is enacted before January 1, 2003, deletes or extends that date.

SECTION 4. Section 16105 is added to the Business and Professions Code, to read:

16105. (a) Any license issued to a business pursuant to this chapter shall be revoked for violation of Section 24185 of the Health and Safety Code, relating to human cloning.

(b) This section shall remain in effect only until January 1, 2003, and as of that date is repealed, unless a later enacted statute, that is enacted before January 1, 2003, deletes or extends that date.

SECTION 5. Chapter 1.4 (commencing with Section 24185) is added to Division 20 of the Health and Safety Code, to read:

CHAPTER 1.4. HUMAN CLONING

24185. (a) No person shall clone a human being.

(b) No person shall purchase or sell an ovum, zygote, embryo, or fetus for the purpose of cloning a human being.

(c) For purposes of this section, "clone" means the practice of creating or attempting to create a human being by transferring the nucleus from a human cell from whatever source into a human egg cell from which the nucleus has been removed for the purpose of, or to implant, the resulting product to initiate a pregnancy that could result in the birth of a human being.

24187. For violations of Section 24185, the State Director of Health Services may, after appropriate notice and opportunity for hearing, by order, levy administrative penalties as follows:

(a) If the violator is a corporation, firm, clinic, hospital, laboratory, or research facility, by a civil penalty of not more than one million dollars ($1,000,000) or the applicable amount under subdivision (c), whichever is greater.

(b) If the violator is an individual, by a civil penalty of not more than two hundred fifty thousand dollars ($250,000) or the applicable amount under subdivision (c), whichever is greater.

(c) If any violator derives pecuniary gain from a violation of this section, the violator may be assessed a civil penalty of not more than an amount equal to the amount of the gross gain multiplied by two.

(d) The administrative penalties shall be paid to the General Fund.

24189. This chapter shall remain in effect only until January 1, 2003, and as of that date is repealed, unless a later enacted statute, that is enacted before January 1, 2003, deletes or extends that date.

* * *

In 2002, California amended the above provisions to make its ban on human reproductive cloning and related provisions permanent, with no automatic repeal date. Additionally, the amendment requires the establishment of an advisory committee to provide guidance on human cloning and similar issues. The amendment reads as follows:

SB 1230, Human cloning.

Existing law, until January 1, 2003, prohibits a person from cloning a human being, and from purchasing or selling an ovum, zygote, embryo, or fetus for the purpose of cloning a human being, and authorizes the State Department of Health Services to levy administrative penalties for violation of these provisions. Existing law, until January 1, 2003, further provides that violation of this prohibition constitutes unprofessional conduct for purposes of the Medical Practice Act, and requires city business licenses and county business licenses to be revoked for violation of the prohibition.

This bill would prohibit a person from engaging in "human reproductive cloning," as defined. It would also delete the January 1, 2003, repeal dates thereby extending the operation of the above provisions indefinitely. The bill, in addition, would require the department to establish an advisory committee, composed of specified representatives, including not less than 3 bioethicists, for purposes of advising the Legislature and the Governor on human cloning and other issues relating to human biotechnology. The bill would require the department to fund the activities of the advisory committee from its existing resources, to the extent that funds are available. It would also require the department, on or before December 31, 2003, and annually thereafter, to report to the Legislature and the Governor regarding the activities of the committee.

THE PEOPLE OF THE STATE OF CALIFORNIA DO ENACT AS FOL-LOWS:

SECTION 1. Section 2260.5 of the Business and Professions Code is amended to read:

2260.5. A violation of Section 24185 of the Health and Safety Code, relating to human cloning, constitutes unprofessional conduct.

SEC. 2. Section 16004 of the Business and Professions Code is amended to read:

16004. Any license issued to a business pursuant to this chapter shall be revoked for a violation of Section 24185 of the Health and Safety Code, relating to human cloning.

SEC. 3. Section 16105 of the Business and Professions Code is amended to read: 16105. Any license issued to a business pursuant to this chapter shall be revoked for violation of Section 24185 of the Health and Safety Code, relating to human cloning.

SEC. 4. Section 24185 of the Health and Safety Code is amended to read:

24185. (a) No person shall clone a human being or engage in human reproductive cloning.

(b) No person shall purchase or sell an ovum, zygote, embryo, or fetus for the purpose of cloning a human being.

(c) For purposes of this chapter, the following definitions apply:

(1) "Clone" means the practice of creating or attempting to create a human being by transferring the nucleus from a human cell from whatever source into a human or nonhuman egg cell from which the nucleus has been removed for the purpose of, or to implant, the resulting product to initiate a pregnancy that could result in the birth of a human being.

(2) "Department" means the State Department of Health Services.

(3) "Human reproductive cloning" means the creation of a human fetus that is substantially genetically identical to a previously born human being. The department may adopt, interpret, and update regulations, as necessary, for purposes of more precisely defining the procedures that constitute human reproductive cloning.

SEC. 5. Section 24186 is added to the Health and Safety Code, to read:

24186. (a) (1) The department shall establish an advisory committee for purposes of advising the Legislature and the Governor on human cloning and other issues relating to human biotechnology. The committee shall be composed of at least nine members, appointed by the Director of Health Services, who shall serve without compensation.

(2) The committee shall include at least one representative from the areas of medicine, religion, biotechnology, genetics, law, and from the general public. The committee shall also include not less than three independent bioethicists who possess the qualifications described in paragraph (3).

(3) The independent bioethicists selected to serve on the committee shall reflect a representative range of religious and ethical perspectives in California regarding the issues of human cloning and human biotechnol-

ogy. An independent bioethicist serving on the advisory committee shall not be employed by, consult with or have consulted with, or have any direct or indirect financial interest, in any corporation engaging in research relating to human cloning or human biotechnology. A person with any affiliation to the grant-funded cloning research programs operated by the University of California or the California State University is also prohibited from serving as a bioethicist on the advisory committee.

(b) On or before December 31, 2003, and annually thereafter, the department shall report to the Legislature and the Governor regarding the activities of the committee.

(c) The activities of the committee shall, to the extent that funds are available, be funded by the department out of existing resources.

SEC. 6. Section 24189 of the Health and Safety Code is repealed.

## Iowa

Section 1. NEW SECTION. 707B.1 TITLE.

This chapter shall be known and may be cited as the "Human Cloning Prohibition Act."

Sec. 2. NEW SECTION. 707B.2 PURPOSE.

It is the purpose of this chapter to prohibit human cloning for any purpose, whether for reproductive cloning or therapeutic cloning.

Sec. 3. NEW SECTION. 707B.3 DEFINITIONS.

As used in this chapter, unless the context otherwise requires:

1. "Fetus" means a living organism of the species homo sapiens from eight weeks' development until complete expulsion or extraction from a woman's body, or until removal from an artificial womb or other similar environment designed to nurture the development of such organism.

2. "Human cloning" means human asexual reproduction, accomplished by introducing the genetic material of a human somatic cell into a fertilized or unfertilized oocyte whose nucleus has been or will be removed or inactivated, to produce a living organism with a human or predominantly human genetic constitution.

3. "Human embryo" means a living organism of the species homo sapiens from the single-celled stage to eight weeks' development.

4. "Human somatic cell" means a cell having a complete set of chromosomes obtained from a living or deceased human organism of the species homo sapiens at any stage of development.

5. "Oocyte" means a human ovum.

Sec. 4. NEW SECTION. 707B.4 HUMAN CLONING—PROHIBITIONS—EXCEPTIONS—PENALTY.

1. A person shall not intentionally or knowingly do any of the following:

a. Perform or attempt to perform human cloning.

b. Participate in performing or in an attempt to perform human cloning.

c. Transfer or receive a cloned human embryo for any purpose.

d. Transfer or receive, in whole or in part, any oocyte, human embryo, fetus, or human somatic cell, for the purpose of human cloning.

2. This section shall not restrict areas of scientific research not specifically prohibited, including in vitro fertilization; the administration of fertility-enhancing drugs; or research in the use of nuclear transfer or other cloning techniques to produce molecules, deoxyribonucleic acid, tissues, organs, plants, animals other than humans, or cells other than human embryos.

3. a. A person who violates subsection 1, paragraph "a" or "b", is guilty of a class "C" felony.

b. A person who violates subsection 1, paragraph "c" or "d", is guilty of an aggravated misdemeanor.

4. A person who violates this section in a manner that results in a pecuniary gain to the person is subject to a civil penalty in an amount that is twice the amount of the gross gain.

5. A person who violates this section and who is licensed pursuant to chapter 148, 150, or 150A is subject to revocation of the person's license.

6. A violation of this section is grounds for denial of an application for, denial of renewal of, or revocation of any license, permit, certification, or any other form of permission required to practice or engage in any trade, occupation, or profession regulated by the state.

## Louisiana

PART XIX. HUMAN CLONING

§1299.36. Legislative intent

It is the intent of the legislature to protect the health and welfare of the citizens of this state through a ban on the cloning of human beings while encouraging the thorough and diligent evaluation required by the profound medical, ethical, and social questions raised by the possibility of human cloning.

§1299.36.1. Definition

As used in this Part, "clone" means the practice of creating or attempting to create a human being by transferring the nucleus from a human cell from whatever source into a human egg cell from which the nucleus has been removed for the purpose of or to implant the resulting product to initiate a pregnancy that could result in the birth of a human being.

§1299.36.2. Cloning of human beings; purchase or sale of ovum, zygote, embryo, or fetus for the purpose of cloning human beings, prohibited

A. No person shall clone or attempt to clone a human being.

B. No person shall purchase or sell an ovum, zygote, embryo, or fetus with the intent to clone a human being.

C. This Section does not prohibit scientific research or a cell based therapy not specifically prohibited elsewhere by this Part.

D. Whoever violates this Section shall be fined not more than ten million dollars or imprisoned, with or without hard labor, for not more than ten years, or both.

§1299.36.3. Administrative penalties

A. For a violation of R.S. 40:1299.36.2, the secretary of the Department of Health and Hospitals may, in accordance with the Administrative Procedure Act, order the levy of an administrative penalty as follows:

(1) If the person is a corporation, firm, clinic, hospital, laboratory, or research facility, a penalty of not more than ten million dollars or the applicable amount under Subsection B, whichever is greater.

(2) If the person is an individual, a penalty of not more than five million dollars or the applicable amount under Subsection B, whichever is greater.

B. If any person derives pecuniary gain from a violation of R.S. 40:1299.36.2, the person shall be assessed a civil penalty of not more than an amount equal to the amount of the gross gain multiplied by two.

C. The administrative penalties shall be deposited into the state treasury.

§1299.36.4. Violation constitutes unprofessional conduct; employment restrictions

A. A violation of this Part relating to human cloning constitutes unprofessional conduct and shall result in the permanent revocation of each license and permit issued pursuant to R.S. 37:1261 et seq.

B. A violation of this Part shall provide, in addition to Subsection A of this Section, the basis for disciplinary action deemed appropriate by the Louisiana State Board of Medical Examiners pursuant to R.S. 37:1261 et seq.

C. Notwithstanding any provision of law to the contrary, a violation of this Part shall be the basis for denying an application for, or an application for the renewal of, any license, permit, or certificate required by this state, or the granting of a conditional license, permit, or certificate required by this state or any department, office, agency, or board of the state in order to practice or engage in a trade, occupation, or profession.

§1299.36.5. Use of state funds prohibited

A. Notwithstanding any other provision of law to the contrary, state funds shall not be used to clone or attempt to clone a human being.

B. Subsection A of this Section does not prohibit the use of state funds for scientific research or cell-based therapies not specifically prohibited by this Part.

C. A person who violates this Section shall be subject to a fine of ten million dollars which shall be deposited into the state treasury.

§1299.36.6. Use of health facility or agency for human cloning prohibited; penalties

A. A health facility or agency shall not allow any individual to clone or attempt to clone a human being in a facility owned or operated by the health facility or agency.

B. Nothing in this Section shall prohibit a health facility or agency from allowing an individual from engaging in scientific research or a cell-based therapy not specifically prohibited by this Part.

C. A health facility or agency that violates this Section shall be subject to administrative penalties provided by law for that facility or agency and to a fine of ten million dollars and loss of each license granted by law to the facility or agency.

D. A fine collected under this Section shall be deposited into the state treasury.

E. This Section does not give a person a private right of action.

## Michigan

MCLS § 333.16274 Human cloning; prohibited acts; exception; violation of subsection (1); private right of action; definitions.

Sec. 16274. (1) A licensee or registrant shall not engage in or attempt to engage in human cloning.

(2) Subsection (1) does not prohibit scientific research or cell-based therapies not specifically prohibited by that subsection.

(3) A licensee or registrant who violates subsection (1) is subject to the administrative penalties prescribed in sections 16221 and 16226 and to the civil penalty prescribed in section 16275.

(4) This section does not give a person a private right of action.

(5) As used in this section:

(a) "Human cloning" means the use of human somatic cell nuclear transfer technology to produce a human embryo.

(b) "Human embryo" means a human egg cell with a full genetic composition capable of differentiating and maturing into a complete human being.

(c) "Human somatic cell" means a cell of a developing or fully developed human being that is not and will not become a sperm or egg cell.

(d) "Human somatic cell nuclear transfer" means transferring the nucleus of a human somatic cell into an egg cell from which the nucleus has been removed or rendered inert.

MCLS § 333.16275 Human cloning; prohibition; exception; violation; penalty; private right of action; "human cloning" defined.

Sec. 16275. (1) A licensee or registrant or other individual shall not engage in or attempt to engage in human cloning.

(2) Subsection (1) does not prohibit scientific research or cell-based therapies not specifically prohibited by that subsection.

(3) A licensee or registrant or other individual who violates subsection (1) is subject to a civil penalty of $10,000,000.00. A fine collected under this

subsection shall be distributed in the same manner as penal fines are distributed in this state.

(4) This section does not give a person a private right of action.

(5) As used in this section, "human cloning" means that term as defined in section 16274.

MCLS §750.430a. Human cloning: prohibition; exception; violation; penalty; "human cloning" defined.

Sec. 430a. (1) An individual shall not intentionally engage in or attempt to engage in human cloning.

(2) Subsection (1) does not prohibit scientific research or cell-based therapies not specifically prohibited by that subsection.

(3) An individual who violates subsection (1) is guilty of a felony punishable by imprisonment for not more than 10 years or a fine of not more than $10,000,000.00, or both.

(4) As used in this section, "human cloning" means that term as defined in section 16274 of the public health code.


### Rhode Island

SECTION 1. Title 23 of the General Laws entitled "Health and Safety" is hereby amended by adding thereto the following chapter:

23-16.4-1. Declaration of Intent and Purpose.

Whereas, recent medical and technological advances have had tremendous benefit to patients, and society as a whole, and biomedical research for the purpose of scientific investigation of disease or cure of a disease or illness should be preserved and protected and not be impeded by regulations involving the cloning of an entire human being; and

Whereas, molecular biology, involving human cells, genes, tissues, and organs, has been used to meet medical needs globally for twenty (20) years, and has proved a powerful tool in the search for cures, leading to effective medicines to treat cystic fibrosis, diabetes, heart attack, stroke, hemophilia, and HIV/AIDS;

The purpose of this legislation is to place a ban on the creation of a human being through division of a blastocyst, zygote, or embryo or somatic cell nuclear transfer, and to protect the citizens of the state from potential abuse deriving from cloning technologies. This ban is not intended to apply to the cloning of human cells, genes, tissues, or organs that would not result in the replication of an entire human being. Nor is this ban intended to apply to in vitro fertilization, the administration of fertility enhancing drugs, or other medical procedures used to assist a woman in becoming or remaining pregnant, so long as that procedure is not specifically intended to result in the gestation or birth of a child who is genetically identical to another conceptus, embryo, fetus, or human being, living or dead.

23-16.4-2. Cloning of human beings prohibited.

(a) No person or entity shall utilize somatic cell nuclear transfer for the purpose of initiating or attempting to initiate a human pregnancy nor shall any person create genetically identical human beings by dividing a blastocyst, zygote, or embryo.

(b) Definitions

(1) "Somatic cell nuclear transfer" means transferring the nucleus of a human somatic cell into an oocyte from which the nucleus has been removed;

(2) "Somatic cell" means any cell of a conceptus, embryo, fetus, child, or adult not biologically determined to become a germ cell;

(3) "Oocyte" means the female germ cell, the egg;

(4) "Nucleus" means the cell structure that houses the chromosomes, and thus the genes, and;

(c) Protected Research and Practices

(1) Nothing in this section shall be construed to restrict areas of biomedical, microbiological, and agricultural research or practices not expressly prohibited in this section, including research or practices that involve the use of:

(a) somatic cell nuclear transfer or other cloning technologies to clone molecules, DNA, cells, and tissues; or

(b) mitochondrial, cytoplasmic, or gene therapy; or

(c) somatic cell nuclear transfer techniques to create animals.

(2) Nothing in this section shall be construed to prohibit:

(a) in vitro fertilization, the administration of fertility-enhancing drugs, or other medical procedures used to assist a woman in becoming or remaining pregnant, so long as that pregnancy is not specifically intended to result in the production of a child who is genetically identical to another human being, living or dead;

(b) any activity or procedure that results, directly or indirectly in two or more natural identical twins.

23-16.4-3. Penalties.

For violations of Section 23-16.4-1 the director of the Department of Health may, after appropriate notice and opportunity for hearing, by order, levy administrative penalties as follows:

(a) If the violator is a corporation, firm, clinic, hospital, laboratory, or research facility, by a civil penalty of not more than one million dollars ($1,000,000), or the applicable amount under subdivision (c), whichever is greater.

(b) If the violator is an individual or an employee of the firm, clinic, hospital, laboratory, or research facility acting without the authorization of the firm, clinic, hospital, or research facility, by a civil penalty of not more than two hundred fifty thousand dollars ($250,000) or the applicable amount under subsection (c), whichever is greater.

(c) If any violator derives pecuniary gain from a violation of this section, the violator may be assessed a civil penalty of not more than an amount equal to the amount of the gross gain multiplied by two (2).

(d) The administrative penalties provided in this section shall be paid to the general fund.

(e) Nothing in this chapter shall be construed to give any person a private right of action.

23-16.4-4. Reauthorization/Sunset Clause.

The prohibition in this legislation shall expire five (5) years from the effective date.

SECTION 2. This act shall take effect upon passage.

### Virginia

§ 32.1–162.21. Definitions.

As used in this chapter, unless the context clearly requires another meaning:

"Cloning" means the production of a precise genetic copy of a molecule, including deoxyribonucleic acid (DNA), or of chromosomes.

"Human cloning" means the creation of or attempt to create a human being by transferring the nucleus from a human cell from whatever source into an oocyte from which the nucleus has been removed.

"Nucleus" means the cell structure that houses the chromosomes and, thus, the genes.

"Oocyte" means the ovum or egg.

"Somatic cell" means a mature, diploid cell, i.e., a cell having a complete set of chromosomes.

"Somatic cell nuclear transfer" means transferring the nucleus of a somatic cell of an existing or deceased human into an oocyte from which the chromosomes are removed or rendered inert.

§ 32.1-162.22. Human cloning prohibited; civil penalty.

A. No person shall (i) perform human cloning or (ii) implant or attempt to implant the product of somatic cell nuclear transfer into a uterine environment so as to initiate a pregnancy or (iii) possess the product of human cloning or (iv) ship or receive the product of a somatic cell nuclear transfer in commerce for the purpose of implanting the product of somatic cell nuclear transfer into a uterine environment so as to initiate a pregnancy.

B. This section shall not be construed to restrict biomedical and agricultural research or practices unless expressly prohibited herein, including research or practices that involve the use of (i) somatic cell nuclear transfer or other cloning technologies to clone molecules, including DNA, cells, or tissues; (ii) gene therapy; or (iii) somatic cell nuclear transfer techniques to create animals other than humans.

C. In addition to any other penalty provided by law, any person violating the provisions of this section shall be liable for a civil penalty in an amount not to exceed $50,000 for each incident.

## FEDERAL BILLS CONSIDERED BUT NOT ENACTED DURING THE 107TH CONGRESS

### Human Cloning Prohibition Act of 2001 (passed by the House and substantially identical to the Brownback-Landrieu bill in the Senate)

SECTION 1. SHORT TITLE.

This Act may be cited as the "Human Cloning Prohibition Act of 2001."

SEC. 2. PROHIBITION ON HUMAN CLONING.

(a) IN GENERAL—Title 18, United States Code, is amended by inserting after chapter 15, the following:

CHAPTER 16—HUMAN CLONING

Sec.

301. Definitions.

302. Prohibition on human cloning.

Sec. 301. Definitions

In this chapter:

(1) HUMAN CLONING—The term "human cloning" means human asexual reproduction, accomplished by introducing nuclear material from one or more human somatic cells into a fertilized or unfertilized oocyte whose nuclear material has been removed or inactivated so as to produce a living organism (at any stage of development) that is genetically virtually identical to an existing or previously existing human organism.

(2) ASEXUAL REPRODUCTION—The term "asexual reproduction" means reproduction not initiated by the union of oocyte and sperm.

(3) SOMATIC CELL—The term "somatic cell" means a diploid cell (having a complete set of chromosomes) obtained or derived from a living or deceased human body at any stage of development.

Sec. 302. Prohibition on human cloning

(a) IN GENERAL—It shall be unlawful for any person or entity, public or private, in or affecting interstate commerce, knowingly—

(1) to perform or attempt to perform human cloning;

(2) to participate in an attempt to perform human cloning; or

(3) to ship or receive for any purpose an embryo produced by human cloning or any product derived from such embryo.

(b) IMPORTATION—It shall be unlawful for any person or entity, public or private, knowingly to import for any purpose an embryo produced by human cloning [or any product derived from such embryo].

(c) PENALTIES—

(1) CRIMINAL PENALTY—Any person or entity that violates this section shall be fined under this title or imprisoned not more than 10 years, or both.

(2) CIVIL PENALTY—Any person or entity that violates any provision of this section shall be subject to, in the case of a violation that involves the derivation of a pecuniary gain, a civil penalty of not less than $1,000,000 and not more than an amount equal to the amount of the gross gain multiplied by 2, if that amount is greater than $1,000,000.

(d) SCIENTIFIC RESEARCH—Nothing in this section restricts areas of scientific research not specifically prohibited by this section, including research in the use of nuclear transfer or other cloning techniques to produce molecules, DNA, cells other than human embryos, tissues, organs, plants, or animals other than humans.

(b) CLERICAL AMENDMENT—The table of chapters for part I of title 18, United States Code, is amended by inserting after the item relating to chapter 15 the following:

301.

SEC. 3. STUDY BY GENERAL ACCOUNTING OFFICE.

(a) IN GENERAL—The General Accounting Office shall conduct a study to assess the need (if any) for amendment of the prohibition on human cloning, as defined in section 301 of title 18, United States Code, as added by this Act, which study should include—

(1) a discussion of new developments in medical technology concerning human cloning and somatic cell nuclear transfer, the need (if any) for somatic cell nuclear transfer to produce medical advances, current public attitudes and prevailing ethical views concerning the use of somatic cell nuclear transfer, and potential legal implications of research in somatic cell nuclear transfer; and

(2) a review of any technological developments that may require that technical changes be made to section 2 of this Act.

(b) REPORT—The General Accounting Office shall transmit to the Congress, within 4 years after the date of enactment of this Act, a report containing the findings and conclusions of its study, together with recommendations for any legislation or administrative actions which it considers appropriate.

### Senate Alternative Version of the Human Cloning Prohibition Act of 2001 (Feinstein et al.)

To prohibit human cloning while preserving important areas of medical research, including stem cell research.

*Be it enacted by the Senate and House of Representatives of the United States of America in Congress assembled,*

**SECTION 1. SHORT TITLE.**

This Act may be cited as the "Human Cloning Prohibition Act of 2002."

## SEC. 2. FINDINGS.

Congress makes the following findings:

(1) Human cloning is unsafe, immoral, and unacceptable.

(2) Federal legislation should be enacted to prohibit anyone from attempting to conduct human cloning, whether using Federal or non-Federal funds.

(3) To deter human cloning, any attempt to create a human clone should be a felony subject to severe punishment.

(4) The National Academies (including the National Academy of Sciences and the Institute of Medicine) and the National Bioethics Advisory Commission recommended that any legislative action undertaken to ban human cloning should be careful not to interfere with important areas of scientific research, such as nuclear transplantation to produce stem cells.

(5) The National Academies found that there are significant differences between human cloning and nuclear transplantation. Specifically, the Academies determined that, unlike human cloning, the creation of embryonic stem cells by nuclear transplantation does not involve implantation of an embryo in a uterus and thus cannot produce a complete, live-born animal (that is, a "clone").

(6) The National Academies found that scientific and medical considerations that justify a ban on human cloning are not applicable to nuclear transplantation.

(7) The National Academies concluded that nuclear transplantation has great potential to increase the understanding and potential treatment of various diseases and debilitating disorders, as well as our fundamental biological knowledge. These diseases and disorders include Lou Gehrig's disease, Parkinson's disease, Alzheimer's disease, spinal-cord injury, cancer, cardiovascular diseases, diabetes, rheumatoid arthritis, and many others.

(8) The National Academies determined that nuclear transplantation research could improve our ability to transplant healthy tissue derived from stem cells into patients with damaged or diseased organs. Such research could greatly reduce the likelihood that a person's body would reject that tissue and also help obviate the need for immunosuppressive drugs, which often have severe and potentially life-threatening side effects.

(9) Based on these expert conclusions and recommendations and other evidence, nuclear transplantation is a valuable area of research that could potentially save millions of lives and relieve the suffering of countless others, and thus should not be banned.

(10) The National Academies recommended that nuclear transplantation experiments should be subject to close scrutiny under the Federal procedures and rules concerning human-subjects research.

(11) Given the need for additional oversight in this area, strict ethical requirements for human subjects research, including informed consent,

safety and privacy protections, and review by an ethics board, should be prescribed for all research involving nuclear transplantation, whether using Federal or non-Federal funds.

(12)

(A) Biomedical research and clinical facilities engage in and affect interstate commerce.

(B) The services provided by clinical facilities move in interstate commerce.

(C) Patients travel regularly across State lines in order to access clinical facilities.

(D) Biomedical research and clinical facilities engage scientists, doctors, and others in an interstate market, and contract for research and purchase medical and other supplies in an interstate market.

**SEC. 3. PURPOSES.**

It is the purpose of this Act to prohibit human cloning and to protect important areas of medical research, including stem cell research.

**SEC. 4. PROHIBITION ON HUMAN CLONING.**

(a) IN GENERAL—Title 18, United States Code, is amended by inserting after chapter 15, the following:

**CHAPTER 16—PROHIBITION ON HUMAN CLONING**

Sec.

301. Prohibition on human cloning.

**Sec. 301. Prohibition on human cloning**

(a) DEFINITIONS—In this section:

(1) HUMAN CLONING—The term "human cloning" means implanting or attempting to implant the product of nuclear transplantation into a uterus or the functional equivalent of a uterus.

(2) HUMAN SOMATIC CELL—The term "human somatic cell" means any human cell other than a haploid germ cell.

(3) NUCLEAR TRANSPLANTATION—The term "nuclear transplantation" means transferring the nucleus of a human somatic cell into an oocyte from which the nucleus or all chromosomes have been or will be removed or rendered inert.

(4) NUCLEUS—The term "nucleus" means the cell structure that houses the chromosomes.

(5) OOCYTE—The term "oocyte" means the female germ cell, the egg.

(b) PROHIBITIONS ON HUMAN CLONING—It shall be unlawful for any person or other legal entity, public or private—

(1) to conduct or attempt to conduct human cloning; or

(2) to ship the product of nuclear transplantation in interstate or foreign commerce for the purpose of human cloning in the United States or elsewhere.

(c) PROTECTION OF RESEARCH—Nothing in this section shall be construed to restrict practices not expressly prohibited in this section.

(d) PENALTIES—

(1) CRIMINAL PENALTIES—Whoever intentionally violates paragraph (1) or (2) of subsection (b) shall be fined under this title and imprisoned not more than 10 years.

(2) CIVIL PENALTIES—Whoever intentionally violates paragraph (1) or (2) of subsection (b) shall be subject to a civil penalty of $1,000,000 or three times the gross pecuniary gain resulting from the violation, whichever is greater.

(3) FORFEITURE—Any property, real or personal, derived from or used to commit a violation or attempted violation of the provisions of subsection (b), or any property traceable to such property, shall be subject to forfeiture to the United States in accordance with the procedures set forth in chapter 46 of title 18, United States Code.

(e) RIGHT OF ACTION—Nothing in this section shall be construed to give any individual or person a private right of action.

(b) ETHICAL REQUIREMENTS FOR NUCLEAR TRANSPLANTA-TION RESEARCH—Part H of title IV of the Public Health Service Act (42 U.S.C. 289 et seq.) is amended by adding at the end the following:

SEC. 498C. ETHICAL REQUIREMENTS FOR NUCLEAR TRANS-PLANTATION RESEARCH, INCLUDING INFORMED CONSENT, INSTITUTIONAL REVIEW BOARD REVIEW, AND PROTECTION FOR SAFETY AND PRIVACY.

(a) DEFINITIONS—In this section:

(1) HUMAN SOMATIC CELL—The term "human somatic cell" means any human cell other than a haploid germ cell.

(2) NUCLEAR TRANSPLANTATION—The term "nuclear transplantation" means transferring the nucleus of a human somatic cell into an oocyte from which the nucleus or all chromosomes have been or will be removed or rendered inert.

(3) NUCLEUS—The term "nucleus" means the cell structure that houses the chromosomes.

(4) OOCYTE—The term "oocyte" means the female germ cell, the egg.

(b) APPLICABILITY OF FEDERAL ETHICAL STANDARDS TO NUCLEAR TRANSPLANTATION RESEARCH—Research involving nuclear transplantation shall be conducted in accordance with subparts A and B of part 46 of title 45, Code of Federal Regulations (as in effect on the date of enactment of the Human Cloning Prohibition Act of 2002).

(c) CIVIL PENALTIES—Whoever intentionally violates subsection (b) shall be subject to a civil penalty in an amount that is appropriate for the violation involved, but not more than $250,000.

(d) ENFORCEMENT—The Secretary of Health and Human Services shall have the exclusive authority to enforce this section.

## NOTES

1. Act of 4 Oct. 1997, 1997 Cal. Stat. 688. The primary statute is found at California Health and Safety Code 24185, Division 20, Chapter 1.4, et seq., although several other statutes are also amended by the act. California subsequently amended this during 2002, in SB 1230, which was signed by the governor on September 23, 2002.

2. R.I. Gen. Laws 23-16.4-1 (1998).

3. Act of 3 June 1998, 1998 Mich. Pub. Acts 108, MCLS 333.16274, 16275; MCLS 750.430a.

4. La. R. S. 40:1299.36.2 et seq.

5. Va. Code 32.1-162.22 (2001).

6. Ia. Code 707B (2002). Approved by the governor April 26, 2002.

7. The legislatures of Alabama, Arizona, Colorado, Delaware, Florida, Illinois, Indiana, Kansas, Kentucky, Massachusetts, Missouri, Nebraska, New Hampshire, New Jersey, New York, Oklahoma, South Carolina, Tennessee, and Wisconsin have all recently formally considered bills to ban or regulate the cloning of humans.

8. Georgia, South Dakota, and California. California's resolution urges a federal ban on human reproductive cloning but not on therapeutic cloning.

9. § 1.217 R.S.Mo. (2001). "No state funds shall be used for research with respect to the cloning of a human person. For purposes of this section, the term 'cloning' means the replication of a human person by taking a cell with genetic material and cultivating such cell through the egg, embryo, fetal, and newborn stages of development into a new human person."

10. R.I. Gen. Laws § 11-54-1(a).

11. National Bioethics Advisory Commission, 2 ETHICAL ISSUES IN HUMAN STEM CELL RESEARCH A-4, A-10 (National Bioethics Advisory Commission 1999).

12. President's Council on Bioethics, *Human Cloning and Human Dignity: An Ethical Inquiry,* chapter 7, note I (July 2002), <http://www.bioethics.gov/cloningreport/fullreport.html>.

13. Michigan's law elsewhere provides that "[a] person shall not use a live human embryo...for nontherapeutic research if...the research substantially jeopardizes the life or health of the embryo," Mich. Comp. Laws § 333.2685 (1), and such experimentation is a felony, §333.2691. However, these provisions do not appear to apply to therapeutic cloning.

14. This is the interpretation of Michigan's law by the President's Council on Bioethics in its 2002 report. *See* President's Council on Bioethics, *supra* note 12.

15. La. Rev. Stat. title 9, §§ 123, 129.

16. La. Rev. Stat. title 9, § 122.

17. *See* President's Council on Bioethics, *supra* note 12.

18. A portion of the proposed (but not enacted) New Hampshire statute reads as follows:

[A]ttempts of "therapeutic cloning" always result in the destruction of human beings at the embryonic stage of life when their stem cells are harvested....The prospect of creating new human life solely to be exploited ("reproductive cloning") or destroyed ("therapeutic cloning") in these ways has been condemned on moral grounds by many, as displaying a profound disrespect for life....The distinction between "therapeutic" and "reproductive" cloning is a false distinction scientifically because both begin with the creation of a human being at the embryonic stage of life, one destined for implantation in a womb, one destined for destructive farming of its stem cells....Regardless of its ultimate destiny, all human embryos are simultaneously human beings. It will be nearly impossible to ban only attempts at "reproductive cloning" if "therapeutic cloning" is allowed because:

(1) Cloning would take place within the privacy of a doctor-patient relationship;

(2) The transfer of embryos to begin a pregnancy is a simple procedure; and

(3) Any government effort to prevent the transfer of an existing cloned embryo, or to prevent birth once transfer has occurred would raise substantial moral, legal, and practical issues....

Based on [these findings], it is the purpose of this act to prohibit the use of cloning technology to initiate the development of new human beings at the embryonic stage of life for any purpose, therapeutic or reproductive.

19. Me. Rev. Stat. title 22 § 1593.
20. National Bioethics Advisory Commission, *supra* note 11, at A-4, A-10.
21. Mass. Gen. Laws ch. 112 §12 J (a) I.
22. Mass. Gen. Laws ch. 112 §12 (J) (a) IV.
23. Minn. Stat. § 145.422.
24. Minn. Stat. §145.421.
25. N.D. Cent. Code § 14-02.2-01(1).
26. National Bioethics Advisory Commission, *supra* note 11, at A-4.
27. Pa. Cons. Stat. title 18 § 3216 (a).
28. Pa. Cons. Stat. title 18 § 3203.
29. S.D. Codified Laws §§ 34-14-16, 34-14-17.
30. S.D. Codified Laws § 34-14-18.
31. S.D. Codified Laws § 34-14-20.
32. H.R. 2505, 107th Cong. (2001). *See* Rick Weiss and Juliet Eilperin, *House Votes Broad Ban on Cloning*, WASH. POST, Aug. 1, 2001, at A1.
33. *Id.*
34. *Id.*
35. *See* Rick Weiss, *Bush Backs Broad Ban on Human Cloning*, WASH. POST, June 21, 2001, at A1. Among the alternative anticloning bills introduced during the 107th Congress were H.R. 1608, H.R. 1644, and S.790. In furtherance of this policy direction, National Bioethics Advisory Commission, *supra* note 11, President Bush named seventeen individuals to serve on a new President's Council on Bioethics. The council made its recommendations concerning a ban on the cloning of humans in July 2002. *See* White House Press Release, *President Names Members of Bioethics Council* (Jan. 22, 2002), <http://www.whitehouse.gov/news/releases/2002/01/20020116-9.html>. Some observers initially anticipated that the council would issue advice consistent with the well-known views of President Bush, but as I shall discuss later, that was not entirely the case. *See* Arthur Caplan, *A Council of Clones*, MSNBC (Jan. 17, 2002), <http://www.msnbc.com/news/689297.asp>.
36. H.R. 2505, Sec. 301(1).
37. *Id.*, Sec. 302(a)(1)–(3).
38. *Id.*, Sec. 302(b).

39. *Id.,* Sec. 302(c)(1).

40. *Id.,* Sec. 302(c)(2).

41. *Id.,* Sec. 302(d).

42. Helen Dewar, *Cloning Foes Consider Moratorium,* WASH. POST, June 12, 2002, at A7; Helen Dewar, *Anti-Cloning Bills Stall in Senate; Vote Unlikely Soon,* WASH. POST, June 14, 2002, at A4.

43. Helen Dewar, *Human Cloning Ban Sidetracked; Senate Vote Deals Amendment Second Setback in a Week,* WASH. POST, June 19, 2002, at A4.

44. *Senators' Bill Details Rules on Cloning Research,* WASH. POST, June 6, 2002, at A3. The bill was drafted primarily by Senators Diane Feinstein (D-Calif.), Edward Kennedy (D-Mass.), Arlen Specter (R-Pa.), and Orrin Hatch (R-Utah).

45. *See* President's Council on Bioethics, *supra* note 12.

46. President's Council on Bioethics, Chapter 8, Policy Recommendations <http://www.bioethics.gov/reports/cloningreport/recommend.html> (July 2002). The ten council members who supported this proposal imposing a moratorium on cloning research are Rebecca S. Dresser, Francis Fukuyama, Robert P. George, Mary Ann Glendon, Alfonso Gómez-Lobo, William B. Hurlbut, Leon R. Kass, Charles Krauthammer, Paul McHugh, and Gilbert C. Meilaender.

47. *Id.* This option was supported by the following seven council members: Elizabeth H. Blackburn, Daniel W. Foster, Michael S. Gazzaniga, William F. May, Janet D. Rowley, Michael J. Sandel, and James Q. Wilson.

48. *See* Jim VandeHei and Jonathan Weisman, *Republicans Poised to Enact Agenda,* WASH. POST, Nov. 7, 2002, at A1 (listing a "ban on human cloning" among the administration's top priorities for the new Congress); Judy Keen and Jim Drinkard, *Shift to GOP Opens Door to Bush's Ambitious Plans,* USA TODAY, Nov. 7, 2002 (same).

49. The House bill goes beyond the Senate version in prohibiting the importation of medical therapies derived from cloned human embryos, as well as the embryos themselves.

50. H.R. 534, Human Cloning Prohibition Act of 2003. *See* Juliet Eilperin and Rick Weiss, *House Votes to Prohibit All Human Cloning; Measure Faces Uncertainty in Closely Divided Senate,* WASH. POST, Feb. 28, 2003, at A6.

51. *Id.* The major competing bill, sponsored by Senator Orin Hatch and others, is entitled Human Cloning Ban and Stem Cell Research Protection Act of 2003, S. 303.

52. *Id.* My research has failed to disclose even one United States Senator or member of the House of Representatives who has publicly declared support for reproductive cloning. Yet there remains no federal law banning it in the United States.

53. Rick Weiss, *Human Clone Research Will Be Regulated,* WASH. POST, Jan. 20, 1998, at A1. See generally Christine Willgoos, *FDA Regulation: An Answer to the Question of Human Cloning and Germline Gene Therapy,* 27 AM. J. L. & MED. 101 (2001).

54. *Id.*

55. United States Food and Drug Administration, PROPOSED APPROACH TO REGULATION OF CELLULAR AND TISSUE-BASED PRODUCTS 6, 9 (United States Food and Drug Administration, 1997).

56. *See* Committee on Science, Engineering, and Public Policy, SCIENTIFIC AND MEDICAL ASPECTS OF HUMAN REPRODUCTIVE CLONING, 81–82 (National Academy Press, 2002) (HUMAN REPRODUCTIVE CLONING); Elizabeth C. Price, *Does the FDA Have Authority to Regulate Human Cloning?* 11 HARV. J. L. & TECH. 619, 694 (1998) (maintaining that the FDA lacks jurisdiction to regulate cloning as a "drug," "medical device," or "biological product"); Willgoos, *supra* note 49, at 119–22. *See also* Rick Weiss, *Legal Barriers to Human Cloning May Not Hold Up*, WASH. POST, May 23, 2001, at A1.

57. *See* Caroline Daniel, *Conflicting Aims Leave the Ban on Human Cloning in Limbo*, WASH. POST, July 26, 1998, at A8.

58. 42 U.S.C. 351(i).

59. *See* Gregory J. Rokosz, *Human Cloning: Is the Reach of FDA Authority Too Far a Stretch?* 30 SETON HALL L. REV. 464, 497 (2000).

60. *See generally* John Charles Kunich, *Mother Frankenstein, Doctor Nature, and the Environmental Law of Genetic Engineering*, 74 S. CAL. L. REV. 807 (2001).

61. *See* FDA Statement, *Use of Cloning Technology to Clone a Human Being*, <http://www.fda.gov/cber/genetherapy/clone.htm> (December 27, 2002).

62. Available on-line at <http://www.fda.gov/cber/ltr/aaclone.htm>.

63. United States v. Lopez, 514 U.S. 549 (1995). The Supreme Court ruled that Congress lacks authority to regulate the possession of firearms near schools in the fifty states. The decision is significant because it signaled a partial reversal of the Court's acceptance, since the New Deal, of Congress's use of the Commerce Clause to regulate many facets of American life.

64. *See* HUMAN REPRODUCTIVE CLONING, *supra* note 52, at 82.

# CHAPTER 3

# International Law and Cloning around the World

The cloning of humans is a worldwide issue, and the United States is by no means unique in determining that some (often drastic) legal measures are necessary. In this chapter, I will discuss some of the legal responses outside the United States. In doing so, I will compare the approaches of other nations to the United States' actions and examine whether there is a model somewhere for the rest of the world to emulate. The full-text version of pertinent provisions of some of these laws is available in appendix 2.

This discussion of foreign law is relevant to the primary thesis of this book for three reasons. First, it will clearly demonstrate the powerful global trend to view the cloning of humans as an obvious and dreadful evil to be preemptively eradicated. This illustrates the urgent need for widespread education as to the facts of life—and of cloning—so that public policy making and law making around the world can be rooted in reality rather than in science fiction. Second, it will demonstrate the diversity of approaches to cloning legislation, nation by nation. Many readers may be surprised to find that the most carefully balanced, meticulously crafted legislation in this cutting-edge area does not come from the largest, wealthiest, oldest, or most technologically advanced nations of the world. This insight is itself evidence that Procrustean, one-size-fits-all, global bans are not necessarily the best approach to follow. And third, nations such as the United States that are still working on their own legislative response can examine in detail the examples from other nations and thus make a more informed decision on which model best fits their national needs, legal system, and overall philosophy.

The world beyond the United States has been active in anticloning legislation for years, both as individual nations and collectively. For example, the 1997 Council of Europe Convention on Human Rights and Biomedicine on the Prohibition of Cloning Human Beings[1] is an international agreement that features a total prohibition on the cloning of human beings.[2] Individual nations have also taken steps to ban the cloning of humans.[3] And in late February 2002, the United States extended its anticloning campaign to the United Nations, proposing a "global and comprehensive ban" on the cloning of humans and on all experimentation involving human embryos.[4] Let us consider some of these in detail, beginning with some influential international statements of policy.

The United Nations Educational, Scientific, and Cultural Organization (UNESCO) issued the Universal Declaration on the Human Genome and Human Rights (Declaration) on November 11, 1997.[5] It contains some sweeping statements as to the lofty significance of "the human genome," including an assertion that the "human genome underlies the fundamental unity of all members of the human family, as well as the recognition of their inherent dignity and diversity. In a symbolic sense, it is the heritage of humanity."[6] Further, "Everyone has a right to respect for their dignity and for their rights regardless of their genetic characteristics," and that dignity "makes it imperative not to reduce individuals to their genetic characteristics and to respect their uniqueness and diversity."[7] Ironically, these latter pronouncements would argue in favor of safeguarding the rights of any cloned person because they would be as entitled as anyone else to respect for their dignity and their rights, irrespective of the fact that they share their nuclear DNA with another person.

However, Article 11 of the Declaration declares that "practices which are contrary to human dignity, such as reproductive cloning of human beings, shall not be permitted." The Declaration, in Article 24, authorizes the International Bioethics Committee to identify any practices that are contrary to "basic notions of human dignity" and in Article 10 mandates that any research involving cloning must give the utmost respect to the integrity of human dignity. However, the Declaration is nonbinding and is intended simply to serve as a model for legislation in member countries.

There is similar guidance on the international front from the World Health Organization (WHO), an umbrella entity with oversight responsibilities for more than seventy international medical organizations. WHO has published a policy statement in which it labeled human cloning as "repugnant to basic ethics" and asked scientists to refrain from cloning humans on a voluntary basis until additional research on the safety, ethics, and morals of the process is conducted.[8] WHO averred that therapeutic/research cloning should be distinguished from reproductive cloning and that the former is an important and legitimate practice to further medical technology and treatment options. WHO lacks any enforcement power, but its policies are widely respected and followed worldwide by most scientists.

Many of the internal anticloning laws of nations other than the United States, and international agreements governing cloning, are based either on declarations by groups such as UNESCO and WHO or on similar basic notions of human rights as reflected in each nation's laws. If a United Nations (UN) treaty on cloning becomes a reality and attracts many signatories, there will be additional pressure on the nations of the world to take anticloning legal action.

Members of the UN were not entirely united on the cloning issue during 2002. France and Germany proposed a global ban on human reproductive cloning, while the United States pressed for a broader treaty that would also prohibit all cloning research involving human embryos.[9] The more all encompassing ban favored by the United States became the focal point of the UN committee responsible for drafting a treaty. The committee deferred debate on the more limited Franco-German proposal until at least late in 2003, while consideration of the sweeping ban proceeds.[10]

At this time, the list of countries that ban human cloning in whole or in part includes some of the oldest and largest nations of the world, and the number is growing. Additionally, some countries have adopted legislation that regulates research involving human embryos and nuclear transfer cloning. I will now discuss some of these in detail. Again, refer to appendix 2 for the full-text version of many of these laws.

## EUROPEAN CONVENTION ON HUMAN RIGHTS AND BIOMEDICINE

The Council of Europe (an instrument of the European Union) established the succinctly named Convention for the Protection of Human Rights and Dignity of the Human Being with Regard to the Application of Biology and Medicine: Convention on Human Rights and Biomedicine (Convention) as a framework for European nations to adopt as a minimum standard to protect human rights and dignity in medical research.[11] Articles 1 and 27 provide that European nations are not allowed to adopt internal regulations less restrictive than those in the Convention, but may enact greater restrictions in accordance with each nation's own values. The Convention, in Article 13, prohibits the modification of the human genome, except for the purpose of prevention or therapy, and then only so long as the descendants' genome is not altered. Article 18.2 bans the "creation of embryos for research purposes. The Convention has attracted the ratifications or accessions of fourteen nations, and the signatures of seventeen more.[12]

Because of the considerable ambiguity in the Convention's language, the Council of Europe on January 1, 1998, adopted an Additional Protocol to the Convention (Protocol).[13] Nineteen nations swiftly signed the Protocol, and thus it became the first binding international legal agreement concerning the cloning of humans.[14] The Preamble and ensuing Article 1 state, in pertinent part:

The member States of the Council of Europe, the other States and the European Community Signatories to this Additional Protocol to the Convention for the Protection of Human Rights and Dignity of the Human Being with Regard to the Application of Biology and Medicine, noting scientific developments in the field of mammal cloning,...Mindful of the progress that some cloning techniques themselves may bring to scientific knowledge and its medical application;...Having noted that embryo splitting may occur naturally and sometimes result in the birth of genetically identical twins; Considering however that the instrumentalization of human beings through the deliberate creation of genetically identical human beings is contrary to human dignity and thus constitutes a misuse of biology and medicine; Considering also the serious difficulties of a medical, psychological and social nature that such a deliberate biomedical practice might imply for all the individuals involved;...[and] aiming to protect the dignity and identity of all human beings, Have agreed as follows:
    Article 1: 1) Any intervention seeking to create a human being genetically identical to another human being, whether living or dead, is prohibited. 2) For the purpose of this article, the term human being "genetically identical" to another human being means a human being sharing with another the same nuclear gene set.

Article 1 of the Protocol thus expressly forbids the "creation of a human being genetically identical to another human being [that is, sharing the same nuclear gene set], whether living or dead." The Protocol prohibits human cloning generically but not any particular cloning technique such as SCNT or embryo splitting. It goes beyond the UNESCO Declaration by seeking an outright ban on the reproductive cloning of humans. However, the Protocol does allow the cloning of isolated cells or tissue and thus would permit at least some forms of therapeutic cloning.

The repeated references in the Protocol to the inherent dignity of humans are mirrored in other international instruments as well, including the preambles to The Universal Declaration of Human Rights,[15] The International Covenant on Economic, Social and Cultural Rights,[16] and The International Covenant on Civil and Political Rights.[17] While all these other UN treaties address the dignity of humans, none deals with the specific subject of cloning human beings.

Once a nation ratifies the Protocol, it must bring its laws into harmony with both the Convention and the Protocol, and must implement sanctions such as fines and/or revocation of medical and research licenses for any violation of the cloning ban. Several of the more influential nations, such as Germany and the United Kingdom, are not signatories to the Protocol, for varying reasons. A total of twelve nations have ratified or acceded to the Protocol as of this writing, and an additional seventeen have signed it.[18]

## EUROPEAN UNION

The European Union (EU) adopted the Fifth Framework Programme on Research and Technological Developments (Framework), which prohibits the governmental funding of any project that uses embryos for human reproductive cloning.[19] The Framework is designed to reinforce respect for ethical and moral principles essential to human rights.

## INDIVIDUAL NATIONS

In the following sections, I discuss a few of the internal domestic laws of nations other than the United States dealing with the cloning of humans. This is not an exhaustive list, and it is only intended to be illustrative of the diversity of legislative approaches to cloning worldwide. In addition to the key provisions mentioned here, please consult appendix 2 for more details.

### United Kingdom

The United Kingdom has had legislation in effect relevant to cloning longer than most other nations. Most recently, on December 4, 2001, the Human Reproductive Cloning Act 2001 was enacted.

This legislation was rushed into place in the immediate aftermath of a High Court ruling on November 15, 2001, that Britain has no laws governing the reproduction of human embryos using cloning technology, despite the 1990 act on embryology that had been touted as a global first. Under the 1990 act, embryos could be destroyed and created for some types of medical research, and in January of 2001, the act was extended to take into account scientific advances, stem-cell experiments in particular. It was specifically worded to allow cloning to create embryos for stem-cell research. Parliament and scientists believed that cloning embryos to reproduce a child remained illegal under the change. But the ProLife Alliance, which opposes all forms of cloning, successfully exposed a loophole in the law, claiming it did not really ban cloning.[20] Thus, Parliament was galvanized into swift action.

The Human Reproductive Cloning Act 2001 provides, in part, the following:

(1) A person who places in a woman a human embryo which has been created otherwise than by fertilisation is guilty of an offence.

(2) A person who is guilty of the offence is liable on conviction on indictment to imprisonment for a term not exceeding 10 years or a fine or both.[21]

This act extends to Northern Ireland and provides for the consent of the director of Public Prosecutions for England, Wales, or Northern Island, as the case may be, in the event of any prosecutions under the act. The statute is extremely brief and contains no definitions for any of its terms, thereby creating the possibility of controversy down the road over the meaning of terms such as "human embryo." But the act was intended to close loopholes in and build upon the foundation laid in 1990 by the Human Fertilisation and Embryology Act (HFEA),[22] which is a much lengthier piece of legislation, complete with definitions of terms.

The HFEA provides, in part, that no person shall bring about the creation of an embryo, or keep or use an embryo, except pursuant to a license. Further, Section 3(3)(d) specifies that a license cannot authorize "replacing a nucleus of a cell of an embryo with a nucleus taken from a cell of any person, embryo or subsequent development of an embryo."[23] This was intended to ban SCNT cloning of humans for reproduction, but because of inartful drafting, the prohibition was held by the British High Court not to apply to the use of enucleated eggs as the recipients of the donor's DNA. Section 5 of the act did, however, establish the Human Fertilisation and Embryology Authority, which, among other things, is to "keep under review information about embryos and any subsequent development of embryos and about the provision of treatment services and activities governed by this Act."[24] A spokesperson for the Human Fertilisation and Embryology Authority explained that the 1990 act was initially an attempt to clarify the law in response to the birth of Louise Brown in 1978, the first baby born through in vitro fertilization. The act "took a long time" he said. "We thought the job was done."[25]

Embryo splitting and nucleus replacement (SCNT) of eggs are not expressly and specifically prohibited by the HFEA, but, because both procedures involve the use or creation of embryos outside the body, they fall within the HFEA and therefore come under the jurisdiction of the Human Fertilisation and Embryology Authority. The HFEA allows, under a license from the Human Fertilisation and Embryology Authority, research involving human embryos (implicitly including therapeutic cloning) within strict limits: the embryos must not exceed the fourteenth day of their development, and embryos used for research must not be implanted in a uterus. The Human Fertilisation and Embryology Authority can license the use of human embryos only where it considers their use to be necessary for the research; thus, animal studies will often be a prerequisite before research involving human embryos will be permitted. In addition, any such research must, in the opinion of the Human Fertilisation and Embryology Authority, be necessary or desirable for one of the following purposes:

to promote advances in the treatment of infertility,

to increase knowledge about the causes of congenital disease or about the causes of miscarriages, or to develop more effective techniques of contraception or methods for detecting the presence of gene or chromosome abnormalities in embryos before implantation.

The secretary of state for health can add to this list, using regulations, provided the new categories are established with a view to increasing knowledge about the creation and development of embryos, or about disease, or with a view to enabling such knowledge to be applied.

The HFEA also contains extensive provisions for the granting and revocation of licenses dealing with human embryos, as well as artificial insemination, surrogacy, and related issues. The act provides for criminal prosecution as well as license revocation for offenses under its terms.

### The Netherlands

The Netherlands has enacted an "Act containing rules relating to the use of gametes and embryos," usually referred to as the "Embryos Act."[26] It is similar in many respects to the British HFEA in that it governs a wide range of practices and issues relevant to human embryos, most of which are not specific to cloning.

The term *embryo* is defined in Division 1, Section 1c of the Embryos Act as "a cell or a complex of cells with the capacity to develop into a human being." Likewise, *gametes* is defined as "human spermatozoa and oocytes," that is, sperm and eggs. By its terms, the act appears to ban all reproductive cloning of humans, as well as therapeutic cloning in which the embryo is allowed to develop past the fourteen-day point. Moreover, the act seems to prohibit therapeutic cloning where the embryo, regardless of duration of development, is created expressly for research purposes (other than initiation of an actual pregnancy). However, this last provision is set to lapse under the terms of Division 8, Section 33.2, "on a date to be determined by Royal Decree," which the act recommends as no later than five years after entry into force. Thus, there is a sunset clause with regard to activities including therapeutic cloning, so long as any resulting embryo does not persist beyond fourteen days.

The Embryos Act, in Division 7, Section 28, provides criminal penalties for its violation. Specifically with regard to the cloning prohibition in Section 24, a prison term of up to one year or a "fourth category" fine is set forth.

### Germany

Section 6(1) of the German embryo protection law (the Federal Embryo Protection Act of 1990, Embryonenschutzgesetz), which has been in force since December 15, 1990, forbids the cloning of human beings in sweeping terms.

It bans the creation of any embryo "genetically identical" to any other embryo, fetus, or any person living or dead, without regard to whether such an embryo is allowed to develop only for a few days, is never implanted in a woman's uterus, or is not intended for reproduction. Thus, both therapeutic and reproductive cloning of humans are illegal in Germany.[27] In large part, of course, the strictness of the German law is reflective of that nation's involvement in horrific experiments during World War II, in which large numbers of human beings were cruelly subjected to involuntary and destructive surgical procedures in the name of scientific inquiry.

This tension between the German approach and that of the Council of Europe is worth noting in light of pressures from some to enact blanket restrictions or bans on human cloning on a uniform global basis, as with a UN-sponsored international treaty. Some nations, like German, for historical reasons have their own unique perspective on human embryo research or forced experimentation on human beings. Other nations have particularly strong constitutional or legislative opposition to governmental intrusion into the private reproductive decisions of their citizens. The spirit of free scientific inquiry is especially vibrant in some countries, a result of a combination of current practices and historical precedent. For all of these reasons, a nation-by-nation approach is preferable to multinational legislation that imposes one method on all.

## Denmark

In Denmark, cloning of humans is governed by Act No. 503 of June 24, 1992, on the Scientific Ethics Committee System and the Examination of Biomedical Research Projects (1992) 43 (4).[28] Act 503, in Section 15, provides that "the following experiments may not be performed: (1) Experiments whose purpose is to enable genetically identical individuals to be produced."

This is complemented by Act No. 460 on Medically Assisted Procreation in connection with medical treatment, diagnosis, and research, enacted in 1997. Act No. 460 specifies that treatment cannot be initiated in areas where a research ban already exists under Act No. 503; it thus implicitly prohibits the creation of human clones, chimeras, and hybrids.[29] It also prohibits the reimplantation of embryos, which have been genetically modified, and embryos that might have been harmed by research activities.

Because the law is phrased in such broad terms, it appears to prohibit all reproductive cloning, irrespective of the method employed. Both SCNT and embryo splitting would arguably "enable genetically identical individuals to be produced" and thus would violate Danish law. Evidently, therapeutic cloning is not banned so long as the purpose of the research is not to bring about reproductive cloning.

## Spain

The Spanish penal code prohibits human reproductive cloning. Under Article 16, "anyone who brings about the birth of identical human beings as a result of cloning or other procedures aimed at the selection of humans is liable for a sentence of one to five years in prison and suspension from his professional activities for six to ten years." Also, Law 35/1988 dealing with medically assisted reproduction, in Chapter VI, Article 20, forbids "(k) the creation of identical human beings, by cloning or any other procedure with the aim of race selection; (l) the creation of human beings by cloning or any other method or any other procedure able to create identical human beings."[30] Violation is punishable by imprisonment from one to five years.

Similarly, with regard to research into reproductive cloning, Law No. 42/1988 of December 28, 1988, on the Donation and Use of Embryos and Fetuses or their Cells, Tissues, and Organs, Section 2 (e), 8(a), prohibits research on the creation or production of "genetically identical human beings."[31] This appears to allow therapeutic cloning, the aim of which is not to produce children.

Of course, it is possible to quibble with such language on the grounds that children of cloning are not truly "identical human beings," even genetically. As I noted in chapter 1, in almost all cases, the person who donated the DNA and the child of cloning will have different mitochondrial DNA, and there will be subtle difference in the nuclear DNA as well. Nonetheless, it was obviously the intent of the Spanish legislature to ban reproductive cloning as well as research into the same. Moreover, as is the case with the Danish law, Spain seems to draw no distinctions on the basis of the method used to create "identical human beings" and therefore would block embryo splitting as well as SCNT for reproductive cloning.

## Norway

On March 25, 1994, the Ministry of Health and Social Affairs presented to the Storting (the Norwegian parliament) a bill relating to the application of biotechnology in medicine. The bill was based on Report No 25 (1992–93) to the Storting, titled "Biotechnology related to human beings" presented by the Norwegian government on March 12, 1993.

The bill was debated in the Storting in June 1994. The government gained a majority for all of its proposals, with the exception of that concerning permission to conduct research on embryos and the use of insemination by a donor in combination with in vitro fertilization. That meant that the preexisting ban on embryo research continued to be in effect in Norway. As codified in Law 56 of 1994 on the use of biotechnology,[32] therefore, research into the cloning of humans is implicitly banned in Norway. There appears to be no distinction made between experimentation using preimplantation embryos and that intended to result in reproductive cloning.

On May 30, 1997, the Norwegian government presented a new amendment to the Law 56, which prohibits the use of techniques for producing genetically identical individuals. Notably, in the remarks accompanying the amendment, it was stated that the amendment covers cloning by embryo splitting and by nuclear transfer techniques as well as other possible techniques, and it includes both medical research and possible applications. Genetically identical individuals are defined as individuals who share the same gene set, and mitochondrial DNA is not included in this definition. The phrase "use of techniques" was used to prevent the prohibition from applying to twins and triplets originating from natural cloning. The amendment was adopted in February 1998 and entered into force at once, as new chapter 3a.[33]

The statute, as amended, is a model of brevity. Chapter 3, Section 3-1 reads, in its entirety, "Research on embryos is prohibited." Similarly, the complete provision on reproductive cloning, Chapter 3a, Section 3a-1, reads, "The use of techniques aimed at the production of genetically identical individuals is prohibited." Violations are punishable by imprisonment for up to three months. It would appear that therapeutic cloning is still permitted, if not intended to lead to reproductive cloning.

### Japan

The Japanese Diet enacted the Law Concerning Regulations Relating to Human Cloning Techniques and Other Similar Techniques,[34] which went into effect in June 2001. Through this law, Japan has made the reproductive cloning of humans a criminal offense and set forth guidelines strictly regulating the creation of human embryos using cloning. Among other things, the law forbids the transfer of a human embryo made through SCNT into the uterus of a human or animal. The key term *embryo* is defined in Article 2(1)1 as "A cell (except for a germ cell) or cells which has/have potential to grow into an individual through the process of development *in utero* of a human or an animal and has/have not yet begun formation of a placenta."

Article 3 prohibits the "transfer" of a human clone embryo into any uterus. With regard to embryo splitting, the law does not absolutely forbid the implantation of a resulting embryo, but in Article 4, it calls for guidelines to be set by the minister of education, culture, sports, science, and technology.[35]

The law specifies procedures for researchers to give detailed advance notice to the minister of education, culture, sports, science, and technology concerning cloned and other "Specified Embryos" and their production or importation. That minister is empowered, under Articles 7 and 12, to order the alteration or cancellation of plans if the method of handling any "Specified Embryos" is "not deemed to comply with the Guidelines." The minister, pursuant to Article 14, "may, to the extent necessary to enforce this Law, ask a person who has given notice…for reports concerning the conditions in which the Specified Embryo was handled and other necessary items related to the notice." Further, Article 15 provides that the minister "may, to the extent necessary to enforce this Law, have a Ministry official access and enter the office or laboratory of a person who has given notice,…inspect documents and other necessary property, and ask questions of the participants." Such a visit, however, is not to "be construed as approved for the purpose of investigation of a criminal offense."

The law provides for severe penalties in the event of violation of Article 3. Imprisonment of up to ten years, or a fine of up to 10 million yen, or both, is authorized under Article 16 for a person who "transfers" any of the "Specified Embryos" into the uterus of a human or animal. Articles 17 through 20 provide lesser criminal sanctions for the violation of other portions of the law.

The law also has a supplementary provision, in Article 2, that, although not truly a sunset clause, does formally recognize that the law may have to be adjusted in fairly short order to reflect the rapidly changing state of our knowledge concerning human reproductive technology. Japan has also been careful not to foreclose work on therapeutic cloning unrelated to reproductive cloning of humans.

### Switzerland

The Swiss Federal Constitution, as amended on August 13, 1982, forbids the reproductive cloning of humans.[36] Article 119, in particular, is a very strong constitutional position against modern assisted reproductive techniques. In addition to banning "all forms of cloning," it also proscribes surrogacy and places limitations on other modern techniques.

Switzerland has considered legislation specifically along the lines mandated by its constitution with regard to banning the cloning of humans. The Federal Bill on Medically Assisted Procreation would explicitly add criminal statutory penalties for human embryo or oocyte cloning to the basic prohibitions already in place in the constitution.

### Australia

Australia, or portions thereof, has banned human cloning in two statutes. First, the Infertility Treatment Act of 1995,[37] Section 47 (titled "Ban on cloning"), provides: "A person must not carry out or attempt to carry out cloning. Penalty: 480 penalty units or 4 years imprisonment or both." The Section 3 definitions state that " 'clone' means to form, outside the human body, a human embryo that is genetically identical to another human embryo or person," and that " 'embryo' means any stage of human embryonic development at and from syngamy [where the chromosomes derived from the male and female pronuclei align on the mitotic spindle]." This would thus apply to therapeutic as well as reproductive cloning, even of preimplantation embryos, with a four-year prison sentence possible for violation.

Exclusive focus on reproductive cloning within Victoria is found in the Gene Technology Act of 2001. Section 192B of that act, titled "Cloning of human beings is prohibited,"[38] states:

(1) A person is guilty of an offence if:

(a) the person engages in conduct; and

(b) the person knows that, or is reckless as to whether, the conduct will result in the cloning of a whole human being.

Maximum penalty: 2,000 penalty units or imprisonment for 10 years.

(2) In this section:

*cloning of a whole human being* means the use of technology for the purpose of producing, from one original, a duplicate or descendant that is, or duplicates or descendants that are, genetically identical to the original.

The Gene Technology Act of 2001 thus applies only to reproductive cloning and, arguably, would apply to both SCNT and embryo-splitting methods. Both techniques can "produce, from one original," others that are in some sense "genetically identical." In the case of SCNT, of course, that original can be anything from an embryo to a fully mature adult, whereas in embryo splitting, the original will be only an embryo. The maximum ten-year prison sentence is evidence of the gravity with which Australia, at least within Victoria, views reproductive cloning compared with the still-onerous but lower four-year maximum for therapeutic cloning.

### Israel

The relevant law in Israel is the Prohibition of Genetic Intervention Law No. 5759 (Cloning of Human Beings and Genetic Modifications for Reproductive Cells), 1998.[39] Passed on December 29, 1988, it establishes a five-year moratorium on reproductive cloning of humans, among other things. The stated intention of the Knesset in enacting the law is as follows:

The purpose of this law is to provide for a limited period of five years, during which certain types of genetic intervention will not be performed on human beings, in order to examine the moral, legal, social and scientific aspects of such types of intervention and their implications on human dignity.

Criminal sanctions are established for violations, in Article 6. A prison sentence of two years is possible, unless an otherwise-forbidden act is performed in accordance with a permit granted under Section 5. No such permits are allowed for human reproductive cloning, however, throughout the five-year moratorium period, which will lapse at the end of 2003.

Therapeutic cloning is not banned, and Israel is only "monitoring" genetic research at present. Specifically, Israel's law allows genetic intervention for medical purposes, such as cloning a healthy organ for donation. Researchers wishing to conduct experiments in human genetics must show an advisory committee that their research does not violate the law, an infraction punishable by two years in prison.[40]

## Peru

The anticloning law of Peru is part of the General Health Law (Law 26842, July 20, 1997). It provides that "fertilization of a human ovum for purposes other than procreation is prohibited, as well as the cloning of human beings."

This provision is punishable under the Peruvian Criminal Code (Amendment for Law 27636, January 16, 2002),[41] which states that "Any person that makes use of any genetic manipulation technique with the purpose of cloning human beings will be punished with imprisonment for not less than six years nor more than eight years."

These provisions constitute a sweeping and permanent ban of reproductive cloning irrespective of the method used (SCNT or embryo splitting). However, although the law in Peru appears to ban the creation of human embryos, via fertilization, for research purposes (as opposed to purposes of procreation), it does not seem to prohibit therapeutic cloning. This is so because therapeutic cloning, via SCNT, would not involve the fertilization of a human egg. Rather, it entails the replacement of the nucleus of an egg with the nuclear material from a cell of a DNA donor. Thus, the net effect of Peru's law is to impose a total and unending ban on all forms of reproductive cloning, while leaving therapeutic cloning legal.

## New Zealand

The New Zealand government has chosen not to put an outright ban on the cloning of humans. Instead, the cloning of humans is recognized as a restricted biotechnical procedure under Part 7A of the Medicines Act 1981.[42] People are prohibited from conducting any specified "biotechnical procedure" (covering all biological material, including the whole or part of any organ, bone, tissue, cell, blood, or body fluids) other than in accordance with an authorization made by the minister of health. A specified biotechnical procedure includes, among other things, any cloning procedure.

These provisions were not intended to be a long-term solution. By its own terms, the law expires on June 30, 2003. However, the law includes the possibility of extending the provisions until June 30, 2005, and it is currently the ministry's intention to seek this extension, by which time a new regulatory regime should be in place.

The relevant portions of New Zealand's Medicines Act, Part 7A, titled "Restrictions on specified biotechnical procedures," include an expansive definition of "cloned human being," which specifically includes zygotes and embryos. It encompasses such beings irrespective of whether their "copied" genetic structure is literally identical to that of any other zygote, embryo, and so on; this definition displays a sophisticated level of knowledge as to the possibility of variations in both nuclear and mitochondrial DNA between DNA donor and recipient in cloning. The definition also includes both embryo splitting and SCNT cloning. However, the key definition of "specified biotechnical procedure" is phrased to include a "cloning procedure," which in turn is defined in terms that would only apply to reproductive, and not to therapeutic, cloning. Because "cloning procedure" only encompasses "the insertion or injection into a human being of a cloned human organism," it would not include any experiments involving "cloned human organisms" at any stage so long as they are not implanted into a woman's uterus.

The Medicines Act goes on to set down permitting provisions regarding "specified biotechnical procedures," as previously defined to include reproductive, but not therapeutic, cloning. In Sections 96C and 96D, the Medicines Act specifies detailed requirements for people who apply for the necessary approval ("authorisation") to conducting procedures including reproductive cloning, as well as for the minister of health to follow in deciding whether to grant such approval. Authorizations may be either conditional or unconditional and are subject to being varied, revoked, or made subject to new or different conditions by the minister at any time, upon written notice to the holder of the permit. Section 96C governs authorization for procedures on a case-by-case basis, whereas Section 96C covers blanket authorization for an entire "class" of procedures.

The act further empowers the minister of health to form a committee, or use an already existing committee or organization, to study and provide advice concerning the various issues to be weighed in granting an authorization to conduct reproductive cloning and other specified procedures. These committees are directed to take into account input from the public and other interested parties before giving advice on any authorization. By this provision, and by including ethical, cultural, and spiritual issues among those that must be adequately addressed in granting an authorization, New Zealand has recognized the complexity of the issues involved and made a significant effort to ensure that all such concerns are given a fair hearing. Moreover, the sunset clause in the act (Section 96J) provides further safeguards against possible long-lasting undesirable consequences of legislation that might prove ill-advised as the state of scientific and technological knowledge continues to progress.

This analysis should suffice to provide some appreciation of the diversity of approaches used by those nations that have enacted a legislative response to the perceived advent of human cloning. The legal spectrum worldwide, thus far, ranges from total, permanent bans on all forms of human cloning to moderate temporary regulatory and permitting measures. As I mentioned here and in chapter 2, the United States has been aiming at the former extreme and may yet achieve it, both in the form of federal legislation and a global UN treaty. In the next chapter, I will discuss the difficult and complex legal issues that any such legislation would implicate in the United States. As we shall see, draconian anticloning laws can touch other legal areas that would appear, at first, to be far removed from the maelstrom of the cloning controversy.

## APPENDIX 2
## SELECTED FOREIGN LAWS APPLICABLE TO HUMAN CLONING

### GERMANY

The German embryo protection law (the Federal Embryo Protection Act of 1990; Embryonenschutzgesetz), which has been in force since December 15, 1990, forbids the cloning of human beings in these terms:

(1) Those who, by artificial means, effect that a human embryo with the same genetic information as another embryo, a fetus, an adult, or a deceased person, is generated, is liable to sentence of imprisonment of up to five years or liable to penalty.

(2) Likewise under liability are those who transfer into a woman an embryo as delineated in Section 1.

(3) The attempt is liable to prosecution.

### ISRAEL

The Prohibition of Genetic Intervention Law No. 5759 (Cloning of Human Beings and Genetic Modifications for Reproductive Cells), 1998, is the applicable law in Israel.

The law, in Article 3, sets down the following prohibitions:

Article 3. Prohibited Genetic Intervention: During the period of time in which this law is in force, no act of intervention in human cells will be carried out, if the purpose of such act is one of the following:

(1)   Cloning human being;
(2)   To bring about the creation of a human being through the use of reproductive cells, which have undergone a permanent intentional genetic modification (Germ-line Gene Therapy).

There is a provision for a limited exception to the latter of these two prohibitions. Article 5(a) describes the requisite circumstances:

Notwithstanding the provision of Section 3 above, if the Minister finds that no harm will be caused to human dignity, he may permit, upon the recommendation of the Advisory Committee, and under conditions, which he shall determine by regulations, the performance of certain types of genetic intervention, which are prohibited according to Section 3(2).

## JAPAN

The Law Concerning Regulations Relating to Human Cloning Techniques and Other Similar Techniques, Article 3 provides:

No person shall transfer a human somatic clone embryo, a human-animal amphimictic embryo, a human-animal hybrid embryo or a human-animal chimeric embryo into the uterus of a human or an animal.

With regard to embryo splitting, the law does not absolutely forbid the implantation of a resulting embryo but in Article 4 calls for guidelines to be set by the minister of education, culture, sports, science, and technology.[43] Such guidelines are required if

there is apprehension that a human split embryo, a human embryonic clone embryo, a human somatic clone embryo, a human-human chimeric embryo, a human-animal amphimictic, an animal-human hybrid embryo or an animal-human chimeric embryo...transferred into a human or an animal uterus could develop to an individual similar to a human clone individual or an amphimictic individual, or affect preservation of human dignity, safety for human life and body, and maintenance of the social order.[44]

The law specifies procedures for researchers to give detailed advance notice to the minister of education, culture, sports, science, and technology concerning such "Specified Embryos" and their production or importation. That minister is empowered, under Articles 7 and 12, to order the alteration or cancellation of plans if the method of handling any "Specified Embryos" is "not deemed to comply with the Guidelines." The minister, pursuant to Article 14, "may, to the extent necessary to enforce this Law, ask a person who has given notice…for reports concerning the conditions in which the Specified Embryo was handled and other necessary items related to the notice." Further, Article 15 provides that the minister "may, to the extent necessary to enforce this Law, have a Ministry official access and enter the office or laboratory of a person who has given notice,…inspect documents and other necessary property, and ask questions of the participants." Such a visit, however, is not to "be construed as approved for the purpose of investigation of a criminal offense."

The law provides for severe penalties in the event of violation of Article 3. Imprisonment of up to ten years or a fine of up to ten million yen or both is authorized under Article 16 for a person who "transfers" any of the "Specified Embryos" into the uterus of a human or animal. Articles 17 through 20 provide lesser criminal sanctions for the violation of other portions of the act.

The law also has a supplementary provision, in Article 2, that states:

The Government shall, within three years of enforcement of this Law, take necessary measures in accordance with the results of its study and examination on the provisions under this Law, on the basis of the results of the study and examination by the Council for Science and Technology Policy, Cabinet Office concerning the method of handling of a human fertilized embryo as the beginning of a human life with consideration to the circumstances in which this Law is enforced or to any change of the situation surrounding the cloning techniques and other similar techniques.

## THE NETHERLANDS

"Act containing rules relating to the use of gametes and embryos," Division 6, "Prohibited uses of gametes and embryos," Section 24:

The following procedures are prohibited:

a. creating an embryo specifically for research purposes other than the induction of a pregnancy and using such an embryo in research or for purposes other than the induction of a pregnancy;

e. allowing an embryo to develop outside the human body for longer than fourteen days;

f. performing procedures with gametes or embryos with a view to the birth of genetically identical human individuals;

g. intentionally modifying the genetic material of the nucleus of human germ-line cells with which a pregnancy is to be induced.

## NEW ZEALAND

New Zealand's Medicines Act, Part 7A, "Restrictions on specified biotechnical procedures" provides as follows, beginning with the pertinent definitions:

96A Interpretation

In this Part, unless the context otherwise requires, biological material means:

(a) the whole or part of any organ, bone, tissue, or cell; or

(b) blood or body fluids

cloned human organism means an artificially formed zygote or an artificially formed embryo whose genetic structure is a copy (whether identical or not) of another zygote or embryo, or of a foetus, or of a dead or living human being, or of a still-born child.

cloning procedure means the insertion or injection into a human being of a cloned human organism.

specified biotechnical procedure means:

(a) any germ-cell genetic procedure; or

(b) any xenotransplantation; or

(c) any cloning procedure

This is an expansive definition of "cloned human being," which specifically includes zygotes and embryos. It encompasses such beings irrespective of whether their "copied" genetic structure is literally identical to that of any other zygote, embryo, and so on; this definition displays a sophisticated level of knowledge as to the possibility of variations in both nuclear and mitochondrial DNA between DNA donor and recipient in cloning. The definition also includes both embryo splitting and SCNT cloning. However, the key definition of "specified biotechnical procedure" is phrased to include a "cloning procedure," which in turn is defined in terms that would only apply to reproductive, and not to therapeutic, cloning. Because "cloning procedure" only encompasses "the insertion or injection into a human being of a cloned human organism," it would not include any experiments involving "cloned human organisms" at any stage so long as they are not implanted into a woman's uterus.

The Medicines Act goes on to set down the following provisions regarding "specified biotechnical procedures," as previously defined to include reproductive, but not therapeutic, cloning:

96B Restrictions on specified biotechnical procedures

(1) No person may conduct a specified biotechnical procedure otherwise than in accordance with an authorisation under section 96C or section 96D.

(2) Subsection (1) applies to a person who continues, after the commencement of this section, to conduct a specified biotechnical procedure that was begun before that commencement.

(3) Every person commits an offence and is liable on summary conviction to imprisonment for a term not exceeding 6 months or to a fine not exceeding $200,000 who contravenes subsection (1).

In Sections 96C and 96D, the Medicines Act specifies detailed requirements for people who apply for the necessary approval ("authorisation") to conduct procedures including reproductive cloning, as well as for the minister of health to follow in deciding whether to grant such approval. Authorizations may be either conditional or unconditional and are subject to being varied, revoked, or made subject to new or different conditions by the minister at any time, upon written notice to the holder of the permit.[45] Section 96C governs authorization for procedures on a case-by-case basis, while Section 96D covers blanket authorization for an entire "class" of procedures. In either situation, the criteria for the granting of an authorization are as set forth in Section 96E:

96E Criteria for authorisations

(1) The Minister may grant or recommend an authorisation sought by an application under section 96G[46] only if satisfied that the application relates to the conduct of a specified biotechnical procedure or class of specified biotechnical procedure that meets each of the following criteria:

    (a) the conduct of the procedure or class of procedure does not pose an unacceptable risk to the health or safety of the public:

    (b) any risks posed by the conduct of the procedure or class of procedure will be appropriately managed:

    (c) any ethical issues have been adequately addressed:

    (d) any cultural issues have been adequately addressed:

    (e) any spiritual issues have been adequately addressed.

(2) A reference in any of paragraphs (c) to (e) of subsection (1) to issues is a reference to issues raised:

    (a) by the conduct of the procedure or class of procedure to which the application relates; and

    (b) by any technology involved in that conduct.

(3) If the Minister is not satisfied that the conduct of the procedure or class of procedure to which the application relates meets any 1 or more of the criteria specified in subsection (1), the Minister:

    (a) may direct that advice on the question whether or not the conduct of the procedure or class of procedure meets that criterion (or, as the case may be, those criteria) be obtained from persons who, in the Minister's opinion, are appropriately qualified, or have the appropriate expertise, to advise on the question; and

    (b) after obtaining that advice, may resume his or her consideration of the application on the basis of that advice.

The act further empowers the minister of health to form a committee, or use an already-existing committee or organization, to study and provide advice concerning the various issues to be weighed in granting an authorization to conduct reproductive cloning and other specified procedures.[47]

These committees are directed to take into account input from the public and other interested parties before giving advice on any authorization. By this provision, and by including ethical, cultural, and spiritual issues among those that must be adequately addressed in granting an authorization, New Zealand has recognized the complexity of the issues involved and made a significant effort to ensure that all such concerns are given a fair hearing. Moreover, the sunset clause in the act (Section 96J) provides further safeguards against possible long-lasting undesirable consequences of legislation that might prove ill-advised as the state of scientific and technological knowledge continues to progress.

## PERU

The Peruvian General Health Law (Law 26842, July 20, 1997) provides as follows:

Every person has the right to use a treatment for his/her infertility, as well as to procreate through the use of assisted reproduction techniques, with the condition that the genetic mother and the birth mother are the same person. A previous written consent from the biological parents is required for the application of assisted reproduction techniques. The fertilization of a human ovum for purposes other than procreation is prohibited, as well as the cloning of human beings.

## SWITZERLAND

The Swiss Constitution includes Article 119, which is titled "Medical Assistance to Procreation and Gene Technology in the Human Field." It provides as follows:

(1) Persons shall be protected against the abuse of medically assisted procreation and gene technology.
(2) The Confederation shall legislate on the use of human reproductive and genetic material. It shall ensure the protection of human dignity, of personality, and of family, and in particular it shall respect the following principles:

   a. All forms of cloning and interference with genetic material of human reproductive cells and embryos is prohibited;
   b. Non-human reproductive and genetic material may neither be introduced into nor combined with human reproductive material;
   c. Methods of medically assisted procreation may only be used when sterility or the danger of transmission of a serious illness cannot be avoided otherwise, but neither in order to induce certain characteristics in the child nor to conduct research. The fertilization of human ova outside a woman's body shall be permitted only under conditions determined by statute. No more

human ova may be developed into embryos outside a woman's body than are capable of being immediately implanted into her;

d. The donation of embryos and all forms of surrogate maternity are prohibited;

e. No trade may be conducted with human reproductive material or with any product obtained from embryos;

f. A person's genetic material may only be analyzed, registered or disclosed with the consent of that person, or if a statute so provides;

g. Every person shall have access to the data concerning his or her ancestry.

## NOTES

1. Council of Europe: Draft Additional Protocol to the Convention on Human Rights and Biomedicine on the Prohibition of Cloning Human Beings, 36 I.L.M. 1415, 1417 (1997), entered into force December 1, 1999. As of November 7, 2002, twelve nations had ratified or acceded to this convention (Cyprus, Czech Republic, Estonia, Georgia, Greece, Hungary, Lithuania, Portugal, Romania, Slovakia, Slovenia, and Spain), and seventeen more had signed but not yet ratified (Croatia, Denmark, Finland, France, Iceland, Italy, Latvia, Luxembourg, Macedonia, Moldova, Netherlands, Norway, Poland, San Marino, Sweden, Switzerland, and Turkey). *See* <http://conventions.coe.int/Treaty/EN/cadreprincipal.htm> for a table of nations signing and ratifying.

2. *See generally* Nati Somekh, Note, *The European Total Ban on Human Cloning: An Analysis of the Council of Europe's Actions in Prohibiting Human Cloning,* 17 B.U. INT'L L. J. 397 (1999); Adam Greene, Note, *The World after Dolly: International Regulation of Human Cloning,* 33 GEO. WASH. INT'L L. REV. 341 (2001).

3. *See, e.g.,* Mark Henderson et al., *Emergency Laws to Ban Human Cloning,* LONDON TIMES, Nov. 16, 2001 (describing British legislative reaction to a judicial decision that exposed a gap in their previous anticloning law, the 1990 Human Fertilisation and Embryology Act). Japan has also banned SCNT cloning of humans, as will be discussed later in this chapter. *See Ministry Bans Cloning Technology for Humans,* DAILY YOMIURI (Japan), July 29, 1998, at 2.

4. *See* Colum Lynch, *U.S. Seeks to Extend Ban on Cloning,* WASH POST, Feb. 27, 2002, at A8. The UN General Assembly has approved negotiations on a treaty along these lines. *Id. See also* Richard Willing, *U.N. Plan Would Ban Cloning to Create Human Baby,* USA TODAY, Sept. 23, 2002, at 3A. A UN committee has begun preliminary work on a treaty governing the cloning of humans. *See* <http://www.cwfa.org/library/life/2002–10–03_un.shtml>. *See also* George J. Annas, Lori B. Andrews and Rosario M. Isasi, *Protecting the Endangered Human: Toward an International Treaty Prohibiting Cloning and Inheritable Alterations,* 28 AM. J. L. AND MED. 151, 166 (2002).

5. *See* United Nations Educational, Scientific, and Cultural Organization, Universal Declaration on the Human Genome and Human Rights, UNESCO, 29th Sess. (Nov. 11, 1997), <http://unesdoc.unesco.org/ulis/> (Declaration). In 1998, the UN General Assembly adopted the declaration. *See* G.A. res. 152, U.N. GAOR,

53rd Sess., Agenda Item 110(b), U.N. Doc. A/53/152/ (1998), <http://www .unesco.org/human_rights/hrbc.htm>.

6. Declaration, Art. 1.

7. *Id.*, Art. 2.

8. *See* Melissa K. Cantrell, *International Response to Dolly: Will Scientific Freedom Get Sheared?* 13 J. L. & HEALTH 69, 91–94 (1998–99).

9. ABC News Online, *U.N. Defers Debate on Anti-Cloning Treaty* (Nov. 8, 2002), <http://abc.net.au/news/scitech/2002/11/item20021108093502_1.htm>.

10. *Id.*

11. Council of Europe, Convention for the Protection of Human Rights and Dignity of the Human Being with Regard to the Application of Biology and Medicine, Apr. 4, 1997, Art. 27, 36 I.L.M. 817 at 824 (1997), <http://conventions.coe.int/ treaty/EN/cadreprincipal.htm>.

12. *Id.*

13. Council of Europe, Additional Protocol to the Convention for the Protection of Human Rights and Dignity of the Human Being with Regard to the Application of Biology and Medicine, on the Prohibition of Cloning Human Beings, Sept. 22, 1997, 36 I.L.M. 1415, 1415–18, entered into force May 1, 1998, <http://conventions.coe.int/treaty/EN/cadreprincipal.htm>.

14. Heidi Forster and Emily Ramsey, *Legal Perspectives on Cloning of Human Beings*, 32 VAL. U. L. REV. 433, 454 (1998).

15. Universal Declaration of Human Rights, G.A. res. 217A (III), U.N. Doc. A/810 at 71 (1948).

16. International Covenant on Economic, Social, and Cultural Rights, G.A. res. 2200 A (XXI), 21 U.N. GAOR Supp. (No. 16) at 49, U.N. Doc. A/6316, (1966), 993 U.N.T.S. 3, entered into force January 3, 1976.

17. International Covenant on Civil and Political Rights (ICCPR), G.A. res. 2200A (XXI), 21 U.N. GAOR Supp. (No. 16) at 52, U.N. Doc. A6316, 999 U.N.T.S. 171, entered into force March 23, 1976.

18. *See* <http://conventions.coe.int/treaty/EN/cadreprincipal.htm>.

19. European Council Decision of 25 January 1999, OJ 1999 L64/105.

20. *See* Tarquin Cooper, *Britain Rushes to Close Legal Loophole on Human Cloning*, CHRISTIAN SCIENCE MONITOR, Nov. 23, 2001, <http://www.csmonitor.com/ 2001/1123/p7s1-woeu.html>.

21. *See* <http://www.hmso.gov.uk/acts/acts2001/20010023.htm>.

22. *See* <http://www.hmso.gov.uk/acts/acts1990/Ukpga_19900037_en_1 .htm>.

23. *See* <http://www.hmso.gov.uk/acts/acts1990/Ukpga_19900037_en_2 .htm#mdiv3>.

24. *See* <http://www.hmso.gov.uk/acts/acts1990/Ukpga_19900037_en_2 .htm#mdiv8>.

25. *See* Cooper, *supra* note 20.

26. *See* <http://www.minvws.nl/documents/IBE/Wetstekst/eng-embry-owettekst.pdf>.

27. For a detailed analysis of the legal and other implications of the German Embryo Protection Act, *see* Council of Research, Technology, and Innovation, *Cloning of Humans: Biological Foundations and Ethico-legal Assessment* (April 1997),

<http://www.dfg.de/aktuell/stellungnahmen/lebenswissenschaften/klonen_e _97.html#text_III_1>.

28. *See* <http://www.all.org/abac/clontx08.htm>.

29. Human-animal hybrids or chimeras may not be familiar to many readers. *Chimera* is a term used in ancient mythology to describe a monster made of parts from several animals, such as a lion, goat, and dragon. In biological terms, it signifies an organism with at least two genetically distinct types of cells.

30. For the full text in Spanish, *see* <http://www.geocities.com/ Eureka/9068/SANIDAD/reproduc.html>.

31. For the full text in Spanish, *see* <http://www.geocities.com/mundodere-cho/SANIDAD/embrion.html>.

32. For the full text in Norwegian, *see* <http://www.lovdata.no/all/hl-19940805-056.html>.

33. The full text, in English, of Law 56 of 1994, as amended, is available at <http://www.helsetilsynet.no/bioweb/05_publikasjoner/bio_act.htm>.

34. For the full text in English, *see* <http://www.mext.go.jp/a_menu/ shinkou/seimei/eclone.pdf>.

35. The English translation of the full text of the guidelines may be found at <http://www.mext.go.jp/a_menu/shinkou/seimei/2001/hai3/31_shishin_e.p df>.

36. For the full text in English, *see* <http://www.uni-wuerzburg.de/ law/sz00000_.html>.

37. *See* <http://www.austlii.edu.au/au/legis/vic/consol_act/ita1995264/>.

38. *See* <http://www.austlii.edu.au/cgi-bin/disp.pl/au/legis/cth/num%5fact/ gta2000n1692000189/s192b.html?query=%7e+clone+cloning>.

39. *See* <http://www.glphr.org/genetic/m_east.htm>.

40. *See* Sari Bashi, *Israel Bans Genetic Cloning* (Dec. 30, 1998), <http://www .gsreport.com/articles/art000048.html>.

41. Código Penal (Modificado por Ley 27636 16 de enero 1/2002), Título XIV-A Delitos contra la Humanidad, Capítulo V Manipulación genética.

42. *See* http://rangi.knowledge-basket.co.nz/gpacts/public/text/1981/an/118 .html.

43. The English translation of the full text of the guidelines may be found at <http://www.mext.go.jp/a_menu/shinkou/seimei/2001/hai3/31_shishin_e.p df>.

44. Hybrids, chimeras, and amphimictics result from combinations of embryos in various ways different from typical sexual reproduction. The law contains specific definitions of each term in Article 2.

45. Section 96C(4) specifies the following:

The Minister may, at any time, by written notice, do any 1 or more of the following in relation to an authorisation granted under subsection (1):

(a) vary the authorisation:

(b) vary or revoke any condition subject to which the authorisation was granted:

(c) make the authorisation subject to new conditions:

(d) revoke the authorisation.

46. That provision, Section 96G, reads as follows:

96G Applications

(1) A person may, by application to the Minister, request the Minister to grant an authorisation under section 96C or to recommend an authorisation under section 96D(1).

(2) An application under subsection (1) must be in a form approved by the Director-General and must be accompanied by the prescribed fee.

(3) If the Minister has, under section 96F(1)(c), requested a person who applies under subsection (1) to obtain any advice, the Minister may defer consideration of the person's application until the person has obtained that advice.

47.

96F Advice on applicability of criteria

(1) For the purpose of obtaining advice of the kind referred to in section 96E(3)(a) in relation to an application, the Minister may do any 1 or more of the following:

(a) establish a committee to advise on the criteria in question

(b) request a body or a committee or an association of persons formed or recognised by or under an enactment to advise on the criteria in question

(c) request the person who made the application under section 96G (in this section referred to as the applicant) to obtain advice on the criteria in question from a committee consisting of persons nominated by the Minister.

(2) A committee or body or an association of persons that is to provide advice for the purposes of section 96E(3)(a) may provide that advice only after it has:

(a) given interested parties and members of the public a reasonable opportunity to make submissions in writing or orally, or both; and

(b) taken any such submissions into account.

(3) Sections 74 to 86 of the New Zealand Public Health and Disability Act 2000 apply, with all necessary modifications, to the establishment and procedures of a committee that is to be established or that has been established under subsection (1)(a) as if it were an inquiry board under that Act.

(4) The Minister may agree with an applicant whose application relates to the work of a committee, body, or association established or requested under subsection (1)(a) or (b) that the applicant will pay, or contribute towards the payment of, any costs incurred or to be incurred by the committee or body or association in the examination of aspects of the applicant's application that, in the Minister's opinion, could have significant commercial benefits (whether or not that examination also benefits the public).

(5) The Minister may agree with an applicant whose application relates to the work of a committee of persons nominated by the Minister under subsection (1)(c) that the Minister will pay, or contribute towards the payment of, any costs incurred or to be incurred by the committee in the examination of aspects of the applicant's application that, in the Minister's opinion, are likely to benefit the public (whether or not that examination also has commercial benefits).

(6) If the Minister is, under subsection (4), attempting to reach an agreement with the applicant, the Minister may direct the committee, body, or association concerned not to consider any matters relating to the applicant's application until agreement under subsection (4) has been reached; and the committee or body or association must give effect to that direction.

# CHAPTER 4

# Galileo in Modern Chains and the Banning of Scientific Research

I now turn again to the United States, with the examples of other nations as a backdrop. Within the United States, there is a variety of legislative approaches in place on the state level and a still-developing federal solution. The laws already in effect, as well as those now being debated in Congress, are important for Americans far beyond the narrow confines of the cloning issue. Even for those citizens who may be utterly uninterested in cloning, the legal trends in the United States on the anticloning front warrant careful attention. Before it is concluded, this debate could easily break out of the cloning box and cause vastly significant changes to American civil liberties in ways that would be astonishing to most laypersons.

Before examining in chapter 5 the highly sensitive issue of reproductive cloning and its implications for our most personal liberties, I want to address another fundamental legal principle, only somewhat less emotionally charged, that is also threatened by some of the more comprehensive bans. I am referring to the First Amendment freedom-of-expression ramifications of cloning legislation.

For example, some of the most sweeping bans (such as the state statutes enacted by Iowa and Michigan, and the federal HCPA passed by the House in 2001 and 2003) include prohibitions on the cloning of humans for any purposes, including "therapeutic" cloning, that is, cloning for purposes of scientific or medical research. A UN committee is currently debating this type of all-encompassing cloning ban as well, with a view toward a global treaty that would ban both reproductive and therapeutic cloning. This worldwide, all-encompassing human cloning ban has been pushed by the United States, over the objections of nations such as France and Germany.[1] But what would a ban on cloning research mean?

Some researchers want to use cloned human cells, presumably limited to early stages of embryonic development, to explore stem-cell options, favorable sources for transplants, and other issues.[2] Such experiments would in no event lead to the birth of a living infant and as such would fall within a different category from the several variants of the "naked clone" scenario discussed in chapter 5. Presumably, there would be no implantation in any woman's uterus and no implication of a woman's privacy and personal autonomy rights. There would be no issues of parental rights, nor of reproductive liberty.

However, there would be important rights implicated in these cases, too.[3] It can be argued that scientific or medical research constitutes a form of expression within the meaning of the First Amendment.[4] If it does, then the courts would entertain First Amendment challenges to limitations or bans on therapeutic cloning.

At least some background on First Amendment law is necessary to understand the constitutional issues regarding a ban or restriction on cloning for research purposes. Unfortunately, First Amendment jurisprudence is among the most complex and convoluted strains in all of constitutional law. Readers who have not enjoyed the dubious benefit of attending law school may be surprised to learn that obtaining the answer to First Amendment questions is not as simple as looking it up in some cookbook-like, well-indexed reference book. Each case is different, developed and decided within the context of a particular place or jurisdiction, at a particular point in time, with its own unique facts and its own individual judge or judges.

Within our common law legal system, rulings from past cases will influence subsequent cases, either as controlling or persuasive authority. In a field as difficult as the First Amendment, there is ample precedent to enable any particular court to rule one way or another on the issue of cloning research. What might appear to be the most obvious, well-established mode of analysis is not necessarily the way any given court will deal with a specific First Amendment issue. Even when the U.S. Supreme Court has ruled on a certain factual and legal issue, expert legal commentators can disagree as to the true meaning of the Court's holding, for many years to come—partially because numerous cases have multiple opinions, including majority or plurality opinions, concurrences, opinions that concur in part and dissent in part, and outright dissents. Even within each opinion, there can be disputes as to whether any phrase or sentence is actually part of the Court's holding and thus entitled to precedential effect, or merely dicta—surplusage, explanatory text, or additional judicial rumination that is not properly deemed to be of controlling import. Indeed, numerous books and countless law review articles have been devoted to the subject of the First Amendment and its myriad intricacies. Notwithstanding, and with apologies to Cliff's Notes and Classics Illustrated comic books, I will now attempt to set forth a very basic introduction to the topic in the short space of the next few paragraphs. This is in no way intended to be a comprehensive, nuanced exegesis of the law of free expression, only an elementary foundation for what will follow.

One cannot get more basic in First Amendment law than to quote the First Amendment itself. It reads, in its entirety:

Congress shall make no law respecting an establishment of religion, or prohibiting the free exercise thereof; or abridging the freedom of speech or of the press; or the right of the people peaceably to assemble and to petition the Government for a redress of grievances.

That is it. But these forty-five words are anything but simple in their application to numberless difficult situations. Under our system of judicial interpretation, the courts have fleshed out the meaning of this text in a bewildering variety of specific contexts. For the purposes of this chapter, I will only consider the way in which freedom of speech has been explicated and will happily leave aside the other knotty First Amendment puzzles such as the Establishment Clause and Free Exercise Clause for others to tackle.

Focusing only on that small portion of this short constitutional amendment that pertains to expression, the First Amendment distills down to this: "Congress shall make no law ... abridging the freedom of speech or of the press." The words seem very clear and the meaning plain and unmistakable. If the text literally meant what it says, any federal statute restricting, let alone banning, freedom of speech would be invalid. But it is not that simple, and it never has been. For one thing, "speech" for purposes of First Amendment analysis has been held to embrace much more than merely the spoken word. For another, there is a lengthy list of situations in which the seemingly absolutist language of the First Amendment has been held to be subject to exceptions allowing governmental restriction and regulation, and even criminal sanction. There is also a diversity of views as to the extent to which the intent of the Framers of the Constitution and those who actually drafted and approved the First Amendment should govern our current interpretation of it.

Legal scholars, lawyers, and judges at all levels disagree even on the underlying purpose of the First Amendment. If we knew the core theory, the bedrock foundation, the animating principle, the central philosophy behind the First Amendment, it would assist us in determining how it applies to any particular set of facts, and it would help us to ensure that our body of case law coalesces around a consistent, unifying theme. But there are several major points of view on this key issue.

Probably the most widely held theory is that the First Amendment is primarily a vehicle for ensuring that the "marketplace of ideas" is well supplied with competing and evolving notions on a wide array of topics at all times.[5] This is a somewhat utilitarian or instrumental view, focused on the value of speech as informing public debate and fueling progress toward truth at manifold levels of society, and some have criticized it as too narrow.[6] There is also a still more limited conceptualization of the First Amendment as principally the guarantor of our political liberties. This school of thought is chiefly devoted to the protection of "political speech," expression related to issues of well-informed self-government, rights, duties, and other public issues, under the supposition that this is the main reason the framers added the First Amendment to the Constitution.[7] Yet another theory is that the First Amendment should further the self-fulfillment, emotional, personal growth and well-being, and self-actualization needs of each individual.[8] This concept holds that the First Amendment is broader and more expansive than allowed by the more utilitarian, concrete results-oriented, intellect-dominated views.[9]

It is possible to find support—sometimes explicit, sometimes implicit—for each of these theories in the many Supreme Court cases explicating the First Amendment, to say nothing of the numerous decisions from the various federal circuit courts, district courts, and state courts. There are also variations on these themes and attempts to combine them,[10] each with its own spin on how the First Amendment should be read, but the views summarized here are the most prominent and the ones most often reflected in the case law. Depending on which school of thought one subscribes to, the First Amendment will tend to be interpreted more or less expansively, protecting more or less expression (and more or fewer types of activities as the equivalent of expression) within its ambit. The fact that experienced, illustrious legal experts still dispute which of these theories is most correct helps to explain the often eccentric, labyrinthine, and baffling First Amendment jurisprudence we have amassed. I will now delve a bit further into some of the most important aspects of First Amendment law.

It is almost obligatory to mention in any discussion of the First Amendment the famous example given by Justice Oliver Wendell Holmes illustrating the illusory nature of its absolute language: "No one has the right falsely to shout 'Fire!' in a crowded theater."[11] This simple, but cogent, example points out how hopelessly unrealistic it is to expect the First Amendment to be read and applied literally by the courts.

There are other notable exceptions to the First Amendment's prohibition of governmental abridgement of expression. Among these exceptions are fighting words,[12] obscenity,[13] and incitement[14] to imminent lawless action. The Supreme Court has carved out exceptions for each of these varieties of "speech" that allow the government to regulate, restrict, and punish. These exceptions may be considered devoid of constitutional protection, although naturally, there are always threshold issues relating to whether a particular type of "speech" properly is classified as one of the exceptions, under the totality of the circumstances in each individual case.

The voluminous First Amendment case law has also recognized the Orwellian concept that aside from the already-named exceptions, some types of speech are more equal than others. Traditionally, political speech has been viewed as at the core of First Amendment protection because it is often thought to be central to the reasons why the framers approved the amendment in the first place: to safeguard the right of the people to speak out against official injustice and tyranny.[15] More recently, there are cases in which the Court has recognized other categories of expression that may be deemed neither completely protected nor utterly without First Amendment protection. Examples are some types of pornography that, although close, fail to meet the legal definition of obscenity,[16] defamation,[17] non-obscene child pornography,[18] and commercial speech,[19] all of which have been held to be afforded some intermediate level of constitutional protection, depending on the circumstances.

Note that some of these types of speech are not really speech at all in the usual sense of the word. Pornography and obscenity certainly include much more than the spoken or written word and often are devoid of words entirely. This therefore leads to another respect in which the First Amendment means both more and less than its simple words would seem to indicate. The jurisprudence identifies many ways in which speech is defined much more expansively than in popular usage.

Speech, fairly obviously, can include written as well as oral expression of words, both spoken utterances (including those made face-to-face in person and more indirect means such as radio, television, and motion pictures) and communications reduced to print or writing (whether in handwritten notes, typed letters, e-mails, laboratory reports, or published newspapers, magazines, pamphlets, and books). All such forms of verbal expression are indisputably classified as "speech" for First Amendment purposes and do not require much intellectual candlepower to illuminate. But less readily apparent, the Supreme Court has held that speech also can be photographs, drawings, and other visual images, devoid of words. Additionally, speech can be conduct, behavior, action—if expression of ideas is part of the event in intent and effect. This last category encompasses such divergent species of expressive or symbolic conduct as flag burning,[20] destruction of a draft card,[21] and wearing a T-shirt bearing a provocative message.[22] Even nude dancing has received support as "speech" in a Supreme Court decision.[23]

The concept of expressive conduct is especially relevant to the topic of the extent to which the act of performing scientific research into the cloning of humans implicates First Amendment protections. Therefore, I will evaluate this somewhat counterintuitive principle of expressive conduct in more detail.

In general, when an activity is "sufficiently imbued with elements of communication,"[24] the conduct in question has been held to be deserving of the same protection afforded "pure" speech under the First Amendment. This protected conduct has been variously called expressive conduct, speech-plus, speech brigaded with action, or symbolic speech. The Supreme Court, however, has recognized limits on the reach of the First Amendment into this area and has rejected "the view that an apparently limitless variety of conduct can be labeled 'speech' whenever the person engaging in the conduct intends thereby to express an idea."[25] The Court has stated that conduct will only be protected under the First Amendment where there is "an intent to convey a particularized message" that would mostly likely be understood by those receiving the message,[26] although this may not be the most accurate statement of the governing principle. As the Court held in *Texas v. Johnson,* flag burning, although certainly "conduct," should be treated as speech because it conveys a message, that is, opposition to the government of the United States, which would be clearly understood by the audience.[27]

Even when conduct is expressive to the requisite extent so as to be entitled to protection under the First Amendment, this protection is not absolute. As the Court stated in *United States v. O'Brien,* "when 'speech' and 'nonspeech' elements are combined in the same course of conduct, a sufficiently important governmental interest in regulating the nonspeech element can justify incidental limitations on First Amendment freedoms."[28] In *O'Brien,* the Court assumed, for purposes of argument, that burning a draft card to protest the Vietnam War was symbolic speech but nevertheless held that punishing such activity was permissible because it advanced an important government interest *unrelated* to the suppression of expression.[29] The Court set forth a four-part test to determine when expressive conduct/symbolic speech could be restricted consistent with the safeguards of the First Amendment:

(1) if it is within the constitutional power of the Government; (2) if it furthers an important or substantial governmental interest; (3) if the governmental interest is unrelated to the suppression of free expression; and (4) if the incidental restriction on alleged First Amendment freedoms is no greater than is essential to the furtherance of that interest.[30]

Under this *O'Brien* test, the government's restriction on the expressive conduct in question must meet *all four* elements to withstand judicial scrutiny and be upheld as constitutional.

In subsequent cases in which the Court has applied the four-part *O'Brien* test, the initial inquiry has focused on the third prong, that is, whether the restriction is unrelated to free expression. As the Court held in the *Texas v. Johnson* flag-burning case, if the basis for the government's regulation is in some sense aimed at the suppression of free speech, the regulation is subject to a "more demanding standard."[31] However, if the symbolic speech is being regulated for reasons unrelated to the message conveyed by the conduct, then the more relaxed *O'Brien* standard applies.[32] In other words, the intermediate level of judicial scrutiny of symbolic speech called for in *O'Brien* is *only* applicable where the government has *not* attempted to regulate such speech because of its expressive content.

For example, in *Tinker v. Des Moines Independent Community School District*,[33] students were suspended after refusing to remove black armbands, which was conduct prohibited by a school policy that had been instituted two days earlier in anticipation of student protests. The school policy was held to be directly related to the expression of the students because the school singled out only political symbols related to opposition to the Vietnam War, and thus, the Court deemed the policy to be aimed at suppression of speech.[34] The *Tinker* case illustrates the Court's general tendency to be especially wary of restrictions that regulate expressive conduct *based on the ideas conveyed* by the conduct. The Court tends to subject such restrictions to a high level of judicial scrutiny that will in most cases result in the restriction being struck down.[35]

If the restriction does not relate to the conduct's expressive message, then the restriction must further an important government interest while placing only incidental restrictions on free expression. In essence, the Court requires that the restriction on symbolic speech be "content neutral," that is, a restriction that regulates the conduct in question rather than the ideas expressed by such conduct. Under this standard, the government has greater latitude to regulate speech.

For example, in *Wayte v. United States*,[36] the petitioner was prosecuted for refusing to register with the Selective Service System. The Court first analyzed the system of passive enforcement under the Selective Service System and concluded that—based on the third prong of the *O'Brien* test—enforcement of the statute was based solely on conduct (failure to register for the draft) rather than expression.[37] Because the statute did not target the expression, the Court analyzed the statute under the four-part *O'Brien* test and held that the enforcement scheme furthered the important government interest of national security and imposed restrictions on free expression no greater than necessary for national defense, and thus, the conviction was affirmed.[38] *Wayte* illustrates that as long as the restrictions on expressive conduct are unrelated to the ideas conveyed, the Court will hold the government to a lesser standard in justifying the restriction on speech, allowing to stand more regulations that indirectly restrict symbolic speech.[39]

As the foregoing discussion indicates, in addition to the intricacies of determining whether something is legally classified as speech, and whether it is within one of the unprotected or less than fully protected varieties of speech, there are important constitutional issues regarding the type of governmental regulation of the speech. Again, there is considerable complexity and nuance evident in the case law, but we can make some useful generalizations.

The courts have emphasized the importance of the purpose of the government's restriction on expression. The standard of review or level of judicial scrutiny to which the regulation is subject turns on whether the regulation is "content based" or "content neutral." In other words, courts must ask whether the governmental restriction is dependent on, or varies with, the specific message of the speech (and is thus content based)[40] or whether the restriction is fairly and evenly applied to all speech across the board, irrespective of the meaning and informational load (and is thus content neutral).[41] The distinction is crucial because the degrees of judicial scrutiny implicated by each category of restriction are so divergent that they are almost invariably outcome determinative; once a court decides which standard of review is appropriate, the end result of that review is virtually a foregone conclusion.

Governmental restriction on speech aimed at suppression or regulation of its specific message and content is subject to strict scrutiny by the courts on review. Such content-based regulation generally will be struck down unless the restriction is narrowly tailored to a compelling state interest.[42] On the other hand, a governmental action that is not directed at particular instances of expression on the basis of their content is permissible if it is, in fact, content neutral and it is narrowly tailored (although not necessarily the least restrictive alternative) to serve a substantial governmental interest. These content-neutral restrictions may have the incidental and indirect effect of constricting the freedom of expression, but they do not have that as their goal and are thus held to a lesser level of judicial scrutiny when challenged in the courts.[43]

The application of these fundamental First Amendment principles, and many other nuances not mentioned here, to the use of cloning for research purposes is not an easy exercise. At the outset, we immediately confront thorny issues regarding conduct that might be deemed expressive and the gathering of, rather than (or in addition to) the expression of, information.

The research process involves a quest for truth, a hunt for more information, which is at the heart of the First Amendment, as an indispensable prerequisite to the more familiar dissemination of information.[44] The notion of a constitutional right or liberty to conduct scientific research—to search for knowledge and truth—has some support in Supreme Court precedent, although the issue has never directly and explicitly come before the Court for decision. Because of this, we are dealing with an area that is anything but settled by binding Supreme Court precedent; instead, we must draw analogies and sometimes rely on dicta in an attempt to divine how the Court would rule if directly confronted with the issue.

As previously noted, the Court has stated in several cases that the First Amendment safeguards a "marketplace of ideas"; if we are to take this metaphor seriously, it makes sense that as with any marketplace, this one must be continually stocked with new supplies (information and ideas), whether obtained by the press or by scientific researchers.[45] The actions of those who produce information and ideas for the marketplace of ideas are arguably deserving of First Amendment protection, at least as much as the actions of those who disseminate information and ideas.[46] Before ideas and information can be expressed, they necessarily must first be created or discovered, by someone. Just as the Court has noted that more speech (not suppression) is the preferred antidote for "bad" or ill-considered speech, more research can properly be the antidote for research the hypotheses, data, methods, or conclusions with which we disagree.

The Court has recognized, in dicta, a Fourteenth Amendment liberty interest in conducting research or inquiry as well,[47] although some lower federal courts have held that there is no fundamental right to conduct research on human fetuses.[48] Substantive and procedural due process have also been postulated as sources of constitutional protection for scientific inquiry.[49] But the First Amendment argument is the most robust, and it is the one on which I will focus here.

It would seem inconsistent and dysfunctional for the Court to maintain its elaborate panoply of First Amendment shields that guard the spreading of information yet refuse to protect the processes by which that information comes into being. If such were the state of the law, the First Amendment could be deprived of its efficacy by a government intent on shutting off ideas and information at their source. The state could stop reporters from collecting news, ban scientists from conducting their experiments, and prevent private citizens from prying into the workings of their government. The freedom to express would be rendered hollow at that point, like a weapon emptied of ammunition. Philosophically, at least, a persuasive case can thus be made in favor of a First Amendment interest in performing scientific research.

The closest the Supreme Court has come to such a ruling is in *Branzburg v. Hayes*,[50] a case involving a news reporter who was communicating with and observing sources of news relating to illegal drug activities. That Court ultimately refused to find that the First Amendment entitled the reporter to a privilege of confidentiality regarding his news sources, reasoning that reporters are not free from incidental burdens generated by general civil or criminal statutes that do not directly target speech.[51] Unfortunately, the Court's opinion is ambiguous, noting that the government had employed the least restrictive means of attaining its objectives and had met the requirements of a "compelling" or "paramount" state interest to justify "even an indirect burden on First Amendment rights."[52] It appears that the *Branzburg* Court recognized First Amendment protection for news gathering (and, presumably, other similar activities, such as scientific research, that are also closely linked preconditions to expression), although the limits of such protection were left hazy at best.[53] Within that haze, it could be argued that there is actually a stronger case for First Amendment protection of scientific research than for news gathering, inasmuch as scientific experimentation has no value or significance if it is not shared with others, especially with other scientists for peer-review purposes so as to test the hypotheses in question.[54]

Another famous but equally ambiguous case that could be posited in support of a First Amendment protection for information gathering is *Buckley v. Valeo*.[55] This case could support the prerequisite theory in that its analysis of the Federal Election Campaign Act of 1971 appears to rely on the assumption that spending money is a necessary precondition of political campaign speech. The *Buckley* Court also deemed the act of contributing money to a candidate as involving the symbolic/communicative act of conveying support to that candidate. However, the Court seemed to give greater protection to the purely facilitative conduct of spending money directly, thus illustrating the constitutional importance of acts that enable expression to take place.[56] *Buckley* also upheld limitations on contributions to a political candidate, while striking down limits on campaign spending, and thus seems to acknowledge some bounds on First Amendment protection of conduct that leads to protected speech as well as symbolic speech itself.[57]

The equation of scientific research with a necessary and constitutionally safeguarded precondition of expression is by no means invulnerable to attack. The principal objection is, in the time-honored phrase, that the argument "proves too much." If research is worthy of First Amendment protection, what about other actions that also are essential links in the chain leading to creation and dissemination of ideas? There may be no clear limit to this line of reasoning, no principled barrier between those actions shielded by the First Amendment and those innumerable others that are just plain actions. Taken to its extreme, the prerequisite argument might urge First Amendment protections on anything that assists a scientist in the pursuit of research, including buying laboratory supplies, getting adequate sleep, and eating. Also, if scientific research is to be placed in a special category, it may be difficult to decide what is and is not scientific; conceivably, the term may be so elastic as to elude demarcation. On these bases, some commentators have criticized the research-as-facilitator theory.[58] However, the law makes distinctions routinely without an iron-clad set of indisputable rules to mandate consistent results in every case, and there is no reason to suspect that the notion of scientific experimentation would prove uniquely dangerous or resistant to principled application in particular instances. There are processes and actions that fall within the generally understood boundaries of "scientific" and that are so intimately, uniquely, and powerfully intertwined with the research/communicative process as to be inseparable from scientific expression.[59]

Leaving aside the issue of First Amendment protection of scientific research as a necessary predicate to communication, there is another credible theory as well. Perhaps the performance of research itself could be viewed as a type of expressive conduct or symbolic speech, along the lines of flag burning, wearing of armbands, and other previously recognized forms of communicative acts. The argument here would be that researchers in general are making the statement that such research is valuable and that the furtherance of knowledge concerning a hypothesis is a worthy aim.[60]

More specifically, scientists working on research into the cloning of humans are arguably making a statement in doing so, at least in part. That statement could be of several different contents, which are not mutually exclusive. The expressive content could be, for example, that (1) enormous good might be achieved through research into the cloning of humans, as an avenue toward relieving human suffering and curing medical conditions; (2) it is important to learn more about the process of cloning humans, as a potential additional form of assisted reproduction technology for infertile people; (3) it is wrong for government to ban scientific inquiry, and the only way such injustice can be overcome is by courageous scientists willing to defy the ban; and (4) even if we never actually clone human beings, there is value in conducting research into the process because it could lead to useful advancements in related areas. But there are substantial objections to this argument of experimentation-as-symbolic-speech.

For the most part, scientists would not be conducting research into the cloning of humans primarily to convey a message to others. Presumably, most scientists, as always, would do research so as to learn more about the subject matter being studied, not to make a statement to observers. However, in an area as novel and controversial as cloning, it is reasonable to suppose that most researchers would have expression as at least a secondary or tertiary purpose for their work, and that may be enough under the scant precedent, as in the nude dancing case.[61]

But the case law seems also to require that the expressive conduct would likely be viewed as such by others (or even have a great likelihood of being so viewed).[62] Here again, it is probable that many, even most, people who learned about scientific research into cloning would not immediately think that the experiments were being done to make a statement, if in fact they were aware of the research at all and could comprehend what it is about; much research is conducted in private, under the radar of the general public, and is highly technical in nature.[63] Instead, the more obvious conclusion of those who knew about the work and who understood it would be that the scientists were doing research because they genuinely wanted to discover new truths and develop new applications of technology. However, it is also likely that observers would discern at least a subsidiary purpose for the work, to express ideas along the lines mentioned earlier. This may again suffice, although it is by no means certain within the sketchy precedential framework we have available.

Courts may be reluctant to adopt the view of research as expressive conduct for the reasons already stated and also because of concerns that there is no clear, logical end point of such a theory. If one takes the theory to extremes, virtually any actions could arguably warrant First Amendment protection. Perhaps the act of driving one's automobile at very high speeds expresses the concept that excessive velocity is a liberating, exhilarating part of being alive. Or using heroin might convey the political thought that drug laws are needless, harmful intrusions by government into the purely private behavior of its citizens. Or refusing to file a federal income tax return could express the political idea that taxation is theft and a coercive abuse of governmental authority over the oppressed masses. Where either or both the primary intent of the actor and the most likely perception of the observer is that conduct is truly conduct, and not expression, courts would be wary of the slippery-slope pitfalls of going too far down that path.

Still, if one accepts either or both of these premises (that scientific research deserves First Amendment protection because of its facilitative role in subsequent expression or that the conduct of research is itself a form of protected symbolic speech), a total ban on *one particular form* of research, that is, that involving the cloning of humans, probably should be considered a content-based restriction on expression, invoking strict scrutiny by the courts.[64] The ban would be explicitly aimed at one specific type of research and the pursuit of "forbidden knowledge," not neutrally applicable to scientific research in general—it would be deliberately and precisely targeted against human clonal experimentation. The gathering and dissemination of scientific data specific to the cloning of humans would be a major, if not the entire, focal point, tantamount to an explicit ban on expressive conduct that proclaims the worthiness of pursuing human clonal research or the uniquely powerful and direct facilitation of such research. Such a deliberate, content-based ban would invoke strict judicial scrutiny.[65]

The outcome of any challenge might turn on whether the reviewing court is willing to accept at face value the intended purpose for the particular ban on therapeutic cloning at issue, that is, the intent as made part of the statute itself or as indicated in accompanying legislative history. Where the legislature has announced a facially legitimate purpose for a law, courts sometimes are reluctant to probe beneath the surface for any other intention.[66] Thus, it might be significant if the anticloning statute were expressly directed at preventing the actual cloning of human beings or the cloning and destruction of human embryos and only banned research insofar as it could lead to these putative evils. But even such a seemingly indirect restriction on research could still be subjected to heightened scrutiny, regardless of whether a court believed the law was intended as a content-based attack on the attainment of scientific knowledge, as illustrated by the Court's handling of the draft-card-burning law in *O'Brien*, where even an incidental impact on speech from a generally applicable law implicated First Amendment analysis.[67]

Along these lines, the government would likely argue that the intent of a ban on therapeutic cloning is not to single out a particular form of research or expression but rather to prevent a grievous harm independent of any expressive issues, such as the production of people as if products or the creation and harvesting of human embryos without regard for their humanity. This line of reasoning could be used either to persuade a court that the ban is content neutral or, if that fails, that the requisite compelling state interest is present to survive judicial review. The government could also assert that cloning bans are akin to the hate-crime statutes upheld by the Supreme Court, wherein laws that enhance criminal penalties because of racial animus on the part of the perpetrator have been held constitutional.[68] Thus, Congress may be entitled to punish some types of arguably symbolic speech both because of its socially disruptive and dehumanizing effects and because of the heavy predominance of conduct over expression in situations such as hate crimes and, perhaps, cloning research.[69]

If a ban on therapeutic cloning is in fact a content-based regulation of expression, it calls for strict scrutiny. In addition to narrowly tailored restrictions, a compelling state interest is required in order to survive strict scrutiny. As I have discussed, it could be difficult to cobble together such an interest in banning cloning, given its similarities to other forms of reproduction and the implausibility of the worst-case arguments. Moreover, it is a bedrock pillar of the First Amendment that government may not ban or punish speech, including expressive conduct, based on its content merely because that content is deemed repugnant, unpopular, or inadvisable.[70]

Is the prevention of reproductive cloning of humans, or the commodification of human embryos, a compelling governmental interest that would survive the very high hurdle of strict scrutiny?[71] The Supreme Court has recognized several interests as "compelling" for purposes of strict scrutiny under the First Amendment. Among these are preventing vote buying;[72] safeguarding the "unique role" of the press and "eliminating from the political process the corrosive effect of political 'war chests' amassed with the aid of the legal advantages given to corporations";[73] protecting voters from confusion, undue influence, and intimidation by electioneers around polling places;[74] ensuring that "criminals do not profit from their crimes" and that victims are compensated by the criminals;[75] "maintaining a stable political system";[76] and safeguarding the right of "members of groups that have historically been subjected to discrimination … to live in peace where they wish."[77]

Although anticloning policies can be stated in terms apparently at least as compelling as most of these, there may be a problem of underinclusiveness. That is, if the evil we fear is the creation and destruction of numerous human embryos, why ban therapeutic cloning while leaving untouched in vitro fertilization or abortion?[78] Or if we want to reserve human reproduction for natural means, apart from intrusive, God-playing, unnatural, laboratory manipulation, why not ban in vitro fertilization, fertility treatments, and various forms of surrogacy, as well as cloning? Such concerns can undermine a ban's ability to weather strict scrutiny on two fronts—both by demonstrating that the government interest is not sufficiently compelling and by showing that the restriction is not sufficiently narrowly tailored to fit that interest. It is also possible that a court would find a blanket ban on both reproductive and therapeutic cloning overinclusive and not the least restrictive alternative if the evil to be prevented is not the attainment of forbidden knowledge (how to clone people) but rather the actual cloning of people. Under that rubric, the least restrictive alternative would be a split ban (such as now is in effect in California), wherein reproductive cloning is banned while research cloning is allowed, subject only to reasonable time, place, and manner regulations. This would avoid the problem of singling out for preemptive legal condemnation the pursuit of a specific category of knowledge, while only banning the application of such knowledge once it is attained. Even in the emotionally heated climate of the cloning debate, courts may be loath to outlaw, in advance, the quest for scientific information as somehow inherently evil, particularly where it does not trammel on the rights of unconsenting postbirth individuals. Indeed, therapeutic cloning does not adversely affect any child, any adult, or any actually born citizen of any age but rather offers them huge benefits.

In the aftermath of *Roe v. Wade*[79] and subsequent abortion-rights cases, most courts would be unlikely to place rudimentary human embryos on the same legal plane as people who have been born. Early-stage embryos comprised of at most a few hundred cells, which have never been implanted in a womb, and which are incapable of existing outside a laboratory, should not be equated under the current law with second- or third-trimester fetuses, let alone postbirth babies, children, and adults. The law readily distinguishes between blastocysts and babies, and judges are accustomed to using this mode of analysis.

To the extent a ban is permanent, rather than a temporary moratorium, that could also cause the restriction to fail as not narrowly tailored or the least restrictive alternative necessary to satisfy the government's compelling interest in the matter. This is so because some (but not all) of the objections to therapeutic cloning are related to uncertainty as to the value of such research, or the number of embryos that would be sacrificed, or other unknowns that could be resolved after the passage of a few years.

This is most emphatically not to say that a court would not find that an explicit ban on therapeutic cloning passes constitutional muster. I have given numerous examples of the abhorrence with which so many people, including members of Congress, the President's Council on Bioethics, and other highly educated people, view the cloning of humans. There is no reason to suppose that judges, even justices of the U.S. Supreme Court, would be any exception. It is entirely possible that a well-meaning Court could uphold a ban on therapeutic cloning by characterizing such cloning as a unique evil in a class by itself, very different from abortion, in vitro fertilization, and the like, and eminently worthy of a preemptive, permanent, sweeping ban. But I have tried to demonstrate that this would not be the most appropriate, most legally defensible outcome, based on a fair application of objective principles to objective facts.

It is seldom that modern events recall the official condemnation and persecution suffered by the renowned seventeenth-century scientist Galileo Galilei, but the bans on research and exploration into cloning have done just that. The Inquisition forced Galileo publicly to deny, under threat of torture, what he had learned through scientific study—that the earth revolved around the sun, that is, the Copernican theory—in order to escape execution for the crime of heresy. Found guilty and sentenced to life imprisonment, he spent the last ten years of his life under house arrest.[80] This infamous travesty was made possible by a society in which the line between Church and State was blatantly breached and a person could be criminally punished for activities that discomforted the religious sensibilities of the dominant elite. When those in power use that power in a preemptive strike to seal off entire categories of learning and inquiry, the loss is unfathomable. No one can ever know what might have been known had the freedom to discover not been denied. Second and third generations of valuable breakthroughs into tangentially related areas might have been gained, but for the prior restraint on research, and again, we can never know what we might have learned. This is a loss without limits.

Scientists have noted that a great deal of value could be gained from research into the cloning of humans, even if reproductive cloning is never pursued.[81] These benefits include potential major advancements in the treatment of serious illnesses, particularly genetic diseases such as cystic fibrosis and Tay-Sachs.[82] Cloning research could also produce invaluable new information about repairing and replacing damaged human tissues and organs, with the potential for the therapeutic transplantation of specific types of "healthy cells, tissues, and organs into people suffering from a variety of diseases and debilitating disorders."[83] People at high risk for diabetes, neurological disorders, cancer, and virtually any disease caused by cellular death or cellular wasting would be good candidates for help through therapeutic cloning.[84] Further, cloning very likely could enable us to realize immense progress in the field of transgenics, in which animals are genetically engineered to produce drugs for the alleviation of an array of human health problems.[85] Such drugs could help fight cancer in humans, and cloning could make the animal testing process much more efficient and rapid.[86]

The 2002 report of the President's Council on Bioethics recognized, in the opinion of some of its members, the positive potential of what they call "cloning-for-biomedical-research," albeit with division among even these members of the council as to the appropriate course of action.[87] Those members who support such research, at least in some form, stated their position as follows:

The moral case for proceeding with the research rests on our obligation to try to relieve human suffering, an obligation that falls most powerfully on medical practitioners and biomedical researchers. We who support cloning-for-biomedical-research all agree that it may offer uniquely useful ways of investigating and possibly treating many chronic debilitating diseases and disabilities, providing aid and relief to millions. We also believe that the moral objections to this research are outweighed by the great good that may come from it. Up to this point, we who support the research all agree. But we differ among ourselves regarding the weight of the moral objections, owing to differences about the moral status of the cloned embryo.[88]

On the other hand, there was significant opposition to therapeutic cloning in any form among other members of the council, amounting to a ten-to-seven majority. Essentially, their position was that "it is morally wrong to exploit and destroy developing human life, even for good reasons, and that it is unwise to open the door to the many undesirable consequences that are likely to result from this research." These members found it "disquieting, even somewhat ignoble, to treat what are in fact seeds of the next generation as mere raw material for satisfying the needs of our own." Their stated reasons for favoring a four-year moratorium on cloning research were as follows:

*Moral status of the cloned embryo.* We hold that the case for treating the early-stage embryo as simply the moral equivalent of all other human cells...is simply mistaken: it denies the continuous history of human individuals from the embryonic to fetal to infant stages of existence; it misunderstands the meaning of potentiality; and it ignores the hazardous moral precedent that the routinized creation, use, and destruction of nascent human life would establish. We hold that the case for according the human embryo "intermediate and developing moral status"...is also unconvincing, for reasons both biological and moral. Attempts to ground the limited measure of respect owed to a maturing embryo in certain of its developmental features do not succeed, and the invoking of a "special respect" owed to nascent human life seems to have little or no operative meaning if cloned embryos may be created in bulk and used routinely with impunity. If from one perspective the view that the embryo seems to amount to little may invite a weakening of our respect, from another perspective its seeming insignificance should awaken in us a sense of shared humanity and a special obligation to protect it.

*The exploitation of developing human life.* To engage in cloning-for-biomedical-research requires the irreversible crossing of a very significant moral boundary: the creation of human life expressly and exclusively for the purpose of its use in research, research that necessarily involves its deliberate destruction. If we permit this research to proceed, we will effectively be endorsing the complete transformation of nascent human life into nothing more than a resource or a tool. Doing so would coarsen our moral sensibilities and make us a different society: one less humble toward that which we cannot fully understand, less willing to extend the boundaries of human respect ever outward, and more willing to transgress moral boundaries once it appears to be in our own interests to do so.

*Moral harm to society.* Even those who are uncertain about the precise moral status of the human embryo have sound ethical-prudential reasons to oppose cloning-for-biomedical-research. Giving moral approval to such research risks significant moral harm to our society by (1) crossing the boundary from sexual to asexual reproduction, thus approving in principle the genetic manipulation and control of nascent human life; (2) opening the door to other moral hazards, such as cloning-to-produce-children or research on later-stage human embryos and fetuses; and (3) potentially putting the federal government in the novel and unsavory position of mandating the destruction of nascent human life. Because we are concerned not only with the fate of the cloned embryos but also with where this research will lead our society, we think prudence requires us not to engage in this research.

*What we owe the suffering.* We are certainly not deaf to the voices of suffering patients; after all, each of us already shares or will share in the hardships of mortal life. We and our loved ones are all patients or potential patients. But we are not only patients, and easing suffering is not our only moral obligation. As much as we wish to alleviate suffering now and to leave our children a world where suffering can be more effectively relieved, we also want to leave them a world in which we and they want to live—a world that honors moral limits, that respects all life whether strong or weak, and that refuses to secure the good of some human beings by sacrificing the lives of others.[89]

But because of the preemptive, door-slamming nature of a permanent ban on research (as in the HCPA), or even a blanket four-year moratorium as advocated by a majority of the President's Council on Bioethics, we can never ascertain exactly what magnitude of a loss the ban would inflict on humanity.[90] In the peripatetic world of biotechnology, even one year can be a very long time. If we attempt to perform cost-benefit analysis on the ban or moratorium, we have a probable enormous cost on one side of the equation, but it is essentially an unknown, a variable with unknowable possible values. That is what happens when the pursuit of knowledge is peremptorily censored. Indeed, there may be a moral obligation *not* to shut down research with such enormous potential to save and enhance so many human lives. One could argue that the preemptive prohibition of this level of medical assistance would be an act of disrespect for human life, an act that refuses to acknowledge the rights and dignity of each person—the very accusations often leveled at those who support cloning.[91]

Indeed, in its 2002 report on human reproductive cloning, the National Academy of Sciences (NAS) reached a very different conclusion regarding therapeutic cloning:

Finally, the scientific and medical considerations that justify a ban on human reproductive cloning at this time are not applicable to nuclear transplantation cloning to produce stem cells. Because of its considerable potential for developing new medical therapies for life-threatening diseases and advancing fundamental knowledge, the panel supports the conclusion of a recent National Academies report that recommended that biomedical research using nuclear transplantation to produce stem cells be permitted. A broad national dialogue on the societal, religious, and ethical issues is encouraged on this matter.[92]

Thus, the NAS did not advocate even a temporary moratorium on therapeutic cloning and also suggested that a ban on reproductive cloning be subject to "review within 5 years" to ascertain whether "new scientific and medical review indicates that the procedures are likely to be safe and effective" and "a broad national dialogue on the societal, religious, and ethical issues suggests that a reconsideration of the ban is warranted."[93]

When the law places Galileo in chains, the entire society of humankind is likewise shackled. We are forced, like Galileo, to kneel before the power of the State and its official orthodoxy and to abjure the reality we have found through so many years of work and sacrifice, pretending instead that modern discoveries were never made. We artificially and arbitrarily close the collective mind of the people to the facts because myths are safer and more familiar to those in command of the coercive force of government. It would require a compelling state interest indeed to justify such a breathtaking curtailment of the freedom of inquiry.

Attempts to find this elusive state interest have led some to liken cloning research to the vilest, most extreme, pseudoscientific examples available in the bottom of the dustbin of history, such as the notorious experiments by Josef Mengele on living prisoners in Nazi concentration camps.[94] But there are such vast differences between the two situations that one scarcely knows where to begin. Legitimate experiments and laboratory procedures involving very early stage human cells are legally and morally indistinguishable from other contemporary activities that are free from governmental censorship. This is not a case of compelling already-born, sentient human beings to diabolical, excruciating, and ultimately fatal surgical procedures to satisfy the perverse curiosity of an evil doctor. There is no legal basis for placing modern cloning research either into an unprotected class by itself or into a locked room with Mengele as the only cell mate.[95]

Some would nonetheless assert that there is a compelling state interest in preventing the creation and use of living human embryos for the explicit purpose of serving as the raw materials for laboratory experiments. In this view, such cloned embryos might be deemed human beings, and the clinical exploitation and commodification of them an evil well within the power of government to ban, with a compelling reason to do so. Notwithstanding the potential benefits that might be reaped from these experiments,[96] the sacredness of human life would stand as an insurmountable obstacle to using cloned human embryos for medical/scientific research. On the other hand, medical breakthroughs derived from such research would save or improve the lives of many people who have actually been born and are indisputably full-fledged human beings imbued with the entire panoply of human rights, while embryos are legally in a different and less-protected category.

A related point deals with the large numbers of failures likely to be endured en route to every successful cloning. This concern applies not only to laboratory research but also to the "naked clone" reproductive cloning scenario, in which parents are seeking to create a live baby. Recall the dismal success rate experienced during the process that resulted in Dolly the cloned sheep. Until and unless massive progress is made toward improving the lopsided ratio of failures to successes, it is possible that every live child of cloning would be outnumbered many times over by embryos that never make it to a live birth, or never survive the earliest stages of infancy, or are deformed. If cloning produces dozens or even hundreds of doomed, damaged, or discarded embryos and infants for every healthy baby, it would spark intense opposition on the grounds that this is an appalling waste of nascent human life.[97] Again, it appears to reduce people to commodities and to accept many dead embryos and deformed babies as just another of the costs of doing business for the production of every viable, normal child of cloning.

There is a certain visceral power to these objections. If the cloning dilemma had developed prior to *Roe v. Wade*,[98] there is little doubt that the opponents of cloning would have prevailed in the courts, including the Supreme Court. There was a long history of legal recognition and protection of unborn human life under the common law.[99] Modern criminal law and tort law also accommodated the interests of the State in the protection of prebirth humans.[100] But the lens through which the judiciary views inchoate human life has been radically altered since *Roe*. The courts have accepted, and indeed ensured, the legality of millions of abortions annually, with myriad embryos and fetuses intentionally eliminated at all stages of gestation, under all circumstances, and for any and all reasons or no reason at all. The process of in vitro fertilization (IVF) is also now well established[101] and is afforded the full complement of legal protections, notwithstanding the significant numbers of unsuccessful attempts to bring about a healthy baby and the frequency with which embryos are frozen or discarded.[102]

Some specific facts are in order. For example, human IVF attempts in the United States in 1998 required one or two embryos only 20 percent of the time; three embryos were transferred in 33 percent of all cases; four embryos were used in 28 percent of the cases; and fully 19 percent of the time, five or more embryos were transferred during the IVF process.[103] And in 1999, the average number of embryos from nondonor eggs transferred per case of IVF, overall, ranged from 3.4 for women under the age of 35 to 3.9 for women over the age of 40.[104] When using fresh embryos from donor eggs, the number of embryos used ranged from 3.3 to 3.4 per individual using IVF, numbers virtually identical to those from cases where frozen embryos were transferred.[105] Of course, in some cases, more than one pregnancy results from the transfer of multiple embryos to one woman simultaneously, and multiple births are not uncommon. But in many instances, the "extra" embryos never lead to a live birth and are lost, destroyed, killed, or otherwise eliminated at some point during the IVF process.

There has not been a tidal wave of restrictive legislation or regulation pertaining to IVF,[106] despite some moral and religious objections.[107] No state has banned it,[108] and the legal measures that are in effect generally require only data collection, certification of practitioners and facilities, and the provision for informed consent.[109] The parallels with cloning are both obvious and significant.[110] Some critics initially predicted that IVF would result in the mass-production of infants.[111] Public outrage at the dawn of IVF was extreme, at least in some quarters, and dire consequences were prophesied.[112] In the early years, legal commentators decried the technology and urged restrictions, and some states attempted to restrict it, as with artificial insemination.[113] Yet, as the reality juggernaut inexorably encroached on speculation, the law has actually moved to protect and foster the use of IVF, primarily because it has been demonstrably successful and a boon to infertile couples and individuals.[114]

Indeed, the many human embryos wasted and destroyed every day through IVF procedures have their "natural" counterpart as well. Some people would be surprised to learn that most of the human embryos created the old-fashioned way, through the chance meeting of egg and sperm inside a woman's body, never survive beyond the very early stages of development. These entirely natural human embryos are spontaneously aborted for a variety of biological reasons and never result in pregnancy, let alone the birth of a live infant. The woman in whose body this sad little drama plays itself out is never even aware that the embryo ever existed. The woman excretes the naturally discarded embryo along with her urine, and it passes through the plumbing into the sewer or septic tank, without any president, pope, or member of Congress arguing that this is an appalling disrespect for the dignity of human life on the part of Mother Nature.

The example of IVF should be instructive to us now in the midst of the cloning controversy. If our response to early furor over a new and, to some, repugnant line of scientific inquiry is to head it off at the pass and kill it before it spreads, then we cannot know what further research might have taught us about the reality as opposed to the fantasy of the new field. Moreover, if unarticulated and unsubstantiated fears are enough to justify the prior restraint of scientific research, where is the line that separates permissible from forbidden science? It may be nowhere other than in the eye of the beholder—or the minds of the legislators. A ban on therapeutic cloning, based on nothing more than the baseless apprehension of so many people, would set a dangerous precedent that could needlessly jeopardize many other potentially salutary lines of scientific investigation. In the process, untold lives could be lost, and many more lives inflicted with great hardship and suffering, all because we hastily acted to foreclose an avenue of science we initially found troubling.

Realistically, it is highly unlikely that the cloning of humans would be attempted by most medical professionals, nor would people want to try it as a form of assisted reproduction, at least until the technology has moved beyond the stage of high failure rates and abnormal births, with or without legislation restricting the practice. It would be prohibitively expensive and ethically dubious to persist in efforts to clone people unless additional experiments involving animals, especially higher primates, dramatically improved the probability of a normal, live birth.

To illustrate by way of another biotechnological phenomenon, consider the case of human-animal hybrids or chimeras. Scientists have had the requisite technological expertise since 1981 to create at least fertilized eggs of some types of such human-animal creatures, when it was found that human sperm can penetrate the protective outer membranes of healthy gibbon eggs.[115] In the case of animal-animal chimeras, viable cross-species hybrids up to and including adulthood have been produced from two distinct but closely related species of mice since 1980, and from a union of sheep and cattle since 1984.[116]

But scientists have not pursued these early leads to their logical (or illogical) conclusion during the ensuing decades. Why not? For essentially the same reasons they would not conduct irresponsible experiments into cloning people: a combination of prudent self-restraint, concern about incurring the disfavor of their professional peers, existing ethical standards governing scientific research, daunting technical obstacles, prohibitively high expenses, aversion to tort liability, and other powerful deterrents to the "mad-scientist" threat.[117]

If you have never been accosted by a latter-day minotaur or centaur while walking down the street, do not thank Congress. There is no federal law in the United States expressly banning the creation of chimeras.[118] The government did not react, or overreact, to the scientific and technological progress underlying hybridization by enacting a statute prohibiting the making of human-animal hybrids. It was unnecessary.

The threat of chimeras, as with the terrifying prospect of monster clones, has literally proven chimerical.[119] No ban was needed explicitly to outlaw chimeras or experiments into creating them. Likewise, a combination of factors would prevent horror-story misuses of human cloning technology, without the need for any new law. By banning that which is self-regulating, we would do something worse than needless, however. In the case of cloning, we would also be throwing out the baby with the bath water...or the water under the burned bridge.

On the pragmatic level, cloning would need to attain something approaching the success rate of IVF before it becomes a real option both for would-be parents and for the medical and technological professionals involved. The process would be self-regulating to a significant degree. And if legislation were narrowly tailored to regulate human reproductive cloning and/or research, perhaps with a very short-term temporary ban (that is, a moratorium) until the requisite progress is achieved through nonhuman research, there could be a legitimate judicial imprimatur as well.

Potentially, courts might draw a distinction between "casualties" unavoidably incurred in the process of cloning a human being for reproductive purposes and cloned embryos intentionally created and "harvested" for the express purpose of scientific/medical research. As explained in chapter 5, the "naked clone" position regarding reproductive cloning is buttressed by powerful additional constitutional rights not available in the research setting, and this might justify greater judicial deference to the former than to the latter. Restrictions and regulations, although probably not an outright permanent ban, properly could be tolerated in the research setting, while cloning for reproduction would be much more fully protected. However, in light of the analogous collateral loss of human embryos during IVF experiments and actual IVF attempts to reproduce and the many millions of prenatal fetuses and embryos deliberately destroyed through various forms of abortion,[120] it is possible that courts would not find an outcome-determinative distinction between the two. We have blazed a path that may lead to even large-scale, intentional sacrifice of research-only cloned human embryos, and a fortiori the unintentional loss of embryos associated with the presumed low success rate of live-birth directed cloning efforts.

Strangely, as I mentioned in chapter 2 and shall discuss again in chapter 5, key states such as California and Virginia, as well as the United States Congress, have been moving in exactly the opposite direction from that which I have just described. I argue that there is an even greater and clearer constitutional guarantee of reproductive cloning rights than of therapeutic cloning, strong though the latter might be. But Congress and states in the California/Virginia mold act as if the situation were completely reversed. To see why, and why this is totally wrong from a constitutional standpoint, we first need to examine the legal issues pertaining to reproductive cloning.

## NOTES

1. ABC News Online, *U.N. Defers Debate on Anti-Cloning Treaty* (Nov. 8, 2002), <http://abc.net.au/news/scitech/2002/11/item20021108093502_1.htm>.

2. *See* Michael A. Goldman, *Human Cloning: Science Fact and Fiction*, 8 S. CAL. INTERDIS. L. J. 103, 109–11 (1998) (discussing various medical-scientific advantages of cloning for research purposes).

3. *See* Paul Berg and Maxine Singer, *Regulating Human Cloning*, 282 SCIENCE 413, 413 (1998) (asserting that legislation is a suboptimal means for the regulation of scientific inquiry and progress). For an interesting compendium of numerous short essays articulating various legal and policy-based arguments against bans on scientific inquiry into the cloning of humans, *see* <http://reason.com/bioresearch/bioresearch.shtml>.

4. *See* Matthew B. Hsu, Note, *Banning Human Cloning: An Acceptable Limit on Scientific Inquiry or an Unconstitutional Restriction of Symbolic Speech?* 87 GEO. L. J. 2399, 2410–16 (1999).

5. *See* David M. Rabban, *The Emergence of Modern First Amendment Doctrine*, 50 U. CHI. L. REV. 1205 (1983); Abrams v. United States, 250 U.S. 616, 630 (1919) (Holmes, J., joined by Brandeis, J., dissenting).

6. *See* Stanley Ingber, *The Marketplace of Ideas: A Legitimizing Myth*, 1984 DUKE L. J. 1 (1984).

7. *See* Alexander Meiklejohn, FREE SPEECH AND ITS RELATION TO SELF-GOVERNMENT (The Lawbook Exchange, Ltd. 1948).

8. *See* C. Edwin Baker, *Scope of the First Amendment Freedom of Speech*, 25 U.C.L.A. L. REV. 964 (1978); Martin H. Redish, *The Value of Free Speech*, 130 U. PA. L. REV. 591 (1982).

9. *See* Whitney v. California, 274 U.S. 357, 375 (1927) (Brandeis, J., joined by Holmes, J., concurring).

10. *See* Thomas Emerson, THE SYSTEM OF FREEDOM OF EXPRESSION, 6–7 (Random House 1970); Steven Shiffrin, *The First Amendment and Economic Regulation: Away from a General Theory of the First Amendment*, 78 NW. U. L. REV. 1212 (1983).

11. Schenck v. United States, 249 U.S. 47 (1919).

12. *See, e.g.,* Chaplinsky v. New Hampshire, 315 U.S. 568 (1942).

13. *See, e.g.,* Miller v. California, 413 U.S. 15 (1973).

14. *See, e.g.,* Brandenburg v. Ohio, 395 U.S. 444 (1969).

15. *See* Whitney v. California, 274 U.S. 357, 375–77 (1927) (Brandeis, J., joined by Holmes, J., concurring). "Those who won our independence believed that the final end of the State was to make men free to develop their faculties. . . . They valued liberty both as an end and as a means. They believed liberty to be the secret of hap-

piness and courage to be the secret of liberty.... [The] freedom to think as you will and to speak as you think" is a "means indispensable to the discovery and spread of political truth" and is essential to "stable government" and "political change."

16. *See, e.g.,* Young v. American Mini Theatres, Inc., 427 U.S. 50 (1976); City of Renton v. Playtime Theatres, Inc., 475 U.S. 41 (1986).

17. *See, e.g.,* Beauharnais v. Illinois, 343 U.S. 250 (1952); New York Times Co. v. Sullivan, 376 U.S. 254 (1964); Gertz v. Robert Welch, Inc., 418 U.S. 323 (1974).

18. *See* New York v. Ferber, 458 U.S. 747 (1982).

19. *See, e.g.,* Virginia State Board of Pharmacy v. Virginia Citizens Consumer Council, Inc., 425 U.S. 748 (1976); Ohralik v. Ohio State Bar Association, 436 U.S. 447 (1978); Central Hudson Gas & Electric Corp. v. Public Service Commission of New York, 447 U.S. 557 (1980); 44 Liquormart, Inc. v. Rhode Island, 517 U.S. 484 (1996).

20. *See, e.g.,* Texas v. Johnson, 491 U.S. 397 (1989).

21. *See* United States v. O'Brien, 391 U.S. 367 (1968).

22. *See, e.g.,* Cohen v. California, 403 U.S. 15, 26 (1971).

23. Barnes v. Glen Theatre, 501 U.S. 560 (1991). In this case, a statute prohibiting nude dancing was upheld in a plurality opinion with four justices dissenting, but the entire Court in various separate opinions agreed that nude dancing was a form of expressive conduct implicating the First Amendment. *See* 501 U.S. at 565–66 (Rehnquist, C.J., plurality opinion) (stating that prior cases suggest that "nude dancing of the kind sought to be performed here is expressive conduct within the outer perimeters of the First Amendment"); 501 U.S. at 572–74 (Scalia, J., concurring) (describing the statute in question as content-neutral with respect to the expression of nude dancing); 501 U.S. at 581 (Souter, J., concurring) (stating that nude dancing contains expressive elements); 501 U.S. at 588 (White, J., dissenting) (stating that nude dancing is expression protected by the First Amendment). This was so despite the fact that the dancers, although they were certainly aware of the sexually stimulating "message" expressed by their dancing, were not intent on conveying any message but only, very pragmatically, wanted to dance nude as a means to earn more money. This implies that the expression of an idea need not be the sole or even primary reason for engaging in the expressive conduct.

24. Spence v. Washington, 418 U.S. 405, 409 (1974). *See* Ronald Rotunda and John Nowak, TREATISE ON CONSTITUTIONAL LAW: SUBSTANCE AND PROCEDURE, VOL 4, § 20.48–20.49 (West Group 3d ed. 1999).

25. United States v. O'Brien, 391 U.S. 367, 376 (1968).

26. Spence v. Washington, 418 U.S. 405, 410–11 (1974).

27. Texas v. Johnson, 491 U.S. 397, 405 (1989). Texas v. Johnson would require that "the likelihood is great that the intended message would be understood by those who viewed it."

28. United States v. O'Brien, 391 U.S. 367, 376 (1968).

29. *Id,* at 376–77.

30. *Id.,* at 377. *See also* Clark v. Community for Creative Non-Violence, 468 U.S. 288 (1984) (regarding demonstrators who slept in a park to call attention to the plight of the homeless).

31. Texas v. Johnson, 491 U.S. 397, 403 (1989).

32. *Id.*

33. Tinker v. Des Moines Independent Community School District, 393 U.S. 503 (1969).

34. *Id.*, at 510–11.

35. *See* Texas v. Johnson, 491 U.S. 397, 403 (1989); *see also* R.A.V. v. City of St. Paul, 505 U.S. 377, 382 (1992) (declaring that "Content-based regulations are presumptively invalid").

36. Wayte v. United States, 470 U.S. 598 (1985).

37. *Id.*, at 611, n.12.

38. *Id.*, at 611–14.

39. *See* Texas v. Johnson, 491 U.S. 397, 403 (1989). It is important to keep in mind, however, that as with restrictions on "pure speech," symbolic speech may also be regulated if the content of the ideas expressed falls within a category of unprotected or low-value speech, such as fighting words, incitement, or obscenity. *See* Chaplinsky v. New Hampshire, 315 U.S. 568, 571–72 (1942).

40. *See, e.g.,* R.A.V. v. City of St. Paul, 505 U.S. 377 (1992); Police Dept. of the City of Chicago v. Mosley, 408 U.S. 92 (1972).

41. *See, e.g.,* Ward v. Rock Against Racism, 491 U.S. 781 (1989).

42. *See* Eugene Volokh, *Freedom of Speech, Permissible Tailoring, and Transcending Strict Scrutiny,* 144 U. PA. L. REV. 2417, 2418–24 (1996).

43. *See, e.g.,* Frisby v. Schultz, 487 U.S. 474 (1988).

44. *See* John A. Robertson, *The Scientist's Right to Research: A Constitutional Analysis,* 51 S. CAL. L. REV. 1203, 1217–18 (1977) (asserting that the scientific method depends on experimentation as an essential prelude to the dissemination of scientific ideas).

45. *See, e.g.,* Branzburg v. Hayes, 408 U.S. 665, 705 (1972) (likening the information production function of the news-gathering press to that of researchers); Buckley v. Valeo, 424 U.S. 1 (1976) (finding First Amendment protection for the financing of political speech). *See* Ira H. Carmen, *Should Human Cloning Be Criminalized?* 13 J. L. & POL. 745, 752 (1997) (arguing that cloning research and other scientific inquiry implicates protected First Amendment values); June Coleman, Comment, *Playing God or Playing Scientist: A Constitutional Analysis of Laws Banning Embryological Procedures,* 27 PAC. L. J. 1331, 1387 (1996) (maintaining that various Supreme Court decisions, when read together, "seem to acknowledge a freedom to conduct research which is anchored in the freedom of speech"); Ira H. Carmen, CLONING AND THE CONSTITUTION 35–36 (University of Wisconsin Press 1986).

46. Gary L. Francione, *Experimentation and the Marketplace Theory of the First Amendment,* 136 U. PA. L. REV. 417, 428–29 (1987) (discussing the recognition by the framers of the Constitution of the "sacred" nature of scientific inquiry).

47. *See* Meyer v. Nebraska, 262 U.S. 390 (1923) (noting that the Fourteenth Amendment guarantees, as part of the right to liberty, the freedom "to acquire useful knowledge … and generally to enjoy those privileges long recognized at common law as essential to the orderly pursuit of happiness by free men").

48. *See* Margaret S. v. Edwards, 488 F. Supp. 181, 220–21 (E.D. La. 1980); Wynn v. Scott, 449 F. Supp. 1302, 1322 (N.D. Ill. 1978), *aff'd sub nom.* Wynn v. Carey, 599 F.2d 193 (7th Cir. 1979). *See also* National Bioethics Advisory Committee, CLONING HUMAN BEINGS: REPORT AND RECOMMENDATIONS OF THE NATIONAL BIOETHICS ADVISORY COMMISSION 6 (National Bioethics Advi-

sory Committee 1997) (NBAC Report) (stating that the freedom of scientific inquiry is not an absolute right and that scientists are expected to conduct their research according to widely held ethical principles, with limits on scientific freedom acceptable at times).

49. *See* Richard Delgado and David R. Millen, *God, Galileo, and Government: Toward Constitutional Protection for Scientific Inquiry,* 53 WASH. L. REV. 349, 394–99 (1978).

50. Branzburg v. Hayes, 408 U.S. 665 (1972).

51. *Id.,* at 684.

52. *Id.,* at 690–91, 695.

53. Roy G. Spece Jr. and Jennifer Weinzierl, *First Amendment Protection of Experimentation: A Critical Review and Tentative Synthesis/Reconstruction of the Literature,* 8 S. CAL. INTERDISC. L. J. 185, 188–90 (1998).

54. Francione, *supra* note 46, at 460–64 (positing and then critiquing this argument).

55. Buckley v. Valeo, 424 U.S. 1 (1976).

56. *See* Robertson, *supra* note 44, at 1218, n.59. *See also* Richard Delgado et al., *Can Science Be Inopportune? Constitutional Validity of Governmental Restrictions on Race-IQ Research,* 31 U.C.L.A. L. REV. 128, 160–61 (1983) (arguing that the nominally nonexpressive aspects of science, including research, are so intimately connected with the scientist's goal of creating and disseminating information that the right of expression would be meaningless without First Amendment protection for research); Natasha C. Lisman, *Freedom of Scientific Research: A Frontier Issue in First Amendment Law,* 35 B.B.J. 4 (1991) (same).

57. *See* Steven L. Carter, *The Bellman, the Snark, and the Biohazard Debate,* 3 YALE L. & POL'Y REV. 358, 375 (1985).

58. *See* John B. Attanasio, *Does the First Amendment Guarantee a Right to Conduct Scientific Experiments?* 14 J.C. & U. L. 435 (1987); Francione, *supra* note 46, at 441–42; Carter, *supra* note 57, at 376–77.

59. *See* Spece and Weinzierl, *supra* note 53, at 213–18; San Antonio School District v. Rodriguez, 411 U.S. 1, 35–37 (1973) (illustrating the Court's willingness to recognize such "nexus arguments" only where there is a uniquely close relationship between the concepts sought to be linked).

60. *See generally* Spece and Weinzierl, *supra* note 53; Steven Goldberg, CULTURE CLASH: LAW AND SCIENCE IN AMERICA 7–9 (New York University Press 1994); Francione, *supra* note 46, at 431–58 (evaluating and critiquing the various ways in which the experiment is itself a form of expressive conduct).

61. *See* Barnes v. Glen Theatre, 501 U.S. 560 (1991).

62. *See* Spence v. Washington, 418 U.S. 405, 410–11 (1974); Texas v. Johnson, 491 U.S. 397, 405 (1989).

63. *See* Steven M. Wise, *Scientific Experimental Conduct Is Not Protected by the First Amendment,* 36 B.B.J. 20, 22–24 (1992); Francione, *supra* note 46, at 448–49.

64. *See* Spece and Weinzierl, *supra* note 53, at 219–20.

65. *See* Francione, *supra* note 46, at 425.

66. *See* United States v. O'Brien, 391 U.S. 367, 381–82, 385 (1968).

67. *Id.,* at 377.

68. *See* Wisconsin v. Mitchell, 508 U.S. 476, 485–88 (1993).

69. However, hate-crime laws deal with behavior that is already criminally punishable, unlike bans on therapeutic cloning, and do not criminalize actions because of their content but because of their effect on others. *See* Hsu, *supra* note 4, at 2427–29.

70. *See* Texas v. Johnson, 491 U.S. 397, 414 (1989) (striking down Texas legislation penalizing those who burn the American flag to express an anti-American viewpoint). *See also* R.A.V. v. City of St. Paul, 505 U.S. 377, 382 (1992) (invalidating a hate-speech law as a content-based restriction).

71. *See* Eugene Volokh, *Freedom of Speech, Permissible Tailoring, and Transcending Strict Scrutiny,* 144 U. PA. L. REV. 2417, 2418–24 (1996).

72. Buckley v. Valeo, 424 U.S. 1 (1976).

73. Austin v. Michigan Chamber of Commerce, 494 U.S. 652 (1990).

74. Burson v. Freeman, 504 U.S. 191, 199 (1992) (plurality opinion).

75. Simon & Schuster, Inc. v. Members of the N.Y. State Crime Victims Bd., 502 U.S. 105, 118–19 (1991).

76. Eu v. San Francisco County Democratic Cent. Comm., 489 U.S. 214, 226 (1989).

77. R.A.V. v. City of St. Paul, 505 U.S. 377 (1992).

78. *See* Florida Star v. B.J.F., 491 U.S. 524 (1989). In other words, the suggestion is that the government itself does not view the interest to be so compelling as to justify a broader ban.

79. Roe v. Wade, 410 U.S. 113 (1973).

80. *See generally* Jerome J. Langford and Stillman Drake, GALILEO, SCIENCE, AND THE CHURCH (St. Augustine Press 1998); Albert Di Canzio, GALILEO: HIS SCIENCE AND HIS SIGNIFICANCE FOR THE FUTURE OF MAN (Adasi Publishing 1997).

81. *See* President's Council on Bioethics, *Human Cloning and Human Dignity: An Ethical Inquiry,* chapter 6 (July 2002), http://www.bioethics.gov/reports/cloning report/fullreport.html>. (listing and discussing such benefits as improving the understanding of human disease, devising new treatments for such diseases; producing immune-compatible tissues for transplantation, and assisting in gene therapy).

82. See Nati Somekh, Note, *The European Total Ban on Human Cloning: An Analysis of the Council of Europe's Actions in Prohibiting Human Cloning,* 17 B. U. INT'L L. J. 397, 411 (1999).

83. *See* Committee on Science, Engineering, and Public Policy, SCIENTIFIC AND MEDICAL ASPECTS OF HUMAN REPRODUCTIVE CLONING 28–31 (National Academy Press, 2002) (HUMAN REPRODUCTIVE CLONING).

84. *See* statement of John C. Fletcher, <http://reason.com/bioresearch/ bioresearch.shtml>.

85. *See* Senate Resolution, Comm. Rep. CA S.J.R. 14 (1997).

86. *See* HUMAN REPRODUCTIVE CLONING, *supra* note 83, at 32–33.

87. This lengthy, detailed document ultimately did not make a clear, unambiguous recommendation. Instead, the council proffered two proposals. Both proposals advocated an immediate and permanent ban on reproductive cloning, or what the report calls "cloning-to-produce-children"; in fact, the council was unanimous (17 to 0) in urging a ban on reproductive cloning. As noted in chapter 2, one proposal that garnered the support of ten members also recommended a four-year

moratorium on therapeutic cloning. *See* President's Council on Bioethics, chapter 8, Policy Recommendations <http://www.bioethics.gov/reports/cloningreport/recommend.html>. The ten council members who supported this proposal are Rebecca S. Dresser, Francis Fukuyama, Robert P. George, Mary Ann Glendon, Alfonso Gómez-Lobo, William B. Hurlbut, Leon R. Kass, Charles Krauthammer, Paul McHugh, and Gilbert C. Meilaender. The other proposal, supported by seven members, argued for continuing to allow research into human cloning to proceed, but with regulation.

88. President's Council on Bioethics, *Human Cloning and Human Dignity: An Ethical Inquiry* (July 2002), <http://www.bioethics.gov/reports/cloning report/index.html>.

89. *Id.*

90. *See* Ronald Bailey, *Split Decision: The Reckless Conservatism of the President's Council on Bioethics,* <http://reason.com/rb/rb071702.shtml> (August 10, 2001).

91. Fletcher, *supra* note 84.

92. *See* HUMAN REPRODUCTIVE CLONING, *supra* note 83, at 99.

93. *Id.*

94. *See generally* Lucette Matalon Lagnado and Sheila Cohn Dekel, CHILDREN OF THE FLAMES: DR. JOSEF MENGELE AND THE UNTOLD STORY OF THE TWINS OF AUSCHWITZ (William Morrow & Co. 1991). Mengele performed forcible, brutal experiments on the prisoners of the Auschwitz death camp, including some 3,000 identical twins, very few of whom survived his horrific operations.

95. *See* Declan Butler, *Calls for Human Cloning Ban "Stem from Ignorance,"* 387 NATURE 324 (1997); Declan Butler and Meredith Wadman, *Calls for Cloning Ban Sell Science Short,* 386 NATURE 8, 9 (1997).

96. *See* Jerome P. Kassirer and Nadia A. Rosenthal, *Should Human Cloning Research Be Off Limits?* 338 NEW. ENG. J. MED. 905, 905 (1998) (arguing that research on SCNT could produce many important benefits, including valuable information on the mechanism of aging, the cause of cancer, and improved treatments of such diseases as diabetes mellitus, leukemia, and genetic disorders).

97. However, as I argue elsewhere in this book, there is no realistic prospect of significant numbers of people trying to clone if the failure rate were high. The costs would be prohibitively high, in terms of money, psychological anguish, and the opprobrium society would heap upon those who courted disaster in such a way. There would also be the risk of ruinous civil liability under the torts system for physicians, scientists, and the institutions where they work, for contributing to the birth of badly deformed children. The system would mostly regulate itself, and there would be no "epidemic" of failures.

98. Roe v. Wade, 410 U.S. 113 (1973).

99. *See* Clarke D. Forsythe, *Legal Perspectives on Cloning: Human Cloning and the Constitution,* 32 VAL. U.L. REV. 469, 485–94 (1998).

100. *Id.,* at 494–513.

101. IVF has become commonplace despite the onerous expenses and inefficiencies involved. *See* Anne Lawton, *The Frankenstein Controversy: The Constitutionality of a Federal Ban on Cloning,* 87 KY. L. J. 277, 328 (1998/1999) (indicating it may cost from $40,000 to $200,000 to have a child using IVF technology); John A. Robertson, CHILDREN OF CHOICE: FREEDOM AND THE NEW REPRODUCTIVE TECHNOLOGIES 100, 116 (1994) (noting that thousands of IVF

attempts are performed every year, and some states require health insurers to cover IVF).

102. *See* Laurence Tribe, *Second Thoughts on Cloning*, N.Y. TIMES, Dec. 5, 1997, at A23. (maintaining that cloning is justified as an "incremental step beyond what we are already doing with artificial insemination, IVF, fertility-enhancing drugs, and genetic manipulation").

103. Centers for Disease Control, *1998 Assisted Reproductive Technology Success Rates, National Summary and Fertility Clinic Reports*, <http://www.cdc.gov/nccdphp/drh/art98/98nation.htm> (1998).

104. Centers for Disease Control, *1999 National Summary*, <http://apps.nccd.cdc.gov/ART99/nation99.asp> (1999). Similar summary tables, and similar statistics, are also available on-line for the years 1995, 1996, 1997, and 1998: <http://www.cdc.gov/nccdphp/drh/art98/index.htm>.

105. *Id.*

106. *See* Janet L. Dolgin, DEFINING THE FAMILY: LAW, TECHNOLOGY, AND REPRODUCTION IN AN UNEASY AGE 62 (New York University Press 1997); Roger J. Chin, *Assisted Reproductive Technologies: Legal Issues in Procreation*, 8 LOY. CONSUMER L. REP. 190, 197 (1996).

107. *See* Roberto Suro, *Vatican Asks Governments to Curb Birth Technology and to Outlaw Surrogates*, N.Y. TIMES, Mar. 11, 1987, at A1.

108. *See* Note, *Human Cloning and Substantive Due Process*, 111 HARV. L. REV. 2348, 2361 (1998).

109. *See* Judith F. Daar, *Regulating Reproductive Technologies: Panacea or Paper Tiger?* 34 HOUS. L. REV. 609, 641–51 (1997).

110. *See* Katheryn D. Katz, *The Clonal Child: Procreative Liberty and Asexual Reproduction*, 8 ALB. L. J. SCI. & TECH. 1, 14 (1997) (concluding that cloning is not as revolutionary as feared and is arguably "more deserving of protection as a means of reproduction than many other techniques").

111. *See A Rush of Test-Tube Babies*, U.S. NEWS & WORLD REP., Aug. 7, 1978, at 22.

112. *See* Lawrence Wu, Note, *Family Planning through Human Cloning: Is There a Fundamental Right?* 98 COLUM. L. REV. 1461, 1512–13 (1998) (citing sources denouncing IVF as "startling as the atomic bomb").

113. *See* Elizabeth Bartholet, FAMILY BONDS: ADOPTION AND THE POLITICS OF PARENTING 202 (1993); Note, *Reproductive Technology and the Procreation Rights of the Unmarried*, 98 HARV. L. REV. 669, 669–70 (1985); HUMAN REPRODUCTIVE CLONING, *supra* note 83, at 68.

114. *See* Dolgin, *supra* note 106, at 9; Chin, *supra* note 106, at 194–99.

115. *See* David Longtin and Duane C. Kraemer, *Cloning Red Herrings*, POLICY REVIEW ONLINE, <http://www.policyreview.org/FEB02/longtin.html> (February 2002).

116. *Id.*

117. *Id. See also* the comedic parody of anticloning fears, including human-animal hybrids or chimeras, in the 2002 Halloween episode of the animated television series *The Simpsons*, which aired on November 3, 2002, on the Fox network.

118. Some other nations, such as Japan and Denmark, have seen fit to enact preemptive bans on experiments involving human-animal hybrids or chimeras, as explained in chapter 3.

119. *See generally* John Charles Kunich, *Chimera: The Illusion of Our Post-Human Future*, ROGER WILLIAMS LAW REVIEW (2003) (analyzing the reasons why pre-emptive bans on speculative biotechnology threats are unconstitutional and imprudent).

120. The Centers for Disease Control statistics indicate that the number of legal abortions performed annually in the United States was consistently well above 1 million per year from 1980 through 1997. *See* <http://www.infoplease .com/ipa/A0764203.html>. For example, in 1996, there were an estimated 1.3 million induced abortions in the United States. *See* <http://www.cdc .gov/nchs/releases/99facts/pregrate.htm>.

# CHAPTER 5

# The Naked Clone and Bans on Reproductive Cloning

In light of the objections to cloning, the reasons people would want to clone, and the multiple pieces of legislation on both the state and federal level that touch on the cloning of human beings, the key question becomes whether anticloning laws are constitutional. Clearly, the answer to this question can only be adumbrated through a process of comparison and analogy, in that there is no case law directly on point at this early juncture in the history of human clonal activity.

I analyze this issue primarily in terms of the Human Cloning Prohibition Act of 2001 (HCPA) because this bill was actually passed by the United States House of Representatives, has the full support of President George W. Bush, was seriously considered by the Senate during the first half of 2002 (although ultimately never brought to a vote), and is sweeping in its scope. After the Republican capture of control in the Senate in the November 2002 elections, a similar bill was reintroduced in both chambers during the 108th Congress and again passed the House in February 2003. Moreover, with regard to a permanent ban on reproductive cloning, it is also completely in accord with the unanimous recommendations of President Bush's Council on Bioethics.[1] The HCPA is a complete and comprehensive ban on the SCNT method of cloning humans irrespective of purpose, and it has no sunset provisions. If the HCPA approach survives constitutional scrutiny, it is reasonable to presume that less-ambitious legislative restrictions would do likewise, along the lines of a ban with provisions for review and reconsideration in five years, as recommended by the National Academy of Sciences report in 2002.[2]

I must emphasize that the following analysis is not an attempt to predict what the current Supreme Court or some future Supreme Court would actually do[3] but rather is a suggestion as to what they should do, to be consistent with stare decisis and the rule of law. My ability to foretell the future has been shaky ever since my Magic Eight-Ball got stuck on "Not at this time" when I was fourteen years old, and I have been unable to find an owl whose entrails are available to be examined. As will be explained, much of the relevant precedent rests on questionable and nontextual constitutional grounds, and has often been produced, case by case, by the narrowest possible majorities or even pluralities. The fragile coalitions that yielded these cases could be shattered if even one justice is replaced by a person of differing judicial views on such matters. Moreover, even the presidents who carefully nominate new U.S. Supreme Court justices are often surprised by how "their" justices vote once on the Court.[4] In an effort to focus on legal principle and not on political maneuvering, I will not essay to foretell the future but only to sort through the doctrinal strands that loosely knit the jurisprudence and see where the threads lead us.

One can hypothesize several ways in which a legal challenge to the HCPA and its state analogues might be mounted. The facts could be arrayed in a variety of patterns, depending on who was attempting to clone a human, the motives for doing so, and the specific governmental response. Indeed, the breadth of many of the anticloning bills and statutes invites legal challenges on multiple fronts and increases the probability that the courts will find constitutional defects. By essaying to ban all cloning of human beings regardless of reason or circumstances, the legislators have made it likely that some cases will be brought in which very earnest, sympathy-attracting people plead for redress of their grievances against a Procrustean anticloning legal regime. It may be that courts would hold some limited restrictions on the cloning of humans permissible, while striking down more sweeping bans. The following sections examine how and why.

## THE NAKED CLONE SCENARIO AND REPRODUCTIVE RIGHTS

First, I will consider the most favorable scenario for a successful legal attack on the anticloning laws. I call this the naked clone situation, the name of which constitutes the title of this book.[5] I use the term *naked clone* to highlight one particularly propitious concatenation of circumstances, in which well-meaning, loving, child-focused people are barred from cloning despite being motivated by some of the best, most altruistic, most basic human impulses. The parents, perhaps already devastated by the terminal illness of their child, would be bereft a second time, having lost the chance to give life another chance through cloning. The child of cloning would be naked in the sense of being devoid of protection, stripped of legal rights, and without any refuge from the government that forbids him or her even to exist. The privacy rights of the parents and child would be subordinated to the state interests, leaving the child of cloning naked and exposed to the dictates of the government.

The naked clone scenario ultimately would probably bring about a holding that invalidates the anticloning legislation. Because the naked clone scenario casts the issue in terms of reproductive rights and personal-privacy concerns, it would push the courts into the same legal territory that embraces the concepts of abortion, contraception, assisted reproduction, and related topics. Modern jurisprudence of the past few decades would pose a formidable obstacle to judges who might find the cloning of humans abhorrent and who would want to uphold the ban.

Is the cloning of a human being a form of reproduction, somewhere in the same category as conventional procreation and in vitro fertilization, and thus a fundamental right—procreative liberty—that can only be circumscribed if the government can demonstrate a compelling state interest in doing so and tailors its restrictions narrowly?[6] Are there satisfactory responses to the various anticloning arguments outlined previously? Does a decision to clone a person implicate privacy rights?[7] Does the recent accretion of abortion, contraception, and assisted reproduction jurisprudence embrace a constitutional right to clone, at least under some circumstances?[8] Is there a moral/normative basis for including cloning within the pantheon of constitutionally protective reproductive rights? The correct answer to all five questions is yes.

The Supreme Court has held, in a long line of cases, that the due process clauses of the Fifth and Fourteenth Amendments, which proscribe the deprivation of "life, liberty, or property, without due process of law," have a substantive component that protects substantive fundamental rights and liberties, both constitutionally enumerated[9] and implied.[10] The Court's substantive due process jurisprudence reflects more robust constitutional protection for rights or liberty interests that implicate particularly important types of choices or "zones of privacy,"[11] which directly involve personal autonomy.[12] Once the Court recognizes such rights, it will uphold legislation impinging on those rights only if it serves a compelling governmental interest and is narrowly tailored to further that interest.[13]

Analysis of fundamental rights under the rubric of substantive due process is complicated by the facts that the recognized rights to date have not always been explicitly mentioned in the actual text of the Constitution and that the Court has employed at least two tests to determine whether fundamental rights exist, neither of which is particularly instructive.[14] One test recognizes as fundamental those rights "that are 'implicit in the concept of ordered liberty,' such that 'neither liberty nor justice would exist if [they] were sacrificed.'"[15] Another test looks to history, recognizing as fundamental those rights that are "deeply rooted in this Nation's history and tradition."[16] The tests are disjunctive, not conjunctive; the lack of a deep historical and traditional foundation can be overcome through the combination of a deeply personal choice and the implications of that choice for firmly established liberty interests.[17] Recently, the Court appears to have added a requirement or a caveat to these tests, that the Court must be careful to describe the asserted fundamental liberty interest.[18]

Although one can easily conclude that the precedent recognizes procreation or reproduction as a firmly established fundamental right,[19] the Supreme Court has never explicitly dealt with its outer boundaries and limitations.[20] When state-of-the-art assisted-reproduction technology meets the primordial procreative process in the Court's chambers, the results are not entirely predictable.

Under all of the rather vague and interrelated tests by which fundamental rights or fundamental liberty interests may be discerned by the Court, the judicial fate of anticloning legislation will turn on the way the Court frames the issue.[21] The question asked predetermines the answer received. The narrow question "Is there a fundamental right to clone human beings for any and all purposes?" would doubtless be but a few paragraphs removed from a resounding "no" in the Court's opinion. Conversely, if the Court asks more expansively, "May the government forbid infertile couples to choose, of their own volition, to use available means of modern technology to have children?" the cloning clinics can confidently begin construction of new facilities. Which question should the Court ask? It depends on which view of cloning as a phenomenon prevails, and this will be determined by the Court's evaluation of the arguments that have been outlined here for and against cloning. This, in turn, depends on how closely the Court's view of the potentialities and limitations of cloning approximates what could actually happen in the real world.

## PSYCHOSOCIAL ARGUMENTS: CLONING IN THE REAL WORLD

Some of the objections to cloning mentioned in chapter 1 are so speculative that they resist analysis, particularly where they hypothesize rampant objectification of children, psychosocial trauma, and slippery-slope catastrophes. I will address the anticloning concerns by focusing on scientific reality and by analogizing cloning to real-world situations with which we are already familiar.

Some commentators have suggested that cloning is fundamentally different from "natural" procreation and even in vitro fertilization.[22] This viewpoint holds that cloning is not reproduction but replication, akin to photocopying, and that the difference is of constitutional importance.[23] Cloning has been excoriated as the moral and perhaps legal equivalent of slavery or incest.[24] But these views reflect both a misunderstanding of cloning itself and an overemphasis on genotypic uniqueness as a prerequisite of personhood.

First, when the SCNT method is used, the mitochondrial DNA is not identical as between the donor of the nuclear DNA and the child of cloning. Their nuclear DNA will be the same, but their m-DNA will be different because the child of cloning will receive his or her m-DNA from the donor of the enucleated ovum. Thus, the two persons would not be truly identical genetically—extremely similar, but not identical. But even if there were absolute, 100 percent, genotypic identity between donor and child, it has never been deemed legally significant that two persons are genetically indistinguishable. All of us in fact have seen or met pairs of people who have exactly the same genetic codes, but these people were not children of cloning. They were "produced" through a much more ancient process.

Identical twins, or even identical siblings of more than two, are referred to as identical because they possess the same genotype. Because of a phenomenon occurring very early in the embryo's development, similar to the embryo-splitting method of cloning, a mother can give birth to two or more children with the same genetic structure and composition. Indeed, identical twins are more alike genetically than a DNA donor and his or her child of cloning because identical twins share the same m-DNA as well as the same nuclear DNA, and yet they are not identical in every aspect of their physical, mental, and behavioral characteristics.[25]

For millennia, human identical twins have been born, lived their lives, and died. They were given individual names, nurtured as are other children, and afforded the same legal rights as all other people. True, identical twins may experience unusual parallels in their lives and life experiences, and they may enjoy particularly powerful relational bonds with one another, but they have not been denied full legal recognition of their personhood. Neither have they been found to lack individuality, dignity, or personal autonomy, despite some (undoubtedly well-intentioned parents) who dressed them alike, taught them alike, disciplined them alike, and continually expressed their expectations that they would fulfill parental expectations in like manner. They have generally managed to endure any teasing and joking, good-natured or otherwise, that was directed at them because of their two-of-a-kind situation.

Certainly, no one has argued that the genetic and environmental identity between identical twins is a reason they should not be allowed to exist. A search of the scholarly legal literature has failed to unearth any article asseverating that identical twins should be preemptively aborted because to allow them to be born would be tantamount to a wrongful life tort. Identical twins, with the identical nuclear DNA *and* the identical m-DNA, who share the same uterus at the same time, who are born within minutes of each other, and who grow up simultaneously in the identical home environment subject to the same parental pressures, are still universally viewed as having lives worth living. They may occasionally chafe at the influence of parents who want them to dress alike or who err on the side of excess in ensuring absolutely identical treatment for both twins in all things, but such are the types of annoyances that all children experience from their parents—no worse, only different. Some quantum of annoyance is the natural state of children with regard to their parents, and vice versa. It comes with the territory.

Furthermore, there is certainly nothing identical about the way identical twins live their lives, despite some similarities. For millennia, identical twins have lived different life spans from one another, pursued different careers, contracted different diseases, and have had different experiences with such important life factors as sexual orientation, substance abuse, mental illness, and marriage.[26] They did not appear to suffer from a crippling sense of diminished personal autonomy.

An example of identical twins from contemporary life may prove illustrative as to just how unalike "identical" twins can be. Major League baseball has recently featured a pair of monozygotic twins, Jose and Ozzie Canseco. Born on July 2, 1964, in Havana, Cuba, the Canseco brothers were as identical genetically as any two people can be. They shared the same DNA in their nuclei, the same mitochondrial DNA, and the same mother's womb at the same time. Moreover, they were reared together, in the same family household, simultaneously, under identical circumstances. Those who fear cloning because it would dehumanize people, reduce humans to designer products, and lead to hordes of identical favored genotypes should consider the "natural cloning" on display in Ozzie and Jose Canseco.

On one level, the fears might seem realistic because both of the twins made it to the Major League level—a feat only attained by a minuscule percentage of all who aspire to that achievement. But if cloning is truly something to be despised and banned, we would expect to see similar performance from both of the twins once they arrived on the big league scene. In the absence of some powerful intervening factor, such as a serious, disabling injury (of which there was none), there should be striking parallels in their Major League records. What does the record show?

Jose played baseball at the Major League level for all or part of seventeen seasons, Ozzie for three. There was no tragic injury that cut short Ozzie's career; lack of talent did that. Here are some key career statistics for both twins:

|  | Jose Canseco[27] | Ozzie Canseco[28] |
| --- | --- | --- |
| Games played | 1,887 | 24 |
| At-bats | 7,057 | 65 |
| Runs scored | 1,186 | 8 |
| Hits | 1,877 | 13 |
| Doubles | 340 | 6 |

| Triples | 14 | 0 |
|---|---|---|
| Home runs | 462 | 0 |
| Runs batted in | 1,407 | 4 |
| Stolen bases | 200 | 0 |
| Walks | 906 | 9 |
| Strikeouts | 1,942 | 17 |
| Batting average | .266 | .200 |
| On-base percentage | .353 | .297 |
| Slugging percentage | .515 | .292 |

Jose Canseco was American League Rookie of the Year in 1986, Most Valuable Player in 1988, and an All-Star six times. He twice led the American League in home runs and once in runs batted in. Needless to say in light of the above table of statistics, Ozzie achieved none of these, nor did he come anywhere remotely close. Even in terms of physical (phenotypic) size, Jose outdid his "identical" twin Ozzie. Jose stood six feet, four inches tall and weighed 240 pounds, whereas Ozzie was six feet, two inches tall and weighed 220 pounds. Quite obviously, there was more to the making of a baseball star than genetic identity in the case of Jose and Ozzie Canseco, who were more alike than any DNA donor and child of cloning could ever hope to be. Would-be evil masterminds of armies of Hitlers or wannabe managers of entire teams of Jose Cansecos, please take note.

As in virtually all aspects of life in which human beings are involved, there is another side to the "problems" faced by identical twins. They may find a great measure of comfort, support, and fulfillment in the ineffable bond they feel to their identical sibling. Perhaps more than most sisters and brothers, they can enjoy a sense of true companionship with one another, an intangible emotional bridge that can span great expanses of time and space. This level of familial union, powerful enough to unite people throughout their lives with a special sense of shared essence, is something many nontwins would envy and covet in their own lives. Would donor and child of cloning enjoy a unique bond as well? Our experience with identical twins suggests that this is a real possibility.

The commentators who theorize that parents would feel and exhibit less emotional bonding to their children of cloning than to other children[29] ignore the special bonds often felt between identical twins.[30] One may safely presume that the majority of people interested in cloning would do so with one of three potential sources of DNA in mind: (1) themselves, (2) their life partner, or (3) their own child. In two of these three naked clone situations, a given parent would have a powerful genetic link to the child, and in the third, the child would possess a profound genetic link to a cherished loved one. Under all of these circumstances, if the evidence regarding identical twins is any indication, parents may feel a stronger emotional link to their children of cloning, not a weaker bond or a commodity-like detachment.[31] These families may reasonably be expected to enjoy a higher level of emotional bonding, greater mutual solicitude, and deeper shared understanding—far from the feared "despotism of the cloners over the cloned," a reversion to the cruel practices of ancient Sparta, and the depersonalized treatment of children as "artifacts" or "products."[32]

The genotypic identity between DNA donor and child of cloning is properly viewed in the same light as identical twins, with, if anything, even more powerful arguments in support of personhood and individuality. As with identical twins, there may eventuate striking similarities in certain aspects of life, but also important differences.[33] Unlike identical twins, the donor and child of cloning would be some years apart in age, often a generation or more apart, with all the cultural and experiential divergences that implies. In all circumstances except the situation in which parents seek to clone their own child, the donor and child of cloning would have different parents, would be carried in different uteri,[34] and would be raised in a different household environment.

The DNA donor and the child of cloning would have different friends and close relatives, would have different teachers, and would be shaped by many divergent environmental factors.[35] They may prefer quite different diets, and the foods they eat, both in terms of type and quantity, would exert a major influence on their appearance, health, lifestyle habits, and longevity. They could have divergent attitudes to such significant life-shaping activities as exercise, nutrition, and proper rest, as well as potentially harmful tobacco use, alcohol consumption, and use of illegal drugs. They may well be more dissimilar than identical twins reared apart.[36]

The fact that DNA donor and the child of cloning have m-DNA from completely different sources also would have a considerable influence on the degree of similarity between the two people. Differences would be expected "in parts of the body that have high demands for energy—such as muscle, heart, eye, and brain—or in body systems that use mitochondrial control over cell death to determine cell numbers."[37] But irrespective of how similar they may be in terms of genotype, phenotype, personality, and preferences, they would be every bit as much individual persons as are identical twins, under the law. Any attempt to elide cloning with mechanical replication would not be capable of formulating a legally significant deficiency in the naked clone.

This is true despite possible parental exertions to rear the child of cloning to be the living replacement of a particular individual or a faithful replica of a living exemplar. Under some of the scenarios envisioned, a person or couple might want to clone in order to give a dying loved one "another chance," or to honor and emulate an admired person, even oneself. In these situations, the caregivers could be expected to make every effort to bring up the new child in the same manner as the DNA donor. They might supply the same bedroom, toys, books, music, clothing, games, lessons, and videos. They could try to re-create many of the same cherished life experiences, such as favorite vacations, outings, activities, and educational opportunities. They might try to narrow the range of options and experiences open to the child. In short, they may do every-thing that countless legions of parents have done throughout the ages in an attempt to live vicariously through their children and to have them carry on the family business and traditions. And they (and their children) may be just as surprised, pleased, and/or frustrated by the results, just as monozygotic twins can look and act very different from one another, notwithstanding the efforts of parents to make them alike in every way.[38]

The same is true for parents who choose to clone in the hope that their child will display outstanding talents in some selected areas of endeavor. Whether their objective is a superstar baseball player, a musical prodigy, a mathematical wizard, or a scientific genius, people who selectively clone on the basis of guaranteeing success in a specific area would understand-ably choose a willing DNA donor whose phenotype and achievements they consider optimal under all the circumstances. Once they secure the best available DNA for their child's genotype, they would rear the child with great emphasis on education, training, exposure, and experience in the chosen field, immersing the child in the subject matter. And again, the results will be as unpredictable (or as predictably diverse) as those obtained by countless other well-meaning but overbearing parents throughout human history. Certainly and inevitably, some parents will be disappointed with the behavior and achievements of their children of cloning in these situations, and the children will be aware of some degree of parental disapproval. But to suggest that this is anything new, or that it would be immeasurably worse than it has been for children and parents from time immemorial, is rank speculation at best.

Because human beings are not sheep, literally or figuratively (with apologies to Dolly), free will is a vital and often unpredictable variable in every life. Regardless of a person's genotype, he or she has the freedom to exercise individual options across a sprawling spectrum of life choices, year by year. Even the staunchest exponents of genetic determinism would admit that there is something ineffable about being human, some-thing that surpasses genetic makeup.[39] If the courts that will grapple with anticloning legislation grasp this, they will inexorably be drawn to the conclusion that SCNT cloning is properly analyzed as another form of human reproduction, different from the others not in the fundamentals but only in the details.

Those who would place reproductive cloning in an unprotected class of one do more than apotheosize the primacy of genetics over all other deter-minants of humanity. They also place emphasis on *how* a person is conceived out of all proper proportion to the importance it legitimately should have, which is to say, none whatsoever.

What relevance does the means by which a person was brought into being have for their personhood, their rights, and their place in society? Does the possibility that some unenlightened people will think less of someone because of the way they begin life support the proposition that they would be better off denied a chance at life altogether? The law makes no distinctions based on whether an individual was created through IVF technology and certainly does not ban them from existing. Moreover, there are no guarantees of noble intentions, love, good parenting skills, sufficient material resources, or emotional maturity inherent in those who can and do have children through traditional coital reproduction. Children are conceived every day by means of acts of sexual intercourse that are loveless, casual, irresponsible, abusive, and even brutally nonconsensual, yet those children are not legislated out of existence by the law.[40] If anything, a child of cloning would be *more* apt, on average, to have parents who deeply and deliberately want to have a child and who have significant financial resources, maturity, and life experience.

The extreme slippery-slope horrors conjured up by some opponents of cloning contain even less substance.[41] As previously pointed out, cloning has nothing to do with mass-production of identical people. Whether the feared outcome is an army of Adolf Hitlers, a *fatwa* spearheaded by thousands of Osama bin Ladens, an NBA overflowing with Michael Jordans, or a Las Vegas showroom full of Elvis Presleys, the fears are unfounded—the stuff of nightmares or pipe dreams.[42] Cloning cannot be carried out in a factory arrayed with row upon row of large test tubes, despite various depictions in popular films such as the *Jurassic Park* series.[43] Every embryo would need to be individually implanted in the uterus of a living woman, one per person, and gestated for the usual nine months, with all the inconveniences, travails, discomfort, and pain that has always entailed.

In addition, it is important to remember that the outcome obtained after all of those failed attempts and after nine months of gestation is a human baby.[44] Cloning does not "produce" a full-formed adult creature such as Frankenstein's monster, ready off-the-shelf to wreak havoc on an unsuspecting world. When any living creature is born through the intervention of cloning, that creature is a human baby, needing to be fed and changed and constantly cared for. The personality, powers, and predilections that will be exhibited by that baby as an adult will not be evident for many years, just as with all other human babies.[45] Thus, anyone who expects to use cloning to create adults for any specific aim, whether benign or evil, would have to be exceedingly patient and ready to work and wait for decades for the eventual result. Will any mad scientist or archvillain be willing or able to change diapers of, breast-feed, and burp the hoped-for army of future henchmen in their infancy? The most active imaginations that have conjured up the specter of cloning as an evil plague would be hard-pressed to visualize any sinister mastermind with the tenacity and capacity to nurse hosts of future accomplices through all the years of teething, 3:00 A.M. nightmares, chicken pox, tantrums, growing pains, puberty, and adolescent rebellion. Even loving parents can sometimes scarcely imagine it.

If in vitro fertilization has not threatened the world with mass-produced people, neither will cloning because no aspect of either one presents the option for assembly-line procreation. If anything, cloning is *less* susceptible to rapid, efficient, large-scale reproduction, owing to the daunting failure rates that are likely to persist for many years. Although we can expect the success rate of cloning to improve with time and further technical advances, there is no reason to presume that it will ever be as high as that associated with coital reproduction. Thus, the Xerox objection is pure fantasy.

Once we move beyond the horror-movie level of argument, the anti-cloning position remains equally unpersuasive.[46] Is there a realistic possibility that children of cloning will be enslaved, used as involuntary organ donors, treated as commodities, or otherwise disproportionately be abused and depersonalized? Will their caregivers consider them subhuman, more akin to property or pets than children, and subject them to a phalanx of physical and psychological assaults? Will families dissolve as parents, having exercised total control over their children's genotypes, somehow feel less emotional attachment to them, feeling no more bond to them than to their cars or sweaters or any other manufactured product? Will the clone-specific abuses spread to such a pervasive extent that the courts will deem it preferable that cloning never take place at all?

To suggest that any of these postulated evils are apt to become more than theoretical threats is to underestimate the humanity of the people who would clone and to overestimate the centrality that knowledge of a clonal origin would occupy in the hearts and minds of the people involved. It also assumes away the force of the rule of law.

There is no question that children born through cloning would be entitled to every legal protection applicable to all other children. There is absolutely no danger that these children would somehow be exempted from the laws prohibiting child abuse, mandating proper care and support of children, requiring the education of children, outlawing the non-consensual harvesting of organs, and banning child labor and involuntary servitude. These laws would be fully applicable and would stand as a deterrent to would-be violators with the same efficacy as in all other circumstances. No legislator, let alone a majority of legislators in any jurisdiction, would take the position that any of these laws should be amended to deprive children of cloning of their coverage. There would be no civilized public policy rationale for doing so, and the manifest injustice of such action would render it political suicide for anyone who attempted it. Once the naked clone is born, he or she would be clothed with every one of the legal rights—from constitutional guarantees to statutory protections—that cover all of us. The feared violation of these existing, indisputably applicable legal safeguards is a poor argument in favor of denying the naked clone the opportunity to live.

Given the complete array of legal strictures, would caregivers nonetheless single out the children of cloning for poor treatment, withheld affection, and depersonalizing abuse? Again, our immersion in popular entertainments has inured us to the suggestion that people, on average, are simply awaiting an opportunity to visit horrors on the children in their homes. In the world outside Hollywood, there are no barbaric hordes eager to use cloning to provide them with helpless subjects for their wretched experiments and abuses. On the contrary, there are multitudes who yearn for an opportunity to nurture a child in their lives.

Irrespective of the primary reason any particular individual or couple might want to have a child through cloning, it is likely among the many reasons people have always wanted children. These reasons are varied, complex, and overlapping and may shift over time. What remains constant is that the desire to have children is one of the most deeply rooted, powerful, and profound of all human aspirations.[47]

The following is a partial list of some of the reasons people might want to have children. The list appears in no particular priority sequence.

1. Perpetuate one's personal or family name, traditions, preferences, and/or business.

2. Transmit some of one's genes to the next generation to achieve a modicum of physical immortality.

3. Provide a source and an object of companionship and love.

4. Supply a source of care, love, companionship, and security in the last years of life.

5. Provide a person whom one can love and nurture and help, long-term.

6. Comply with religious, familial, and/or societal expectations.

7. Provide a deeper source of meaning in life, a reason for being.

8. Secure a beneficiary of and heir to one's lifetime accumulation of savings and other material goods, both during life and upon death.

9. Satisfy the desire to enjoy a child-inclusive life, featuring caring, play, teaching, and shared exploration of the wonders of existence.

10. Relive treasured memories from one's own childhood.

11. Rectify perceived deficiencies and missed opportunities from one's own childhood.

12. Vicariously experience aspects of life, including career decisions and making certain choices among life's options, one regrets never experiencing firsthand.

13. Altruistically devote oneself to a cause greater than self.

14. Create more connections with relatives and other people.

15. Make an impact on the future that will live beyond one's own life, perhaps by rearing one's children to enter specific professions or excel in specific fields.

16. Secure an heir apparent to an actual or perceived throne or position of power and privilege, whether in government or in business.

17. Obtain an in-family source of help with the family's farm or other business.

Most people, of course, do not approach the decision to have children with a checklist in hand. Even the archetypal rational utility maximizer would be far more likely to tackle the procreation question with heart, not spreadsheet. The reasons for having children are so numerous and so basic to the human condition—indeed, to all sentient life—that they generally do not require articulation. They are understood on a subconscious level and are deeply felt. But to the extent it is possible to parse these reasons rationally and methodically, let us consider how the decision to clone compares with other decisions to have children.

Whatever the mode of reproduction, people will differ as to which reasons are most important and which are secondary or even entirely absent—and this is true without factoring in the cloning option. For example, reason number 2 is extremely powerful for some people and moves them to endure great exertions and tremendous personal expense in the pursuit of in vitro fertilization or surrogacy while eschewing the adoption option. And since the beginnings of civilizations, it has been paramount for some parents to rear a child who will live, work, and act in a certain predetermined manner, whether to carry on the family business or avenge some wrong or achieve ambitions left unrealized in the parents' lives. Such people have always treated, educated, pressured, and trained their children to fit within their template, with mixed results—some successes and some unfortunate consequences for both parent and child. So reasons 1, 12, and 15 are not new and are not unique to would-be cloners. Moreover, although some of the reasons on the list may be considered utilitarian, even manipulative or exploitative, one hopes that it is a rarity where one chooses to have children, does have children, and rears those children solely for selfish, calculated, personal profit. Love and affection, and the other altruistic or mutually supportive reasons, would usually accompany the utilitarian approach, if not dominate it.

It appears that every one of the listed reasons for having children applies with at least equal force to cloning as to other alternatives. None of the reasons would fail to apply to cloning, and some might apply even more strongly than usual. But as with other ways of having children, people interested in cloning would typically have a complex and evolving amalgam of motivations. Certainly in the naked clone scenario and its variants, love would be the predominant motivator, just as it usually is in other forms of reproduction.[48] In fact, love may be more universally the prime factor in cloning than in traditional procreation, for the simple reason that it is not possible to clone unintentionally, whereas it is possible to become pregnant despite a desire to the contrary, through failure of contraceptives, irresponsible unprotected sex, or rape.[49] We can rest assured that people would not endure the expense and effort of cloning unless they truly wanted to have a child. There would be no surprise, accidental, or otherwise unwanted children of cloning.[50]

Thus, the factors that spur people to clone would be very similar to the traditional reasons for wanting children and might differ from case to case only to the same degree that motivations have always differed among those who wish to adopt versus procreate through coital reproduction versus the use of assisted reproduction, including in vitro fertilization and surrogacy.[51] The means of reproduction are varied, but the ultimate goals are harmonious if not utterly indistinguishable.

These factors also constitute a formidable moral/normative reason that cloning should not be legally segregated from all other forms of human reproduction and subjected to sweeping bans. The naked clone scenario and its variants present us with people, whether married or single, heterosexual or homosexual, who want to have children with some biological tie to them and to nurture these children. Presumably, many of these people would be unable to have their own biological children through any other means because of infertility of one or both members of the couple, lack of a partner, presence of serious genetic problems within one of both members, absence of an opposite-sex partner, or other circumstances. Yet they would have all of the reasons any traditional procreative couple has for wanting children, as well as an equal commitment to and capability of nurturing their children to maturity and independence. Why, then, should they be denied? Morally, they should be afforded the opportunity to have and care for their own biologically related children, by the only means left available to them by the vagaries of life.

There are one or two additional reasons for cloning that are not on the general list. As mentioned previously, some might want to clone themselves to secure a potential source of compatible nonessential organs, blood, and other bodily components. Even if this were the primary motivator in some cases, as where the DNA donor is afflicted with a serious medical condition, it is probable that additional motivators would soon begin to evolve and even overwhelm the original utilitarian impetus. After all, an infant child of cloning is still a baby and would presumably be equally as appealing and endearing to adults as babies have always been. Adults seem to be instinctively drawn to infants and driven to care for them and nurture them. And as adult and child share experiences over time, it is virtually inevitable that mutual love and genuine bonding would supplement or replace other motivations. Likewise, a desire to replicate as exactly as possible oneself, a lost loved one or an admired third party would be apt to give way to love, as reality interferes with the theory that led to the cloning decision.[52]

Might the cloning situation constitute an especially extreme or potentially abusive strain of some of the motivators, such as reasons 1, 12, and 15? This is unlikely. People have traditionally seemed to believe their children were the veritable reincarnation of themselves, even when another person contributed half of the DNA. Cloners could scarcely be more zealous in their efforts to ensure that their children adhere to the desired path in life than some parents have always been in seeking to direct their progeny's lives. That does not mean it is right for parents to treat their children this way, only that the human race has a long history of both success and failure, triumph and tragedy, along these lines. Again, in most cases, love is more powerful and enduring than ego, ambition, or any other selfish motivator. In short, cloning is properly viewed as one more alternative in the choice to reproduce, akin to all the others in its array of advantages and disadvantages. It is a form of human reproduction, not mechanical replication or the malevolent plaything of mad scientists, and should be recognized as such by the law.

Those who, Cassandra-like, foresee calamitous and ruinous abuses of the new powers made possible by cloning have forgotten that technology is both created by and ruled by people—people with common decency and common sense. Fears of cloning becoming rampant and seriously diminishing genetic diversity or undermining familial love or spawning a recrudescence of slavery are of a type that is not new. It was not long ago that the birth control pill was a novel and powerful scientific advancement, with the power to bring human reproduction to a halt. The widespread availability of birth control pills could have brought to pass the extinction of the human race in one generation...in theory. But that theory would have required a world in which people abandon their core instincts to have children and subvert their highest impulses to the mindless service of a technological tool. That world exists only on paper, on film, and in the imagination. Decades after the advent of the birth control pill, procreation has not ended, and the fact that you are here to read these words is evidence on behalf of the real world.

Of course, it is possible that some courts, including the Supreme Court, will be sufficiently determined in their personal opposition to the cloning of humans that they will find a way to distinguish cloning from other forms of reproduction. Particularly powerful religion-based or morality-rooted aversion could move judges and justices to construct a legal and policy justification for upholding anticloning laws. Arguably, such factors moved the Court narrowly to define the issues in post-*Roe* controversial cases involving sodomy and assisted suicide and to rule in a manner inconsistent with the broader principles evident in the jurisprudence.[53] Uncritical acceptance of some of the more horrific worst-case slippery-slope scenarios, coupled with personal religious or moral beliefs, might lead judges to uphold the bans. But adherence to stare decisis and the rule of law should generate a line of judicial decisions in which bans on the cloning of humans are consistently struck down.

Would it be legally significant that some people might want to clone for reasons some judges find repugnant? For example, consider situations different from the naked clone scenario, but not so extreme as to run afoul of existing laws against murder or child abuse. Perhaps the most intense egocentric motivations for cloning would offend judges as megalomaniacal self-glorification and the apotheosis of self. A yearning for personal fame and/or physical immortality would be far less sympathetic to many jurists than the desire of couples and individuals to use cloning as a form of assisted reproduction for more traditional reasons for family building. But absent manifestations that cross preexisting and well-established legal lines, such as cloning for involuntary harvesting of organs or for slavery or sexual abuse, the law should not intervene to prevent people from using cloning for reasons judges personally consider improper.[54]

The courts generally have not seen fit to interject themselves into reproductive decision making, so as to substitute their judgment for that of would-be parents in deciding whether to have a child. The few exceptions, of questionable validity in their own right, are limited to extreme cases such as compulsory sterilization of mentally challenged persons[55] and prisoners denied conjugal visits or the use of artificial insemination with their spouses.[56] There is certainly no justification for expanding these dubious doctrines to ban cloning.[57] The reasons people desire to have children, as listed previously, include some that offend the personal morals of certain people. We may think it is morally wrong for someone to want a child mainly to carry on the family business or to provide a way for the parent to live again vicariously through the child or to take care of the parent during enfeebled old age. But would-be cloners did not invent, and have no monopoly on, such unappealing motivations; others beat them to the punch by several tens of thousands of years. People have chosen to have children for these and other arguably ignoble reasons since the dawn of humanity. And yet the law does not empower the government to forbid its citizens to reproduce on this basis. Government cannot ask couples or individuals to explain and justify the reasons they want to reproduce—whether through cloning or any other means. As the time-hallowed saying goes, it is none of their business.

Some may be dismayed by this result. But decades of Supreme Court holdings have left little doctrinal daylight between cloning and other facets of the reproduction, abortion, contraception, and privacy construct.

## THE ROLE OF LOVE IN TYING TOGETHER THE DOCTRINAL STRANDS

In chapter 4 I posited the somewhat less robust, but still formidable, case in favor of some level of First Amendment protection for clonal research involving humans. In this chapter thus far, I have attempted to explain why a ban on reproductive cloning should not survive judicial scrutiny. I want to add some much-needed big-picture perspective before leaving this issue.

Even if only one viable infant is produced from 277 enucleated eggs, as in the case of Dolly,[58] there is no principled legal reason under the established jurisprudence to use a low success rate to uphold a permanent and total ban on the reproductive cloning of humans along the lines of the bans in effect in California, Iowa, Louisiana, and Virginia. Short-term regulation and limitation linked to success rate, not blanket and unending prohibition, is the most that should be upheld by the courts.[59] The same is true regarding the prospect that cloning of humans, at least until the process is improved, may cause significant numbers of babies to be born with grotesque deformities, gigantism, and a very short life span. We crossed, and burned, that bridge long ago. It is proper and constitutionally defensible for Congress to enact legislation that places health and safety restrictions on cloning, perhaps even including a temporary, self-expiring moratorium, pending evidence of sufficient scientific and technological progress. But the debate thus far has been dominated less by such legitimate short-term concerns than by unending, unfounded prejudice and ignorance.

The same penumbras and emanations that have been divined by the Supreme Court in the context of abortion rights must also embrace the naked clone. Indeed, there is a stronger public policy rationale buttressing the naked clone situation, in that it has as its aim the propagation of human life. Crucially important as a person's privacy rights and personal autonomy are, the naked clone scenario presents an even more satisfying final outcome: a loved and wanted living child, rather than an aborted fetus or embryo. Whereas abortion rights safeguard a woman's right *not* to reproduce, the naked clone represents a woman's (and man's) right *to* reproduce. The jurisprudence that recognized the former must necessarily and at least as vigorously support the latter.[60]

It is not the strength of the doctrinal foundation underlying the abortion decisions that guarantees the naked clone rights but its fragility. The Court, often by the narrowest of majorities, has been unwilling to concede the existence of several rather minor and specialized limitations on abortion rights because of concern that the exceptions would expose the brittle doctrinal and historical support[61] for abortion rights in general and undermine the entire structure. The same premonitions that led the Court to invalidate laws requiring parental consent for abortions sought by their unemancipated minor children,[62] providing that second-trimester abortions take place only in hospitals,[63] mandating parental notification that their unempancipated minor children are seeking an abortion,[64] or restricting partial-birth abortions[65] would drive the Court to strike down legislation banning the cloning of humans in the naked clone situation. Any judicial approval of a legitimate, even compelling governmental interest in preventing the destruction and exploitation of inchoate human life in the cloning context readily could be turned against abortion rights in the next case.

Although some commentators have argued that abortion rights are in a class by themselves, with similar legal support unavailable to cloning, this is unpersuasive. While it is true that some cases contain language identifying abortion as distinct from some other issues,[66] this is an artifact of the subtext that acknowledges the fundamental weakness of the constitutional underpinnings of the abortion rights.[67] The line of abortion cases does not stand for the principle that the practice of abortion is inherently noble or good. On the contrary, the abortion jurisprudence rests on the more foundational precept that a woman has the right to make her own decisions as to whether to reproduce, to carry to term a fetus within her body, not that the law must favor abortion over birth. The inventive and highly controversial judicial reasoning that led to the creation of abortion rights and the invalidation of dozens of antiabortion statutes in the states has survived intense legal and political criticism from the outset not because abortion is a palpable public or private virtue but because it implicates other virtues that are central to human rights. Those virtues—the liberty of free, autonomous individuals to decide whether to have children, the privacy rights that prevent the government from restricting or dictating reproductive options, the personal autonomy and dominion over procreative processes taking place within a woman's own body—are abundantly manifested in the case of cloning, at least as much as within the abortion context.[68]

The creation and exploitation of human clone embryos solely for research purposes is a closer case, but here, too, modern jurisprudence favors only limited regulation, not an outright ban. A blanket and total prohibition such as set forth in the HCPA is probably violative of First Amendment rights. It would be more appropriate to regulate cloning-related research in a manner consistent with other federal restrictions on biomedical research involving human subjects. Requirements for researchers to submit proposals to expert panels prior to conducting studies, with federal guidelines used to assess the proposals, are well established and available.[69] Additionally, when the researchers are the recipients of federal funding, there is a risk-benefit analysis, a requirement of informed consent, and protections for vulnerable populations.[70]

It is interesting and ironic, in light of the foregoing analysis, that there are some indications that Congress might opt to ban reproductive cloning entirely and permanently but permit therapeutic cloning under some circumstances.[71] Some influential states, such as California, have already done this. But if anything, the established jurisprudence embraces and protects reproductive cloning even more firmly than it does therapeutic cloning. The naked clone scenario, which brings the world a new living baby, should properly be viewed as constitutionally secured, more so than a laboratory procedure that produces, subjects to experimentation, and then discards cloned human embryos solely for utilitarian purposes of scientific/medical research. Yet such is the degraded quality of the public debate on cloning that the exact opposite approach has been enacted into law by California and is being seriously considered by the United States Senate.[72]

What are the implications of a federal statute that completely and permanently bans reproductive cloning but permits therapeutic cloning under some set of controlled circumstances, along the lines of the Feinstein bill, cited in chapter 2, which was considered by the Senate but not voted on during spring 2002? Where would the law draw the line between the legal use of cloning for therapeutic/scientific/medical research purposes and the illegal use of cloning to facilitate the live birth of a human baby? Would the law tolerate therapeutic cloning so long as no cloned human embryo is implanted in a woman's uterus? Or would it allow therapeutic cloning to proceed past implantation, so long as the embryo is not permitted to gestate past a certain stage? Would the law turn on whether embryos are only allowed to progress up to but not past the development of the so-called primitive streak, that is, the fourteenth day of existence, at which time early forms of the nervous system appear?

This legal dichotomy between therapeutic and reproductive cloning highlights a situation heretofore unknown in modern human experience: such a law would create a *legal duty* to destroy the developing human embryo before the embryo progressed too far. This is very different from the situation with regard to abortion rights, in which the courts have (often very reluctantly) recognized a woman's *right* to decide for herself whether she will carry an embryo within her own body to term. The abortion rights cases, controversial and often decided by narrow majorities, found constitutional protection for a woman's *choice* to abort. But the laws that ban all reproductive cloning while allowing some therapeutic cloning shift the operative legal environment from choice to requirement.

A researcher working in the field of therapeutic cloning under this legal regime would be compelled by law to terminate, destroy, kill—use whatever word you will, the effect is the same—the developing human embryos. If the researcher did not, and a living human baby were born, the researcher would be subject to arrest, arraignment, prosecution, trial, conviction, and imprisonment as a criminal for failing to abide by the legal duty created by the ban. This duty to destroy nascent human life is both novel and repugnant and could pose an enormous threat to existing reproductive liberties when it is challenged in the courts...as it inevitably will be.

A court faced with a challenge to this split ban (allowing some therapeutic cloning but banning all reproductive cloning) might decide that this is the bottom of the slippery slope we began sliding down in *Roe v. Wade* and that enough is enough. A legal duty to terminate developing human life goes far beyond the intensely personal concerns centered around a woman's control over her own body that allowed our abortion rights jurisprudence to become as tolerant as it is—and even those rights continue to be in jeopardy and could fall if one or two key members of the United States Supreme Court are replaced. In this manner, the split ban, with its "clone and kill" requirement,[73] could be a legal Trojan Horse that leads to the destruction of far more than the anticloning legislation alone.

Could the proponents of a split ban be unaware of its implications? Or might at least some of them be fully cognizant of these issues and secretly hoping to use it as a Trojan Horse to overturn *Roe v. Wade*? Adherents of the Critical Legal Studies school of jurisprudence[74] would argue that this type of political manipulation is very familiar in our legal system. It is difficult to believe that the intelligent legislators and staffers who have proposed a split ban are oblivious to the perverse strictures it would place on researchers and the indirect risk it poses to reproductive liberties. Yet this may be exactly the case, given the staunch abortion rights record of many of the supporters of the split ban, such as Senators Feinstein and Kennedy, who would undoubtedly be horrified by the suggestion that their law could jeopardize reproductive freedom. On the other hand, there are some pro-life senators who also support the split ban, including Senator Hatch. It is not impossible that some pro-life advocates may have carefully chosen the split ban as an ideal way to undermine the precarious judicial supports of relatively unrestricted abortion on demand.

They may be well aware that unpopular, unappealing litigants and causes have historically been a vehicle for the courts to go far beyond the particulars of the case before them to establish much more wide ranging legal precedent, as in the infamous First Amendment cases of the World War I, 1920s era.[75] In those cases, popularly disfavored anarchists and communists provided a ready way for the Supreme Court to curtail freedom of expression for all Americans.[76] It was decades before a differently staffed Court, with different and more sympathetic parties before it (mostly civil rights activists) could undo the damage. The split ban on cloning could do the same for our reproductive liberties now. Highly controversial, widely unpopular, and commonly misunderstood people and principles facilitate bad precedent setting by judges who, knowingly or subconsciously, allow their decisions to be influenced by such extraneous factors. As the saying goes, "Bad facts make bad law." If there ever was a classic example of this, it is the human cloning turmoil, in which science and fact so often are overwhelmed by superstition and fear.

This is the core significance of the legal battle over cloning. Cloning itself, although fascinating, would probably never be even as common as IVF, no matter how favorable the legal climate, because of technological hurdles, exorbitant costs, and widespread personal aversion. But cloning could be extremely momentous as the instrument for courts to use to overturn *Roe v. Wade* and its progeny. Regardless of our political and personal religious and ethical beliefs concerning legal abortion, we must be alert to the links between cloning rights and abortion rights. A battle over the former could easily spill over into the latter.

It is difficult to conjure up a more extreme, worst-case example of the reproductive liberties line of case law begun with *Griswold*[77] and *Roe* than this: medical researchers, under a split ban, are subject to criminal penalties unless they destroy developing human embryos. If their work leads to even a single living, breathing, crying human infant, the researchers can go to prison. But if they deliberately, efficiently, and methodically end the life processes underway in hundreds or thousands or millions of human embryos, they are entirely on safe legal ground. This goes quite beyond the situation the law has tolerated in IVF, where many failed attempts are accepted as the unavoidable and very regrettable price to be paid for each successful pregnancy and live baby. The bottom-line goal with IVF is the intentional facilitation of the birth of a living human infant, whereas the split ban on cloning ("clone and kill") forces the intentional destruction of all cloned human embryos in the laboratory to permit medical/therapeutic research unrelated to—and in fact, mutually exclusive of—the birth of any baby.

Similarly, the abortion rights case law has been predicated in large part on a woman's personal privacy concerns and autonomy to decide for herself whether she will or will not carry to term an embryo within her own body. Her right to make such a deeply personal and individual decision regarding the fate of one developing embryo inside her own uterus is very different—different in kind, not just in degree—from the duty of a laboratory researcher to avoid implanting any cloned embryo into a woman's uterus and to destroy every such embryo before it ever enters a woman's body. The split ban's duty to destroy is not directly tied to personal reproductive autonomy. For the government to arrogate to itself the power to compel such rampant destruction of inchoate human life, under pain of criminal penalty, is a chilling exercise of raw state power. One need not be a libertarian to be troubled by this level of intrusion of government into fundamental human liberties.[78]

Of course, the courts may strike down a split ban altogether and permit both reproductive and therapeutic cloning, under reasoning along the lines I have set forth in this book that is consistent with continued judicial recognition of established reproductive liberties. If a woman has the right to terminate the existence of a human embryo within her uterus, and thus give birth to no baby, she should have the right to have a human embryo (cloned or not) implanted in her uterus for purposes of bringing a new baby into the world. A woman's autonomy and personal privacy concerns regarding her own body and its reproductive processes are at least equally at work in the latter situation as in the former. But if courts are not persuaded by this logic and are ruled by repugnance (toward cloning, abortion, or both), the outcome could be very different. The courts could, in the process of invalidating the split ban on cloning, rely on a different strand of judicial reasoning, one that drastically curtails the broader categories of reproductive liberties. The end of reproductive cloning could thus also spell the end of much more.

Alternatively, the courts might uphold the split ban and by distinguishing cloning from abortion rights, leave the latter undisturbed. I have attempted to make it clear that this is not the appropriate outcome under the facts and the existing case law, but it would be unrealistic to suggest that a court could not rule in this way. If a court concentrates on some of the more extreme moral and ethical arguments against the cloning of humans and draws from the many sources that depict this as a horrific abuse of scientific power with appalling potential dangers for the future of humanity, it could cabin off cloning from the reproductive rights jurisprudence and treat it as a discrete, exceptional evil that can be banned in isolation from abortion, contraception, IVF, surrogacy, and all other reproductive issues.

As renowned constitutional scholar Laurence Tribe has written: "A society that bans acts of human creation that reflect unconventional sex roles or parenting models (surrogate motherhood, in vitro fertilization, artificial insemination, and the like) for no better reason than that such acts dare to defy 'nature' and tradition (and to risk adding to life's complexity) is a society that risks cutting itself off from vital experimentation and risks sterilizing a significant part of its capacity to grow."[79] Yet that is precisely what the United States, key states such as California, and many of the other nations of the world are doing. The best of intentions do not guarantee the wisest of actions.

The debate in Congress concerning HCPA and its Senate analogues is powerful evidence that intelligent, well-educated people are entirely capable of holding and acting upon this opinion. I do not argue that a split ban will necessarily and ineluctably provoke an overturning of reproductive rights apart from reproductive cloning itself, only that this is one possible outcome, serious enough and of sufficiently significant probability that we cannot blithely dismiss it out of hand with impunity.

Apart from the weighty constitutional ramifications of a split ban, there are practical considerations as well. The Department of Justice has advocated a complete rather than partial ban on the cloning of humans, largely because it views a partial ban as unenforceable.[80] Partial bans such as the Feinstein bill the Senate considered in early 2002 and the Hatch bill in 2003 would allow certain therapeutic cloning activities and prohibit only "implanting or attempting to implant the product of nuclear transplantation into a uterus or the functional equivalent of a uterus." In the opinion of a Department of Justice spokesperson who testified before Congress, since transferring an embryo to a uterus is permitted and is performed regularly in fertility clinics, there is no observable difference between what would be allowed and prohibited. "Law enforcement would be in the unenviable position of having to impose new and unprecedented scrutiny over doctors in fertility clinics and/or research facilities to ensure that only fertilized embryos were being transferred to would-be mothers."[81] And a complete, all-or-nothing ban along the lines of the HCPA would at least not confront researchers (and judges) with the first entire class of (arguably) human beings whom American civilian citizens have an affirmative legal duty to destroy.

The state laws described in chapter 2 are vulnerable to essentially the same legal challenges as the HCPA and the Feinstein split ban because of the applicability of the relevant constitutional provisions to the states through operation of the due process clause of the Fourteenth Amendment.[82] Both the First Amendment implications of a ban on therapeutic/research cloning and the reproductive liberty, personal autonomy, and privacy concerns pertinent to a ban on reproductive cloning could be brought before a court in an action arising out of a state law. In fact, in the absence of any federal statute on point, the first opportunities for judicial review of anticloning legislation may come from legal challenges to these state bans. Iowa and Michigan (and arguably, Rhode Island and Louisiana) have enacted HCPA-like sweeping bans on both reproductive and therapeutic cloning (and others, including Colorado, Illinois, Massachusetts, and New Hampshire, have considered it), while some states (including California and Virginia) have only banned reproductive cloning, similar to the Feinstein bill's and Hatch bill's split ban.

No state has formally considered the converse type of split ban, that is, banning therapeutic cloning while permitting reproductive cloning. However, because of state laws regarding experiments using human embryos, that is the net effect in some states that have not directly addressed the cloning of humans. In states with no ban on reproductive cloning but with laws on the books with respect to human embryo experimentation, there is a situation tantamount to unregulated reproductive cloning and banned therapeutic cloning. Maine, Massachusetts, Minnesota, North Dakota, Pennsylvania, and South Dakota appear to be in this category.

From this variety of restrictions and bans passed by the states, we could get our initial indications as to how the courts at various levels will deal with cloning. It will be interesting to see how the courts handle the Galileo and naked clone situations that come before them in the form of state laws.

One final, rather remote, possibility deserves mention. Some people might want to use cloning to produce viable human embryos or infants, but with no intention of rearing them. This presumably would be a rare situation, one that includes certain of the more objectionable scenarios posited by the opponents of cloning. If someone engages in cloning and then sells the embryos to others to gestate, or pays others to gestate the embryos, and the babies are eventually brought up by others, it is likely that reasons beyond many or all of the usual reasons for having children are fueling the process.[83] There could be a compelling governmental interest in regulating or banning cloning under these circumstances, owing to the unconventional motivations at work and the dissevering of embryo formation, gestation, and rearing. Legal intervention to prevent nefarious forms of cloning is entirely proper, as it has been when it has also proscribed the selling of children, infanticide, enslavement of children, child abuse or neglect, child pornography, and other evils that touch on reproductive liberties and the rights to have and rear children. It is where cloning would take place for worthy reasons harmonious with or indistinguishable from those that always have motivated people to have children—the naked clone situation—that the law should not pose an obstacle.

The debate concerning the cloning of humans has swirled around wildly, with far-fetched horror-story monstrosities crowding out sound science and common sense. The mad dance of the horribles has also obscured a key factor that truly resides at the heart of the matter, both literally and figuratively: love. Love is a word rarely mentioned by those who would outlaw cloning with a sweeping ban, but it is actually the most important part of the entire issue. Among all the reasons people might want to have children, including children of cloning, love is paramount.

Cloning calls to mind the legend of Brigadoon, as immortalized in the musical play by Alan Jay Lerner and Frederick Loewe. In the play, a remarkable little village only comes to life and becomes accessible to outsiders for a single day every 100 years. After that one day, Brigadoon and everyone in it vanishes again for another century. A visitor can only remain in Brigadoon if he or she loves someone within it very much because "if you love someone deeply enough, anything is possible—even miracles." So too, with cloning, there are people for whom having children through their own biological processes has been an impossible dream, mostly out of sight and out of mind for virtually everyone but those directly affected. Now, with the intervention of modern science, there is a window about to open that might make the dream come true for some people. But those who would ban all cloning of human beings per-

manently are on the verge of slamming and locking the window and closing the shutters, blocking out the sunlight, and bringing about the end of
the day. If we care enough about these would-be parents and the children
they could nurture, there may yet be a way to prevent their dreams from
disappearing. Cloning, in the real world, would not be a horror story but
a love story, made possible through the miracle of scientific advancement.
As in Brigadoon, with sufficient love, even miracles are possible.

## NOTES

1. President's Council on Bioethics, *Human Cloning and Human Dignity: An Ethical Inquiry,* (July 2002), Panel's Conclusions and Recommendations, <http://
www.bioethics.gov/reports/cloningreport/fullreport.html>. Although the council was deeply divided (10 to 7) on the issue of therapeutic cloning, all seventeen
members favored a permanent, no-exceptions ban on reproductive cloning.

2. *See* Committee on Science, Engineering, and Public Policy, SCIENTIFIC
AND MEDICAL ASPECTS OF HUMAN REPRODUCTIVE CLONING 98–99
(National Academy Press 2002) (HUMAN REPRODUCTIVE CLONING).

3. *See* Katherine D. Katz, *The Clonal Child: Procreative Liberty and Asexual Reproduction,* 8 ALB.L. J. SC. & TECH. 1, 44 (1997) (noting that the Court's view of the
cloning of humans, as with other issues of reproductive freedom, may be "particularly vulnerable to the vicissitudes of personnel changes of the Court").

4. Well-known examples include the unexpectedly liberal voting patterns of
Justices William Brennan, Harry Blackmun, and David Souter, who were nomi-
nated by Republican presidents Dwight Eisenhower, Richard Nixon, and George
H.W. Bush, respectively.

5. Throughout this book, I have attempted to use the phrase "child of cloning"
rather than "clone" to refer to a human being who begins life through the cloning
process. I believe "child of cloning" is preferable because it emphasizes the personhood of the individual rather than the process by which he or she came into
being. To call a person a "clone" is akin to calling someone conceived through in
vitro fertilization an "IVF" or a "test tube." However, when I use the phrase
"naked clone," I opt for the word "clone" intentionally to highlight the negative
prejudices, ignorant misconceptions, and pejorative use of quasi-scientific language that have so often accompanied the debate on the cloning of humans. In
actuality, if one wishes to be perfectly accurate, there is another term preferable
even to "child of cloning" when referring to a child born through the cloning process. That term is "child."

6. Strict scrutiny has been the standard of review when fundamental rights are
affected, under which a governmental regulation of a fundamental right will only
be upheld if narrowly tailored and necessary to achieve a compelling governmental interest. *See* Shaw v. Reno, 509 U.S. 630 (1993).

7. *See generally* Jed Rubenfeld, *The Right of Privacy,* 102 HARV. L. REV. 737,
740–52 (1989) (outlining the development of the right to privacy in the courts, case
by case).

8. *See* Katz, *supra* note 3, at 40–51. *See generally* Lawrence Wu, Note, *Family
Planning through Human Cloning: Is There a Fundamental Right?* 98 COLUM.L. REV.

1461 (1998); Stephanie J. Hong, Note, *And "Cloning" Makes Three: A Constitutional Comparison between Cloning and Other Assisted Reproductive Technologies,* 26 HASTINGS CONST. L. Q. 741 (1999).

9. *See, e.g.,* Mapp v. Ohio, 367 U.S. 643, 655–57 (1961); Duncan v. Louisiana, 391 U.S. 145, 147–48 (1968).

10. *See, e.g.,* Loving v. Virginia, 388 U.S. 1, 12 (1967).

11. *See* Carey v. Population Servs. Int'l, 431 U.S. 678, 684 (1977); Griswold v. Connecticut, 381 U.S. 479, 484 (1965).

12. *See* Planned Parenthood v. Casey, 505 U.S. 833, 852 (1992).

13. *See* Roe v. Wade, 410 U.S. 113, 155 (1973).

14. Anne Lawton, *The Frankenstein Controversy: The Constitutionality of a Federal Ban on Cloning,* 87 KY. L. J. 277, 332–34 (1998/1999).

15. Bowers v. Hardwick, 478 U.S. 186, 191–92 (1986), *quoting* Palko v. Connecticut, 302 U.S. 319, 325–26 (1937).

16. Bowers v. Hardwick, 478 U.S. 186, 192 (1986), *quoting* Moore v. East Cleveland, 431 U.S. 494, 503 (1977) (Powell, J.).

17. *See* Planned Parenthood v. Casey, 505 U.S. 833, 852 (1992) (upholding a substantive due process claim despite powerful countervailing historical traditions).

18. Washington v. Glucksberg, 521 U.S. 702, 720 (1997).

19. Within its substantive due process body of case law, the Supreme Court has described procreation, the process of having children, as "one of the basic civil rights of man." Skinner v. Oklahoma ex rel Williamson, 316 U.S. 535, 541 (1942). Human reproduction has been considered not only a fundamental personal liberty but also a vital interest at the center of privacy rights. *See* Griswold v. Connecticut, 381 U.S. 479 (1965); Cleveland Bd. of Educ. v. LaFleur, 414 U.S. 632, 639–40 (1974); Eisenstadt v. Baird, 405 U.S. 438, 453 (1972), ("If the right to privacy means anything, it is the right of the individual, married or single, to be free from unwarranted governmental intrusion into matters so fundamentally affecting a person as the decision whether to bear or beget a child"); Carey v. Population Servs. Int'l, 431 U.S. 678, 684–85 (1977) ("This right of personal privacy includes...personal decisions 'relating to marriage, procreation, contraception, family relationships, and child rearing and education' " [citations omitted] [quoting Roe v. Wade, 410 U.S. 113, 152–53 (1973)]). More recently, the Court has recognized that the liberty interest safeguarded by the due process clause includes the right "to have children." Washington v. Glucksberg, 521 U.S. 702, 720 (1997); Planned Parenthood v. Casey, 505 U.S. 833, 857 (1992) (reaffirming the "recognized protection accorded to liberty relating to intimate relationships, the family, and decisions about whether or not to beget or bear a child").

20. *See* John A. Robertson, CHILDREN OF CHOICE: FREEDOM AND THE NEW REPRODUCTIVE TECHNOLOGIES 35–40 (Princeton University Press 1994) (tracing the history of the legal right to reproduction and arguing that the right applies to methods other than traditional procreation as well). *But see* Ann MacLean Massie, *Regulating Choice: A Constitutional Law Response to Professor John A. Robertson's Children of Choice,* 52 WASH. & LEE L. REV. 135, 162 (1995) (arguing against the extension of constitutional protection to assisted reproduction in general).

21. *See* Laurence H. Tribe and Michael C. Dorf, *Levels of Generality in the Definition of Rights,* 57 U. CHI. L. REV. 1057, 1065–71 (1990) (analyzing the difference

between the majority and dissent in Bowers v. Hardwick, 478 U.S. 186, 187–97, 199–214 [1986], as turning on the level of narrowness or generality employed to frame the issue in light of precedent).

22. *See* Lori B. Andrews, *Surrogate Motherhood: The Challenge for Feminists,* 16 L., MED. & HEALTH CARE 72 (1988) (positing that unconventional forms of reproduction such as in vitro fertilization and surrogate motherhood should not be banned on the basis of speculative harms).

23. *See,* e.g., George J. Annas, *Human Cloning: Should the United States Legislate Against It?* A.B.A.J., May 1997, at 80; Lori B. Andrews, *Is There a Right to Clone? Constitutional Challenges to Bans on Human Cloning,* 11 HARV. J. LAW & TECH. 643, 666, 669 (1998) (distinguishing cloning from in vitro fertilization and surrogacy).

24. *See* Andrews, *supra* note 23, at 667–69; Francis C. Pizzuli, Note, *Asexual Reproduction and Genetic Engineering: A Constitutional Assessment of the Technology of Cloning,* 47 S. CAL. L. REV. 476, 481 (1974).

25. *See* Gerald E. McClearn et al., *Substantial Genetic Influence on Cognitive Abilities in Twins 80 or More Years Old,* 276 SCIENCE 1560, 1562 (1997) (finding that 62 percent of general cognitive abilities in elderly identical twins was attributable to genetic influences, but 38 percent was due to environmental factors). *See also* Richard Cohen, *The Mad Scientist Bogeyman,* WASH. POST, August 7, 2001, at A15 (deriding popular and political opinions on the evils of cloning).

26. *See* Dorothy C. Wertz, *Cloning Humans: Is It Ethical?* 1 THE GENE LETTER, no. 5 (Mar. 1997), <http://www.geneletter.com/archives/cloning1.html>.

27. *See* <http://www.baseball-reference.com/c/cansejo01.shtml>.

28. *See* <http://www.baseball-reference.com/c/canseoz01.shtml>.

29. *See,* e.g., Clarke D. Forsythe, *Legal Perspectives on Cloning: Human Cloning and the Constitution,* 32 VAL. U.L. REV. 469, 536–40 (1998); Leon R. Kass, *The Wisdom of Repugnance,* NEW REPUBLIC, June 2 1997, at 21.

30. *See* Nancy L. Segal, *Behavioral Aspects of Intergenerational Human Cloning: What Twins Tell Us,* 38 JURIMETRICS J. 57, 60, 65 (1997) (reporting the special emotional bonds enjoyed by many identical twins and the additional richness and closeness this brings to the twins' lives).

31. *See* John A. Robertson, *Liberty, Identity, and Human Cloning,* 76 TEX. L. REV. 1371, 1412 (1998).

32. Kass, *supra* note 29, at 21.

33. *See* Segal, *supra* note 30, at 63 (discussing divergences among identical twins in such features as physical characteristics, intellectual abilities, vocational interests, and social attitudes, presumably due to the differential environments experienced at the prenatal, perinatal, and postnatal stages); National Bioethics Advisory Committee, CLONING HUMAN BEINGS: REPORT AND RECOMMENDATIONS OF THE NATIONAL BIOETHICS ADVISORY COMMISSION 33, 82 (National Bioethics Advisory Committee 1997) (NBAC Report).

34. The first of many environments that affect human development is the uterus, and there is scientific evidence adumbrating the many effects of the uterine environment on traits as important as intelligence. *See* B. Devlin et al., *The Heritability of IQ,* 388 NATURE 468, 469 (1997). Of course, the uterine environment and the eventual human infant can be profoundly altered by such stressors as maternal alcohol and tobacco use during pregnancy. *See* LAURA E. BERK, CHILD DEVELOPMENT 92–102 (4th ed. 1997).

35. *See* Michael A. Goldman, *Human Cloning: Science Fact and Fiction*, 8 S. CAL. INTERDIS. L. J. 103, 112–13 (1998) (discussing the importance of many prenatal and postnatal environmental variables in determining the phenotypic expression of even identical genotypes).

36. *See* Committee on Science, Engineering, and Public Policy, SCIENTIFIC AND MEDICAL ASPECTS OF HUMAN REPRODUCTIVE CLONING 26 (National Academy Press 2002) (HUMAN REPRODUCTIVE CLONING).

37. *Id. See also* D. K. Simon et al., *Mitochondrial Disorders: Clinical and Genetic Features*, 50 ANN. REV. MED. 111–27 (1999); J. G. Hall, *Genomic Imprinting: Nature and Clinical Relevance*, 48 ANN. REV. MED. 35–44 (1997).

38. *Id.* Even identical (monozygotic) twins are not fully identical in either their genes or their appearance and behavior, in part because "mutations, stochastic developmental variations, and varying imprinting effects (parent-specific chemical marks on the DNA) make different contributions to each twin. *See also* A. W. Chan et al., *Clonal Propagation of Primate Offspring by Embryo Splitting*, 287 SCIENCE 317–19 (2000); J. G. Hall, *Twinning: Mechanisms and Genetic Implications*, 6 CURR. OPIN. GENET. DEV. 343–47 (1996).

39. *See* Dena S. Davis, *What's Wrong with Cloning?* 38 JURIMETRICS J. 83, 83–84 (1997); Bonnie Steinbock, *The NBAC Report on Cloning Human Beings: What It Did— and Did Not—Do*, JURIMETRICS J. 39, 42–43 (1997) (analyzing the extent to which opponents of cloning overestimate the centrality of genetics as a determinant of human individuality).

40. *See* President's Council on Bioethics, *supra* note 1, chapter 5, at note vi ("We are, of course, well aware that many children are conceived in casual, loveless, or even brutal acts of sexual concourse, including rape and incest").

41. *See* Lee M. Silver, *Popular Cloning versus Scientific Cloning in Ethical Debates*, 4 N.Y.U. J. LEGIS. & PUB. POL'Y 47, 49 (2000/2001) (listing some of the imagined horrible misuses of human cloning).

42. Horrific visions of armies of mass-produced, malevolent clones have long held a special fascination for filmmakers. *Star Wars Episode II: Attack of the Clones* is one of the latest and most ubiquitous of these fantasies. *See generally* James Warren, *Hollywood and Cloning: An Old Pairing*, CHI. TRIB., Sept. 29, 1997, at 5.

43. One memorable line from the *Jurassic Park* films does, however, seem particularly apposite to the issue of cloning: "Life will find a way."

44. *See* NBAC Report, *supra* note 33, at 82. ("Should this type of cloning proceed, however, any children born as a result of this technique should be treated as having the same rights and moral status as any other human being"); Richard Dawkins, *Thinking Clearly about Clones: How Dogma and Ignorance Get in the Way*, FREE INQUIRY, June 22, 1997, at 13.

45. *See* Silver, *supra* note 41, at 52–53.

46. Some notable opponents of cloning have gone so far as to imply that irrespective of actual evidence, cloning is wrong because it feels wrong to us. *See* Leon R. Kass and James Q. Wilson, THE ETHICS OF HUMAN CLONING 19 (AEI Press 1998) ( "We are repelled by the prospect of cloning human beings not because of the strangeness or novelty of the undertaking, but because we intuit and feel, immediately and without argument, the violation of things that we rightfully hold dear"). This, of course, is more properly categorized as bias, baseless fear, unarticulated emotion, or religious sentiment than law or logic.

47. *See* Silver, *supra* note 41, at 53.

48. *See* John A. Robertson, *Two Models of Human Cloning,* 27 HOFSTRA L. REV. 609, 624 (1999) (arguing that at least with the benefit of appropriate counseling, people who raise a child of cloning will probably be competent and loving parents committed to their child's best interests and unique identity).

49. *See* James Q. Wilson, *Sex and Family,* in Leon R. Kass and James Q. Wilson, THE ETHICS OF HUMAN CLONING 89, 94 (AEI Press 1998) (likening cloning to IVF, where there is no evidence that IVF had a harmful effect on the children's mental or psychological status or their relationships with parents); Segal, *supra* note 30, at 61–62 (stating that children conceived through assisted reproduction "did not differ from naturally conceived children in emotions, behavior, or quality of family relations"). *Id.,* at 62 (indicating that adoptive parents and those conceiving children through assisted reproduction "expressed greater warmth and emotional involvement with children, as well as greater satisfaction with parenting roles, relative to birth parents").

50. *See* Sarah S. Brown and Leon Eisenberg, *Unintended Pregnancy and the Well-Being of Children and Families,* 274 J.A.M.A. 1332, 1332 (1995) (noting that nearly 60 percent of the pregnancies in the United States are unintended at the time of conception, whether because they occur at a suboptimal time or are entirely unwanted).

51. *See* Katz, *supra* note 3, at 23–27 (discussing the argument in favor of cloning as a form of reproduction).

52. *See* James Q. Wilson, *The Paradox of Cloning,* in Leon R. Kass and James Q. Wilson, THE ETHICS OF HUMAN CLONING 63, 64–65 (AEI Press 1998) ("Parents, whether they acquire a child by normal birth, artificial insemination, or adoption, will, in the overwhelming majority of cases, become deeply attached to the infant and care for it without regard to its origin").

53. *See* Bowers v. Hardwick, 478 U.S. 186, 190 (1986) (narrowly framing the core issue as "whether the Federal Constitution confers a fundamental right upon homosexuals to engage in sodomy" rather than as a fundamental privacy right); Washington v. Glucksberg, 521 U.S. 702, 720 (1997) (narrowly framing the issue as "whether the 'liberty' specially protected by the Due Process Clause includes a right to commit suicide," not as a fundamental right to privacy). *See* Lawton, *supra* note 14, at 333–34.

54. *See* Katz, *supra* note 3, at 31–35.

55. Buck v. Bell, 274 U.S. 200, 207 (1927). *See* Paul A. Lombardo, *Three Generations, No Imbeciles: New Light on* Buck v. Bell, 60 N.Y.U. L. REV. 30 (1985) (debunking the factual underpinnings of the case).

56. *See* Goodwin v. Turner, 908 F. 2d 1395 (8th Cir. 1990) (holding that an inmate's status as a prisoner was sufficient to justify the prison's policy of prohibiting the inmate from artificially inseminating his wife); Anderson v. Vasquez, 827 F. Supp. 617 (N.D. Cal. 1992) (holding that an inmate on death row lacked the right to conjugal visits and was not entitled to compel the prison to furnish him with artificial insemination services), *aff'd in part, rev'd in part,* 28 F. 3d 104 (9th Cir. 1994).

57. *See generally* Jacqueline B. DeOliveira, Comment, *Marriage, Procreation, and the Prisoner: Should Reproductive Alternatives Survive during Incarceration?* 5 TOURO L. REV. 189 (1988); Kristin M. Davis, Note, *Inmates and Artificial Insemination: A New*

*Perspective on Prisoners' Residual Right to Procreate,* 44 WASH. U. J. URB. & CON-TEMP. L. 163 (1993).

58. In later SCNT experiments involving mice, the results have been somewhat better, although still not approaching a high success rate. One experiment resulted in 10 mice surviving from 800 embryos transferred, and a subsequent trial yielded 5 mice surviving from 298 embryos. *See* T. Wakayama et al., *Full-Term Development of Mice from Enucleated Oocytes Injected with Cumulus Cell Nuclei,* 394 NATURE 369, 371 (1998). Even more encouraging, recent work involving cows has found that cloned cows are as healthy as their conventionally bred counterparts, and researchers have claimed an 80 percent success rate among those cows that survived gestation, although many embryos were spontaneously aborted during gestation. *See* John Whitfield, *Cloned Cows in the Pink,* NATURE SCIENCE UPDATE, <http://www.nature.com/nsu/011129/011129–1.html, 2001> (November 23, 2001); Robert P. Lanza et al., *Cloned Cattle Can Be Healthy and Normal,* 294 SCIENCE 1893–94 (2001). With the successful cloning of a calico cat named "cc" (for "Copy Cat") by a Texas company named Genetic Savings and Clone in late 2001, the number of mammalian species cloned through SCNT reached six: sheep, mice, cattle, goats, pigs, and cats. It is interesting to note that "cc" did not have the same physical appearance as the DNA donor cat because of postfertilization factors that contribute to phenotypic expression. *See* Rick Weiss, *Copy Cat Is First Cloned Pet,* WASH. POST, Feb. 15, 2002, at A1.

59. There is reason to believe that "improvements in animal cloning indicate that safety concerns may be only a temporary barrier to reproductive [use of cloning] in humans." *See* Ethics Committee Report, *Human Somatic Cell Nuclear Transfer (Cloning),* FERTILITY & STERILITY, Nov. 2000, at 873.

60. *See* Lifchez v. Hartigan, 735 F. Supp. 1361, 1376–77 (N.D. Ill. 1990), *aff'd mem.,* 914 F.2d 260 (7th Cir. 1990). The district court held that an Illinois law banning embryo and fetal research and prohibiting embryo donation, embryo freezing, and experimental prenatal diagnostic procedures was impermissibly vague and an unacceptable infringement on a woman's fundamental right to privacy. The court stated, "It takes no great leap of logic to see that within the cluster of constitutionally protected choices that includes the right to have access to contraceptives, there must be included within that cluster the right to submit to a medical procedure that may bring about, rather than prevent, pregnancy." The case involved an infertile couple's efforts to avail themselves of medically assisted reproduction, including the use of a donated embryo and IVF. *See also* Lindley v. Sullivan, 889 F.2d 124, 130 (7th Cir. 1989) (opining that there is a fundamental interest in having children, citing Eisenstadt and other cases); Cameron v. Board of Educ., 795 F. Supp. 228, 236–37 (S.D. Ohio 1991) (citing Eisenstadt and LaFleur in support of a holding that a single woman has a fundamental "constitutional privacy right to…become pregnant by artificial insemination").

61. *See* David Kader, *The Law of Tortious Prenatal Death since Roe v. Wade,* 45 MO. L. REV. 639, 652–53 (1980).

62. Planned Parenthood of Central Mo. v. Danforth, 428 U.S. 52 (1976).

63. Akron v. Akron Center for Reproductive Health, Inc., 462 U.S. 416 (1983).

64. Hodgson v. Minnesota, 497 U.S. 417 (1990).

65. Stenberg v. Carhart, 530 U.S. 914 (2000).

66. Abortion has been described as "inherently different from marital intimacy, or bedroom possession of obscene material, or marriage, or procreation, or edu-

cation, with which Eisenstadt and Griswold, Stanley, Loving, Skinner, and Pierce and Meyer were respectively concerned" (Roe v. Wade, 410 U.S. 113, 159 [1973]) and "a unique act" (Planned Parenthood v. Casey, 505 U.S. 833, 852 [1992]). These statements are literally true but can hardly support a suggestion that abortion is a right exalted above all others or utterly beyond comparison.

67. Planned Parenthood v. Casey, 505 U.S. 833 (1992). The four dissenting justices argued that "Roe was wrongly decided" and "should be overruled." Chief Justice Rehnquist declared that the decision to abort is "different in kind" from other recognized privacy rights such as those involving contraception and procreation because abortion "necessarily involves the destruction of a fetus." *Id.*, at 952 (Rehnquist, C.J., concurring in part and dissenting in part) (citations omitted). Justice Scalia's opinion asseverated that "the best the Court can do to explain how it is that the word 'liberty' must be thought to include the right to destroy human fetuses is to rattle off a collection of adjectives that simply decorate a value judgment and conceal a political choice." *Id.*, at 983 (Scalia, J., concurring in part and dissenting in part).

68. Indeed, there are important cases recognizing a privacy right or related fundamental rights in personal autonomy contexts quite distinct from either abortion or contraception. *See, e.g.,* Meyer v. Nebraska, 262 U.S. 390 (1923) (upholding parental autonomy in choosing a mode of education for their children); Pierce v. Society of Sisters, 268 U.S. 510 (1925) (same); Loving v. Virginia, 388 U.S. 1 (1967) (holding the right to interracial marriage is a fundamental right); Moore v. City of East Cleveland, 431 U.S. 494 (1977) (protecting the right of the family to determine its own living arrangements); and Zablocki v. Redhail, 434 U.S. 374 (1978) (recognizing as a fundamental right the right to marry).

69. *See* Henry T. Greely, *The Control of Genetic Research: Involving the "Groups Between,"* 33 HOUS. L. REV. 1397, 1399 (1997).

70. *Id.,* at 1401–2.

71. *See* Wesley J. Smith, *Close the Door on Cloning,* NATIONAL REVIEW ONLINE, <http://www.nationalreview.com/comment/comment-smith011402 .shtml> (January 14, 2002).

72. *Id.* The House of Representatives and President Bush, of course, both favor total bans on the cloning of humans for any purpose whatsoever. *See* Rick Weiss, *Mass. Firm's Disclosure Renews Cloning Debate; Bush Reiterates Support for Ban on Use of Embryos,* WASH. POST, Nov. 27, 2001, at A3.

73. The phrase "clone and kill" has a visceral, repellant impact and is oddly similar to the fishing phrase "catch and release." *See* <http://www.cwfa.org/ library/life/2001-12-11_un-cloning.shtml>.

74. *See generally* Roberto Mangabeira Unger, THE CRITICAL LEGAL STUDIES MOVEMENT (Harvard University Press 1983); James Boyle (ed.), CRITICAL LEGAL STUDIES (New York University Press 1992). The Critical Legal Studies view, in a nutshell, is that rules do not decide cases or determine legal outcomes. Rather, the key stimuli are political power, hierarchical disparities in wealth and influence, the personal self-interest and predilections of the decision makers, and other similar factors relating to the domination of some individuals, groups, and nations by others.

75. *See, e.g.,* Schenck v. United States, 249 U.S. 47 (1919); Abrams v. United States, 250 U.S. 616 (1919); Gitlow v. People of New York, 268 U.S. 652 (1925); Whitney v. California, 274 U.S. 357 (1927).

76. Often, these cases upheld criminal prosecutions of antiwar activists and political dissidents under "criminal syndicalism" statutes, finding in the expressive conduct of the defendants a "clear and present danger" that their communications would lead to violence or harm to the United States government. Despite that the expressive behavior was clearly political, and thus within the very core of expression traditionally thought to be safeguarded by the First Amendment to the United States Constitution, this series of cases carved out significant exceptions in that protection. The result was expanded governmental power to silence, and even criminally punish, citizens for "dangerous" speech for decades to come.

77. Griswold v. Connecticut, 381 U.S. 479 (1965).

78. The libertarian magazine *Reason* has provided a forum for discussion of the cloning issue, focusing on such issues. An extensive collection of short essays is available on-line at <http://reason.com/bioresearch/bioresearch.shtml>.

79. *See* Laurence Tribe, *On Not Banning Cloning for the Wrong Reasons*, in Martha Nussbaum and Cass Sunstein, CLONES AND CLONES: FACTS AND FANTASIES ABOUT HUMAN CLONING 321 (Norton, 1998).

80. *See* Wendy Wright, *Partial Ban on Cloning Is Unrealistic, DOJ Says* <http://www.cwfa.org/library/life/2002–05–28_cloning.shtml> (May 28, 2002).

81. *Id., quoting* DOJ spokesperson Daniel Bryant, assistant attorney general for the Office of Legislative Affairs.

82. Gradually, in a series of decisions over the span of years, the U.S. Supreme Court has held, little by little, that most of the rights specifically guaranteed by the first eight amendments are as fully applicable to the states as to the federal government through their "incorporation" into the due process clause of the Fourteenth Amendment, which provides that no state shall deprive "any person of life, liberty, or property, without due process of law." *See, e.g.,* Duncan v. Louisiana, 391 U.S. 145 (1968); Malloy v. Hogan, 378 U.S. 1 (1964); Benton v. Maryland, 395 U.S. 784 (1969); Pointer v. Texas, 380 U.S. 400 (1965); Schilb v. Kuebel, 404 U.S. 357 (1971); and Robinson v. California, 370 U.S. 660 (1962).

83. *See* John A. Robertson, *supra* note 31, at 1398–99.

# CHAPTER 6

# The Proper Role of Law in Cloning

Fear and misunderstanding have spawned extreme, and extremely vocal, opposition to the cloning of human beings. This opposition has taken root in the form of several highly restrictive state laws and threatens to become a federal ban as well. But cloning is properly viewed as one more form of human reproduction, both different from and similar to the others.

Modern advances in the science and technology of cloning have produced some startling headlines and emotional reactions, as successes of varying degrees have been reported in cloning sheep, mice, and cows. More than all the other examples, the recent announcement of the first tentative, limited breakthrough in cloning a human being ignited a firestorm of denunciations and vows to ban such cloning permanently, under all circumstances and for all purposes. Two presidents of the United States, the pope, numerous senators and members of Congress of both major political parties, and hosts of world leaders have spoken with virtually one voice in decrying the cloning of humans, irrespective of the motives of those involved and the potential benefits that could be realized. But as Clarence Darrow noted in his immortal closing argument in the *Leopold and Loeb* trial, when the people speak with one voice it is often out of "pure prejudice" and a demand for killing, rather than love and mercy.[1] Darrow was arguing against the death penalty in a case in which it seemed all the world was united in clamoring for the execution of his two young defendants. The point he made there is fully applicable in the naked clone context, decades later: unanimity of public opinion does not equate to justice. Most often, it is a sign of rampant prejudice.

Much of the intense animosity has been on the level of unfounded fear, science-fiction fantasy, moralistic bias, and slippery-slope prognostications. Opponents of cloning imagine a horror-story world in which mad scientists and evil geniuses mass-produce hordes of identical warriors, slaves, or monsters ready to effectuate their malevolent purposes. They see cloning as the doorway to a world in which human beings are reduced to mere commodities, their vital organs forcibly harvested from them for profit or the personal benefit of their master. They prophesy of a world in which people clone themselves and others, in conjunction with genetic engineering, to create legions of designer offspring, made to specification like, and treated like, products, not people. But this world does not exist, and could not exist, even in the absence of any legislation regulating or banning cloning. These specters of doom are either scientifically impossible or already illegal or both.

Even if it were somehow possible to use (or misuse) cloning technology to bring about evil results, that would be no reason to outlaw further scientific progress. Specific misuses can be regulated and punished, if and when they become a reality, without banning the entire line of inquiry. The flowering of modern germline technology as a powerful therapeutic tool was not preemptively shut down because of tragic misapplications of primitive eugenics methods by Nazis, Soviet Lysenkoists, and even American authorities during the first half of the twentieth century.[2] If it had been, countless human lives would have been lost or degraded because we were too hasty in painting, with a very broad brush, the words "PERMANENTLY CLOSED" on the laboratory door.

If the United States Congress ultimately succeeds in passing a bill such as the HCPA, and the president eagerly signs it into law, the government will have succeeded, but not in protecting human life and dignity. On the contrary, it will have successfully ensured that an infertile woman who uses cloning to have a baby can be prosecuted, tried, and convicted in federal court and sentenced to ten years in a federal prison. The government will have succeeded in subjecting a physician to a ten-year prison sentence for the federal crime of using cloning-based therapy to help desperately ill patients—and in sending those patients to prison as well, although they probably would not live long enough to serve their full ten-year sentences. Success will also come in the form of millions of dollars in fines imposed against universities and hospitals that try to find ways of saving lives through cloning research; of course, all of the doctors and scientists who actually commit these heinous crimes would again be subject to imprisonment for ten years. And success will come as the parents who clone their dying child—the only child they could ever have—are incarcerated for ten years, while their new baby grows up knowing that she came into this world, in the eyes of her own government, as an illegal product.

Sadly, as the discussion in chapter 3 shows, the HCPA would not be alone in the world as a national law totally and permanently banning the reproductive and therapeutic cloning of humans. Germany has led the field in this regard, for example. Chapter 3 lists several examples of nations—including the United Kingdom, Spain, and Japan—that have already enacted permanent bans on reproductive cloning while declining to sweep away therapeutic cloning entirely. And certain key states, including California, have also passed permanent bans. But the United States could derive some "lessons learned" from some other nations in crafting cloning legislation.

Israel, for example, built in a sunset clause for its ban on reproductive cloning so that it expires of its own terms in five years. And Japan, by mandating periodic review of its cloning legislation, with expert input on recent advances in science and technology, has acknowledged that the law must in some manner remain appropriately tailored to the state of the art in these other disciplines on an issue of this magnitude.

New Zealand's Medicines Act of 1981, Part 7A, may be the best example of a reasonable, balanced approach to regulating reproductive cloning. This law has several notable and positive features that other nations, including the United States, would do well to emulate. First, there is no permanent ban; the law contains an expiration date that, even if extended, would not allow the law's provisions to continue in effect beyond June 30, 2005. Second, even during its effective period, the law does not ban reproductive cloning outright but rather makes it subject to a flexible "authorization" process overseen by the minister of health. Third, authorizations to conduct reproductive cloning can have specific conditions attached, tailored to the particular circumstances of each individual case, and those conditions can either be revoked, amended, or added upon as required in light of subsequent developments. Fourth, the minister can direct applicants who seek authorizations for reproductive cloning to obtain the expert advice of either a committee formed for that specific case or from a preexisting committee or organization; the advice of such a presumably well qualified group can be incorporated into the terms and conditions of any authorization. Fifth, the advisory group is required to gather and take into account input from interested parties and members of the general public, which helps ensure that the group does not make its decisions in isolation or in secret. Sixth, the criteria under which an application for authorization is to be evaluated are explicitly crafted to include health and safety issues as well as more intangible ethical, cultural, and spiritual issues. In light of the myriad complex issues implicated by human reproductive cloning, this is both prescient and appropriate. In short, New Zealand has handled cloning with a rational, fair, balanced, and flexible set of legislative measures. It stands out as almost unique in this regard.

A frequently cited attack on cloning is titled "The Wisdom of Repugnance."[3] The unintentional irony of that title perfectly summarizes the deeply flawed reasoning that usually has been proffered in opposition to the cloning of humans. Repugnance is endowed with no inherent wisdom.

On the contrary, when we feel an inexplicable, ill-defined loathing for someone or something, divorced from reason and rationality, that revulsion is not wisdom but prejudice. We may concede that there is a common tendency of people to hate without reason, and a powerful urge to destroy that which, through misunderstanding, is hated. Again, this human penchant to demonize and demolish the chimerical unknowns that frighten us is not wisdom to be celebrated. It is unarticulated, baseless fear and hatred, and we should seek to overcome it, not to enshrine it. Many "right-thinking" people in the distant and not-so-distant past have felt repugnance for practices ranging from inoculation to artificial insemination to organ transplantation to dissection of human cadavers, but that critical mass of opinion did not, in a sort of alchemy, transform their repugnance into wisdom.

Many people are understandably disturbed by what they have read and heard about cloning. In some ways, this may fit within the category of a "discontinuity," that is, one more example of ways in which human beings were once thought to be in a unique class by themselves and now no longer seem so utterly above the rest of nature. Bruce Mazlish has argued that previously there have been at least three such discontinuities whereby notions of human uniqueness were ultimately destroyed by scientific theories, each of which was traumatic to many people.[4] First, when Galileo theorized that the earth revolved around the sun, the idea that life here was unique and separate from the rest of the universe was overturned. Then, Charles Darwin postulated that humans evolved from other forms of life, and the discontinuity that people were separate from animals was destroyed. The third discontinuity occurred when Sigmund Freud asserted that human action was guided by irrational forces and that even rational human thought was based on irrational motivations. In Mazlish's view, the fourth discontinuity, that is, the separation between humans and the computers we create, is now being threatened by advancements in artificial intelligence. This could force the realization that intelligence is not an attribute that makes humans unique.[5] In like manner, the advent of cloning could confront people with dramatic evidence that they, along with other life forms, are not beyond genetic manipulation. And this is a message that many are finding to be most unpleasant, as were the other discontinuities. But should this be so?

Cloning is utterly incapable of mass-producing people, just as are in vitro fertilization, artificial insemination, and all the other modern forms of assisted reproduction. In fact, this book has noted several ways in which cloning could be both physically safer and legally less problematic than some other well-established modes of reproduction. Moreover, the reasons individuals might want to use cloning are very consonant with the reasons people have always chosen to have children throughout the world's history. Cloning, like all other types of latter-day assisted reproduction, is at its core a process that would result in the birth of a baby, who, by virtue of an array of environmental and developmental factors, would grow up to be a unique individual, a fully human being.

This is reproduction, not replication. Genetics are not everything; differing environments produce different people, even among identical twins. When people are cloned, they would be genetically *less* similar than identical twins because they have different mitochondrial DNA. They would also experience, and be shaped by, quite divergent environmental influences, beginning within the mother's uterus and extending through all the formative years in the familial milieu. They each would be distinct and unique—and entitled to all human rights.

The overwhelming majority of people who would endure the great expense and effort to have a child through cloning would do so for much the same reasons people have babies through coital reproduction, in vitro fertilization, artificial insemination, and surrogacy—and those reasons have as their epicenter love.

In this book I have posited the naked clone situation to describe those instances in which people earnestly desire to have a child and choose, for their own very personal reasons, to use cloning to realize their dream, and yet they find the legal system standing as a barricade in their path. The anticloning laws single out and ban the cloning choice while other modes of human reproduction and family building remain legal, respectable, honorable, and even hallowed. Traditional procreation, adoption, foster parenting, in vitro fertilization, and the use of various forms of surrogacy are all accommodated by contemporary jurisprudence. But the anticloning laws would, without justification, leave the naked clone in an unprotected class of one.

I mentioned Clarence Darrow's renowned closing argument in *Leopold and Loeb* and its resonance now, decades later, in a very different context. It is fitting to conclude this book as Clarence Darrow ended his ultimately triumphant plea for the lives of his young clients, by quoting from *The Rubiyat of Omar Khayyam*:

> So I be written in the Book of Love,
> I do not care about that Book above;
> Erase my name or write it as you will,
> So I be written in the Book of Love.[6]

We have seen that sweeping anticloning laws are inconsistent with Supreme Court precedent recognizing a fundamental right to have children, as well as the cases acknowledging a constitutional right to privacy and personal autonomy. Even within the context of therapeutic cloning for purposes of medical/scientific research, the bans may fail to withstand judicial scrutiny as an impermissible infringement on First Amendment rights of free expression and inquiry.

Cases finding fundamental rights to marry, educate our children, use contraceptives, and abort also support the general right to make our own reproductive choices. Thus, the naked clone situation of reproductive cloning implicates fundamental rights—the right of couples and individuals to bear and beget children and to be free from governmental intrusion in matters involving intensely personal decisions regarding the creation of new life. Encroachment on such rights invokes strict scrutiny by the judiciary, and the arguments arrayed against cloning fail to constitute the requisite compelling governmental interest, whether in isolation or in the aggregate. And certainly, any sweeping, permanent ban is not narrowly tailored to achieve whatever governmental interest might exist.

Proponents of permanent, Procrustean bans along the lines of the HCPA insist that there is really no harm in enacting them because laws once enacted can always be repealed later if and when circumstances change. They make the valid point that reproductive cloning of humans is, at present, apt to be extremely dangerous for the mother, fetus, and child alike. But they want to legislate away all aspects of cloning so broadly and comprehensively even to include any research into the technology. But what about a year from now, or three or five or ten years from now, when progress in other nations has made the risks tolerable? They dismiss objections with assurances that the bans can simply be repealed if that were to happen.

The reality is again at odds with the theory. Legislation, once on the books, tends to take on a life of its own. Absent a sunset clause, mere inertia often suffices to protect statutes from repeal, even for decades after they have become outmoded and useless. Even today, long-antiquated laws remain in effect in many states, at best an embarrassment, at worst a counter-progressive impediment, all the while staying under the legislature's radar year after year. Legislatures in every state, as well as the United States Congress, always have ample concerns on their plate, and it is easy to forget about repealing outdated laws. Indeed, in its 1997 report on cloning, the National Bioethics Advisory Commission stated that, "while it is true that a ban could always be removed by a vote to repeal the prohibition, such an effort would take a strong interest group lobbying for change."[7] Thus, any anticloning statute without a built-in expiration date is liable to be with us for a very long time, irrespective of dramatic changes in science and technology.

If the United States ultimately enacts such a ban, and if there remains any nation in the world that does not do likewise, the effect will be to allow cloning to proceed without meaningful American leadership. Leading scientists and doctors from the United States and all other ban-happy countries will move to the places where they remain free to do their work. Advancements, and even major breakthroughs, will find a hospitable nurturing environment outside the United States, and we will be prohibited—under threat of criminal prosecution—even to import the resulting benefits. Already, the states of Michigan, Louisiana, and Iowa within the United States have criminalized human reproductive cloning, and many more are actively considering this drastic measure. Such laws will have consequences—often unforeseen and destructive consequences—even at the state level, but much more so at the national and international levels. If the United Nations' comprehensive anticloning treaty (as urged by the United States) becomes a reality, any nations that remain nonsignatories will become havens for biotechnology in the future.

A better approach would be to regulate, not to ban. Constitutionally sound regulation would provide safeguards and require demonstrably adequate success rates and healthy offspring in animal tests before allowing full-scale reproductive human cloning. Powerful incentives already exist—both financial and emotional—to proceed with caution and prudence. These incentives are already in place, independent of any legislation, because reasonable, rational people will not spend huge sums of money to subject themselves and their children to formidable physical risks. If at all, legislation is only advisable to address those few anomalous cases that might result in premature and irresponsible cloning initiatives.[8]

A temporary restriction on reproductive cloning, particularly if carefully balanced along the lines of the New Zealand law, would likely survive judicial scrutiny, and much more justifiably than any permanent ban. It is undeniable that there are formidable hurdles remaining in the path of human reproductive cloning at present. It may be many years, even decades, before there is sufficient experimental and experiential evidence that cloning is safe, both in near- and long-term, for both mother and offspring in higher nonhuman primates.

For example, the possibility of accelerated aging might not be thoroughly studied and addressed until several generations of cloned primates have a chance to live their complete lifetimes. And although I consider the phenomenon to be almost entirely self-regulating (because of prohibitively high costs, moral qualms, fear of tort liability, professional/scientific obloquy,[9] and other concerns), a legislatively imposed set of temporary restrictions would ensure that the few anomalous instances in which someone prematurely—and without official authorization—attempts reproductive cloning would be confronted by an additional powerful disincentive to do so. But any such legislation should have a very short expiration period—no more than five years—because we can reasonably anticipate that the science and technology of mammalian cloning will be increasingly a rapidly moving target. The law must remain able to adjust in response to changes and new developments as swiftly and easily as possible, unencumbered by either permanent bans or moratoria with far-distant expiration dates.

Ultimately, we cannot prevent the reproductive cloning of humans, no matter how much we fear that prospect, and despite all the laws we might enact. To try to hold back a scientific advancement with so much promise to improve the lives of people is the modern-day equivalent of legendary King Canute futilely commanding the ocean not to let the tide come in.[10] It will happen somewhere in the world, and it will not be far in the future. When it does, the babies born through the intervention of cloning technology will grow, celebrate birthdays, go to school, make friends, become annoying teenagers, and probably be completely indistinguishable from any child born through in vitro fertilization, artificial insemination, surrogacy, fertility treatment, or good old-fashioned unaided sexual reproduction. We cannot stuff the genie back in the bottle, and we cannot legislate away biotechnological advancements. Witch-hunts and clone-hunts do not do anyone much good—certainly not those people who are hunted, but not the hunters or their society as a whole either. The antidote to fear and ignorance is accurate information and understanding, not poorly considered bans.

People have always feared the unknown and resisted the unfamiliar. During its early years, in vitro fertilization also was the target of bitter attacks and predictions of disaster. It has now become virtually commonplace, and the world still turns on its axis. Despite all the sensationalist films and novels, cloning is not an evil force from a hostile planet. It is one more in a series of new opportunities made possible by the best that science has to offer. It is the chance for people to have children of their own, where before there was no chance, only an impossible dream.

## NOTES

1. *See* Arthur Weinberg (ed.), ATTORNEY FOR THE DAMNED: CLARENCE DARROW IN HIS OWN WORDS 20, 85–86 (University of Chicago Press 1957).

2. *See* statement of Michael Lind, <http://reason.com/bioresearch/bioresearch .shtml>.

3. *See* Leon R. Kass, *The Wisdom of Repugnance,* NEW REPUBLIC, June 2, 1997, at 17 (detailing the ethical case against the cloning of humans).

4. *See generally* Bruce Mazlish, THE FOURTH DISCONTINUITY (Yale University Press 1993).

5. See Matthew B. Hsu, Note, *Banning Human Cloning: An Acceptable Limit on Scientific Inquiry or an Unconstitutional Restriction of Symbolic Speech?* 87 GEO. L. J. 2399, 2420–21 (1999).

6. *See* Weinberg, *supra* note 1, at 87. The meaning of the verse is essentially that it is more important to devote oneself to love here on earth in this lifetime than to be preoccupied with any heavenly ledger in which the names of people entitled to an eternal reward are recorded. The verse may be read as implying that the successful pursuit of the former necessarily leads toward the latter as well.

7. *See* National Bioethics Advisory Committee, CLONING HUMAN BEINGS: REPORT AND RECOMMENDATIONS OF THE NATIONAL BIOETHICS ADVI-

SORY COMMISSION 101 (National Bioethics Advisory Committee 1997) (NBAC Report).

8. One such example is arguably Clonaid, which self-identifies as "the first human cloning company." Clonaid was founded in February 1997 by a person known only as Raël. Raël is the leader of the Raelian Movement, an international religious organization that claims that life on Earth was created scientifically through genetic engineering by a human extraterrestrial race named Elohim. The Raelian Movement also claims that Jesus was resurrected through an advanced cloning technique performed by the Elohim. The movement seeks to use Clonaid to clone human beings as soon as possible, with a view toward attaining eternal life. *See* Rick Weiss, *First Human Embryos Are Cloned in U.S.*, WASH. POST, Nov. 26, 2001, at A1 (mentioning an announcement that Clonaid had succeeded in preliminary experiments on cloning humans). *See* Clifford Krauss, *Earthlings, the Prophet of Clone Is Alive in Quebec*, N.Y. TIMES, Feb. 24, 2003, at A4; Richard Jerome et al., *Maybe Baby; History or Hoax? A Bizarre Sect That Believes in Space Aliens Announces the Birth of the First Human Clone, a Girl Named Eve*, PEOPLE, Jan 13, 2003, at 58. *See generally* Raël, trans. Marcus Wenner, YES TO HUMAN CLONING: ETERNAL LIFE THANKS TO SCIENCE (Raelian Foundation, 2001); <http://www. clonaid.com/>.

9. *See* David Longtin and Duane C. Kraemer, *Cloning Red Herrings*, POLICY REVIEW ONLINE, <http://www.policyreview.org/FEB02/longtin.html> (February, 2002) (arguing that scientists have, for years, possessed the capability to create some very early stage human-animal hybrids using techniques quite apart from cloning but have not exercised that capability because of a combination of self-restraint, concern about incurring the disfavor of their peers, existing ethical standards governing scientific research, etc.).

10. *See* <http://www.inspirationalstories.com/0/91.html>.

# List of Cases

Stenberg v. Carhart, 530 U.S. 914 (2000).

Texas v. Johnson, 491 U.S. 397 (1989).

Tinker v. Des Moines Independent Community School District, 393 U.S. 503 (1969).

United States v. O'Brien, 391 U.S. 367 (1968).

Virginia State Board of Pharmacy v. Virginia Citizens Consumer Council, Inc., 425 U.S. 748 (1976).

Ward v. Rock Against Racism, 491 U.S. 781 (1989).

Washington v. Glucksberg, 521 U.S. 702 (1997).

Wayte v. United States, 470 U.S. 598 (1985).

Whitney v. California, 274 U.S. 357 (1927).

Wisconsin v. Mitchell, 508 U.S. 476 (1993).

Wynn v. Scott, 449 F. Supp. 1302 (N.D. Ill. 1978).

Young v. American Mini Theatres, Inc., 427 U.S. 50 (1976).

Zablocki v. Redhail, 434 U.S. 374 (1978).

# Glossary

**Allele:** One member of a pair or series of genes that are situated in a certain position on a specific chromosome.

**Amphimictic:** Capable of freely interbreeding and producing fertile offspring, as do members of the same species.

**Asexual reproduction:** Production of offspring without the union of egg and sperm cells; reproduction without coitus.

**Blastocyst:** In mammals, the mass of cells produced by cell division shortly after fertilization of an egg by a sperm, prior to implantation in the female's uterus; blastula.

**Blastomere:** A cell resulting from cell division or cleavage of a fertilized egg, very shortly after fertilization.

**Cell:** The smallest structural unit of an organism that is capable of independent functioning, typically consisting of at least one nucleus, plus cytoplasm and various organelles, all surrounded by a semipermeable membrane.

**Chimera:** An organism, organ, or part consisting of two or more tissues of different genetic composition, produced as a result of organ transplant, grafting, or genetic engineering; a bizarre human-animal amalgam or hybrid.

**Chromosome:** A threadlike strand of DNA and associated proteins in a cell that carries genetic information and that functions in the transmission of hereditary information.

**Clone:** A cell, group of cells, or entire organism descended from and essentially genetically identical to a single common ancestor, such as a bacterial colony whose members arose from a single original cell; also, an organism descended asexually from a single ancestor, such as a plant produced by layering or a polyp produced by budding.

**Cloning:** A form of asexual reproduction in which the offspring has a genetic composition substantially identical to that of the source of the DNA.

**Cytoplasm:** The protoplasm outside the nucleus of a cell.

**DNA:** Deoxyribonucleic acid; the double-helixed nucleic acid molecule that is primarily responsible for acting as the repository and transmitter of hereditary genetic information from one generation to the next.

**Embryo:** A prebirth organism at an early stage of development; in humans, the prefetal product of conception from implantation in the uterus through the eighth week of development.

**Embryo splitting:** A type of cloning in which a fertilized egg at a very early stage of cell division (blastomere) is artificially separated into multiple individual cells for subsequent implantation into the uteri of females of the same species; a form of artificially twinning.

**Enucleated egg:** An egg cell (oocyte or ovum) that has had its nucleus removed through microscopic surgery.

**Eugenics:** The study of hereditary improvement of the human race through controlled selective breeding, often associated with Nazi Germany but also practiced in other nations.

**Fertilization:** The union of gametes (egg and sperm cells) in sexual reproduction to form a zygote.

**Fetus:** In human reproduction, the prebirth young from the end of the eighth week after conception until birth; a postembryonic stage.

**First Amendment:** In the Bill of Rights, the first of the amendments to the United States Constitution. It provides for freedom of speech and of the press, as well as the free exercise of religion, prohibition of establishment of an official federal religion, and freedom of association.

**Freedom of expression:** Free speech rights secured by the First Amendment to the United States Constitution.

**Gamete:** Nonsomatic reproductive cell, either egg or sperm, with half the normal complement of chromosomes (haploid), capable of fusing with a gamete from the opposite sex in fertilization.

**Gene:** A hereditary unit consisting of a sequence of DNA that occupies a specific location on a chromosome and determines a particular phenotypic characteristic in an organism.

**Genetic engineering:** The process of altering the DNA of an organism to produce offspring with certain desired traits; in modern biotechnology, this can include splicing certain portions of the DNA from one species into that of another species.

**Genotype:** The genetic composition or combination of alleles of an organism that determines its specific characteristics or traits, as distinguished from phenotype.

**Judicial review:** The process by which appellate courts determine whether the specific holdings of lower courts will be upheld or overturned on appeal, within the United States common law system.

**Mitochondrion:** An organelle within the cytoplasm of nearly all cells, which functions as a center for energy production and other important aspects of cellular metabolism; plural form: mitochondria.

**Mitochondrial DNA (m-DNA):** Genetic material contained within the mitochondria of a cell, as opposed to nuclear DNA within the cell's nucleus; mitochondrial DNA is inherited only from an organism's biological mother, with no genetic contribution from the biological father.

**Monozygotic twins:** Identical twins; twins produced from early stage separation of a zygote into two (or more) genetically identical individuals.

**Mutation:** A change, usually not intentionally induced, of the DNA sequence within a gene or chromosome of an organism resulting in the creation of a new phenotypic characteristic or trait not found in the parental type.

**Naked clone:** A human being born through reproductive cloning by well-intentioned parent(s), who would be stripped of all legal rights, include the right to exist, by the sweeping, permanent bans on such cloning currently in vogue in many nations.

**Nucleus:** A large, membrane-bound, usually spherical protoplasmic structure within a living cell, containing the cell's hereditary material and controlling its metabolism, growth, and reproduction.

**Oocyte:** A cell from which an egg cell or ovum develops by meiosis; a female gametocyte, or future gamete.

**Ovum:** Egg, female gamete; plural form: ova.

**Personal autonomy rights:** Rights not explicitly mentioned in the text of the United States Constitution but recognized in decisions of various federal courts, to the effect that human beings are entitled to certain zones of privacy, personal dignity, and independence from unwarranted governmental intrusion. Some examples might be the rights to marry, have children, use contraceptives, and make one's own decisions on abortion of a fetus within one's body.

**Phenotype:** The observable physical and biochemical manifestation or expression of both the genetic information in one's genotype and any environmental influences.

**Pleuripotent:** Capable of developing into anything, even a full adult organism; totipotent.

**Privacy rights:** Rights not explicitly mentioned in the text of the United States Constitution but recognized in decisions of various federal courts, to the effect that human beings are entitled to freedom from unwarranted governmental interference in certain private areas of their lives, such as reproductive choices.

**Protoplasm:** The complex, semifluid, translucent substance that constitutes the living matter of plant and animal cells and manifests the essential life functions of a cell. Composed of proteins, fats, and other molecules suspended in water, it includes the cell's nucleus and cytoplasm.

**Reproductive cloning:** Cloning to produce children; the use of cloning technology with the aim of bringing a living baby into the world, as opposed to therapeutic/research cloning.

**Reproductive liberties:** Rights not explicitly mentioned in the text of the United States Constitution but recognized in decisions of various federal courts, to the effect that human beings are entitled to freedom from unwarranted governmental interference with their decisions to have children, use contraceptives, or have an abortion.

**Somatic cell:** A body cell, as opposed to a gamete; any cell other than an egg or sperm.

**Somatic cell nuclear transfer (SCNT):** A method of cloning in which microscopic surgery is used to remove the nucleus of an egg cell and replace it with the nucleus from a somatic cell. In reproductive cloning, the resulting reconstituted cell can then be implanted in the uterus of a female of the same species as that of the egg donor and nucleus donor, to undergo gestation.

**Species:** One of the most fundamental units of taxonomic classification, ranking below the level of genus or subgenus and consisting of related individual organisms capable of interbreeding and producing fertile offspring.

**Spermatozoan:** A male gamete, or sperm cell; plural form: spermatozoa.

**Stem cell:** An unspecialized or undifferentiated cell that can give rise to a specific specialized cell.

**Strict scrutiny:** A particularly rigorous standard of judicial review, which will generally result in a particular example of governmental action or regulation being invalidated by a court. In First Amendment jurisprudence, this is the standard of review used when the government restricts protected speech because of the specific content and message of the speech. Such restrictions will only be upheld if narrowly tailored to a compelling governmental interest.

**Symbolic speech:** A form of expression in which actions are used either in lieu of or in conjunction with words to convey a particular message to others. Flag burning and public destruction of a draft card are typical examples.

**Therapeutic cloning:** Cloning conducted solely for purposes of medical or scientific research and not to produce a child.

**Totipotent:** Capable of giving rise to differentiated cells of any type, including an entire organism or major parts thereof.

**Transgenic:** Genetically altered through artificial means for a particular purpose; genetically modified or genetically engineered.

**Uterus:** A hollow muscular organ located in the pelvic cavity of female mammals in which the fertilized egg is implanted and subsequently develops; womb.

**Xenotransplantation:** The artificial surgical transfer of cells, tissues, or entire organs from a member of one species to a member of a different species.

**Zygote:** The cell formed by the fusion of two gametes (egg and sperm) in the process of fertilization, before the product of conception begins dividing/cleaving.

# Index

## About the Author

**JOHN CHARLES KUNICH** is Associate Professor of Law at the Roger Williams University School of Law in Bristol, Rhode Island. He is the author of *Entomology and the Law: Flies as Forensic Indicators* with Bernard Greenberg (2002) and *Ark of the Broken Covenant: Protecting the World's Biodiversity Hotspots* (2003).